DISCARDED

# SOLVING PROBLEMS IN SECONDARY SCHOOL ADMINISTRATION

# SOLVING PROBLEMS IN SECONDARY SCHOOL ADMINISTRATION

## A HUMAN ORGANIZATION APPROACH

*Bill R. Hampton*

Principal, McCluer North High School

*Robert H. Lauer*

Southern Illinois University at Edwardsville

ALLYN AND BACON, INC.

BOSTON  LONDON  SYDNEY  TORONTO

Copyright © 1981 by Allyn and Bacon, Inc., 470 Atlantic Avenue, Boston, Massachusetts 02210. All rights reserved. No part of the material protected by this copyright notice may be reproduced or utilized in any form or by any means, electronic or mechanical, including photocopying, recording, or by any information storage and retrieval system, without written permission from the copyright owner.

**Library of Congress Cataloging in Publication Data**

Hampton, Bill R   1934-
  Solving problems in secondary school administration.

  Includes index.
  1. High schools—Administration. I. Lauer,
Robert H., 1933-    joint author. II. Title.
LB2822.H29      373.12      80-18033
ISBN 0-205-06951-7

Printed in the United States of America

*To*
*The Faculty of McCluer North High School*
*Sine Qua Non*

# Contents

*Preface* xi

**INTRODUCTION: Confronting the Dilemmas of the Modern High School** 1

Our Troubled Schools 2

*General Atmosphere: Learning or Surviving? Violence in the Schools What's Happening to Achievement? The Public's Opinion The Dilemmas of Contemporary Education*

The Human Organization 10

*The Social Psychological Basis Organizational Theory and the Human Organization*

The High School as a Human Organization 22

Can It Work? 24

**PART 1 ADVISEMENT: A PARTICIPATORY SYSTEM** 29

**1 Goals and Tasks of Participatory Advisement** 31

Responding to the Challenges 33

*The Initial Response—Guidance Counseling Participatory Advisement as a Response The Tasks of Participatory Advisement Participatory Advisement and the School Year Additional Handbook Materials: An Example*

Summary 50

**2  Implementing Participatory Advisement   52**

Organizational Change   53

*Change as a Multistage Process   Initiating Change   The Nature of
Resistance   The Human Approach   Conclusion: Principles of Change*

Initiating Participatory Advisement   62

*Gathering Information   The Sources of Information   Forming
Attitudes and Making a Decision*

Implementing Participatory Advisement   68

*Decisions About People   Decisions About Time
Decisions About Space   Decisions About Resources*

Summary   84

**3  The Role of Counselors   87**

The Background—Historical Developments   88

*The Changing High School*

What Counselors Are Trained to Be   92

*The Counselor's Ideal Role   Theories of Counseling*

What Counselors Are   100

*The Counselor as Administrative Assistant   Counselors as Student
Advocates   Counselors as Trouble-Shooters   Counselors as Therapists
and Facilitators   Forces That Shape the Role*

The Counselor in a Participatory Advisement System   106

*The Counselor as Model Advisor   Counselors as Support Person-
nel   Counselors as Deliberate Psychological Educators   Counselors as
Information and Program Specialists   The Counselor's Workload*

Summary   115

**PART 2   THE CURRICULUM: A RESPONSIVE SYSTEM   119**

**4  Designing a Responsive Curriculum   121**

The Curriculum in the Comprehensive High School   122

*The Influence of Conant   The Ideas of Trump
Individualized Education*

Curriculum Design for Optimum Choice and Flexibility   128

*The Traditional Curriculum and Its Problems   The Design of a
Responsive Curriculum*

General Criteria for Curriculum Design   141

Ongoing Evaluation and Changes in Curriculum   142

*Participants in Evaluation and Change   The Process of
Evaluation and Change*

Summary   145

**5  Nontraditional Options  148**

The Roots of Nontraditional Options  149

*Accidental Education  Learning by Living*

Current Options  153

*Some Typical Options  Some Atypical Options*

Deliberate Psychological Education  157

*Background and Nature of the Program  An Example:*
*Community Outreach*

Community Learning Program  169

*Functions of the CLP Supervisors  Implementing a Community*
*Learning Program  Useful Forms and Materials*

Merits of Out-of-School Learning  175

*Effects on Community Sponsors  Effects on the Parents*
*Effects on Students*

Some Additional Options  181

Summary  182


**PART 3  ADMINISTRATION: MANAGING A**
**HUMAN ORGANIZATION  185**

**6  Decision Making: Freedom and Responsibility  187**

Authoritarian Organizations and Alienation  189

*Authoritarian Organizations  Authoritarianism and Alienation*
*Treating the Symptoms*

The Elements of Democratic Decision Making  193

*A Caveat  Organizing for Shared Decision Making*
*Time and Opportunity  Information Training*

Building a Structure for Shared Decision Making  199

*The Instructional Improvement Committee  Other Decision-Making*
*Groups  Advisement Team Leaders  Department Chairpeople*
*Students  Special Ad Hoc Committees  Parents*
*A Concluding Comment*

Summary  217


**7  Discipline in a Human Organization  220**

What Is Discipline?  222

*Discipline as Conformity to Rules  Discipline, Self-Discipline,*
*and Order*

The Process of Disciplining  225

*Guidelines for Rule Enforcement  The Question of*
*Suspension  Evaluating the Discipline Process*

Preventing Discipline Problems  236
*Maintain Open Communication   Keep Discipline Private
Give Students Responsibility   Praise Good Behavior   Build Good
Human Relations*
Summary  247

8  Rewarding Excellence  251

Equality and Excellence  253
*An American Dilemma   A High School Dilemma*
Rewarding Excellence  257
*The Basis: Diverse Competencies   Rewarding Academic
Excellence   Rewarding Other Competencies   Rewarding the
Gifted   Rewards as Public Recognition*
Motivating To Excellence  267
*The Reward System as Motivation   Realistic Opportunities   Teacher
Expectations   The Advisory System*
Effects of Rewarding Excellence  271
Evaluating the Reward System  273
Summary  274

9  Space: The Architecture of a Human Organization  278

Significance of the Physical Environment  279
*The Physical Environment as Meaning   The Building as
Environment   Spatial Arrangements as Environment*
The High School as Physical Environment  284
Architectural and Spatial Themes in a High School  288
*Interaction   Participation   Flexibility and Forgiveness   Aesthetic
Pleasantness   A Concluding Comment*
Summary  299

ENVOI  302

*Index  307*

# Preface

This book is designed to provide an organizational model for the high school. It shows how a high school can be a human organization and thereby address some of the problems and dilemmas confronting the contemporary school. The book is intended to be used as a professional reference by educational administrators in secondary school institutions and as a text for college undergraduate or graduate level courses.

Predicting the future is a hazardous undertaking. In 1899, *The Literary Digest* magazine predicted that the automobile would undoubtedly become available to a greater number of people, though it would certainly never be as common as the bicycle. A famed electronics pioneer, Lee DeForest, asserted in 1926 that television was a commercial and financial impossibility, and so we need not waste our time dreaming about it.

We could compile a considerable list of predictions that have similarly proved false in a short time. Both the famous and the infamous, the experts and the amateurs, have boldly described a future that never came to pass. We are fully aware of the mistaken visions of others. Nevertheless, we offer our own prediction with some confidence: the kind of school that we describe in this book is the school of the future, at least of the near future. No one knows what schools will be like in another century, but we see signs that the near future will witness the development of many schools along the lines of the model contained in this book.

In the Spring of 1979, the authors attended a conference on the advisement system described in the first part of this book. Over 200 secondary educators from various parts of the nation attended the conference. Some came from states that had already mandated the advisement system for all their schools. Others came because they were convinced that the system could greatly improve the quality of education in their schools. Interest in the kind of school we describe is widespread and growing. This book addresses that interest in both a practical and a theoretical way. It shows the social scientific basis for a humane school, and it describes the kinds of procedures, programs, and policies necessary for creating such a school. We intend the book to be useful both to practicing educators and to those in the universities and colleges who are training, or training to be, future educators.

A number of people were involved in the early development of some of the ideas contained in this book, including Frederick Wood, Jon Paden, Jon Kinghorn, and Keigh Hubel. We would also like to recognize the contributions of the following personnel in the Ferguson-Florissant School District who have worked hard to develop the kind of school described here: Warren M. Brown, Henry Prokop, Robert Cowles, Mary Louise Hawkins, M. Delores Graham, Martin Tempel, Shirley Salmon, Robin Johnson, Nancy Adelsberger, Susan Benassi, Robert Chamberlain, Dale Davis, Robert Deckert, Patricia Dick, Kathleen Dombrink, Marilyn Edds, Joyce Evans, Michael Herring, Margaret Keeser, Larry Kreyling, Carole Mulliken, Joseph Naumann, Neta Pope, David Roth, Raymond Schoch, Guy Schuermann, Pamela Shenberg, Pamela Sidener, Charles Steevens, Billie Teneau, Michael Thacker, Corinne VanderMeulen, James V. Waldo, Richard Wallace, Peter Wetzel, and Carl Yochum. Finally, we would like to express our thanks to those who read the initial manuscript and made valuable suggestions for improving it—Dr. James Lipham, University of Wisconsin; Dr. Samuel Ersoff, University of Miami; and Dr. Lester Ball, University of North Carolina.

# Introduction:

# Confronting the Dilemmas of the Modern High School

Historically, Americans have considered education to be an important tool for resolving social problems and for maximizing the well-being of individuals. But a chorus of voices in the 1970s has proclaimed that modern education is more of a problem than a solution. For example, Fred Hechinger, a noted writer on education, said in 1976 that our nation is in "headlong retreat from its commitment to education." This retreat, he argued, reflects the fact that "political confusion and economic uncertainty have shaken the people's faith in education as the key to financial and social success." He also warned that a retreat from a strong commitment to education threatens the survival of democracy.[1]

Both professional and popular sources have expressed concern about education. In late 1977, the cover story of *Time* magazine dealt with the high school. "American education in the '70s is in deep trouble," according to the report, and "nowhere are the difficulties more acute than in the 25,300 public high schools, junior and senior, in the U.S., which enroll 19 million students and carry a million teachers on their payrolls."[2] The article identified such things as declining performance, rising violence, spreading shutdowns, teacher troubles, and

1

mounting absenteeism as evidence that the American high school —whether in large urban, small town, or rural setting—is "in deepening trouble."

While it is true that education, like all social institutions, has always had critics and prophets of doom, we believe that there is some validity to the concerns expressed above. In this chapter we will note some evidence of troubles in the nation's high schools. Then we will discuss briefly some of the dilemmas that contribute to these troubles, and conclude with a theoretical resolution and the outline of a practical model based on the theory. The model we propose has been successfully implemented at the secondary level. We believe that it is broadly applicable to all high schools.

## OUR TROUBLED SCHOOLS

During the past few decades, a number of problems have been identified that are common to secondary schools. Some of these problems are recurrent in American history. All of them reflect the troubled nature of the high school today. It is not our intention here to probe these problems in depth nor to provide an exhaustive list of the problems faced by the schools. Rather, we want to note a few of the problems that are widespread in the schools and that form the basis for the current concern.

### GENERAL ATMOSPHERE: LEARNING OR SURVIVING?

Some critics have argued that the bulk of America's schools involve more survival than learning behavior, that the atmosphere of the school requires the student to focus on merely getting through with body and sanity intact. A part of such an atmosphere is violence in the schools. Violence has become such a large issue, however, that we shall discuss it separately below. For while violence contributes to a survival-focused atmosphere, it is not the only culprit.

Even if there is no violence in a school, the general atmosphere can be stultifying to the minds of students. In a well-known critique, Silberman charged that public schools "mutilate" the spirit of children:

> It is not possible to spend any prolonged period visiting public school classrooms without being appalled by the mutilation visible everywhere—mutilations of spontaneity, of joy in learning, of pleasure in creating, of sense of self. The public schools . . . are the kind of institution one cannot really dis-

like until one gets to know them well. Because adults take the schools so much for granted, they fail to appreciate what grim, joyless places most American schools are, how oppressive and petty are the rules by which they are governed, how intellectually sterile and esthetically barren the atmosphere, what an appalling lack of civility obtains on the part of teachers and principals, what contempt they unconsciously display for children as children.[3]

Even if one would argue that Silberman overstates the case, it is undeniable that many schools have policies and practices that impose a heavy burden of conformity on both teachers and pupils. There is, of course, variation in the extent to which schools are structured by rules. Some allow considerable flexibility for teachers and pupils. But others require almost total conformity to rules, which means rigid schedules, approved and disapproved kinds of behavior, standardized and inflexible patterns for learning, and so forth. In such a school, curiosity and interest on the part of pupils may be stifled in the name of a schedule or a rule of some kind. Pupils may find themselves struggling to endure rather than striving to learn.

Rigidity in schools has certain useful functions, of course. It means that everyone is treated the same and that the administration is closely controlling the entire educational process. But it ignores the fact that equality does not demand uniformity. To say that every child should have an equal opportunity for quality education does not mean that every child should be treated to the same schedule and curriculum as every other child. In fact, that kind of "equality" is inequality because it ignores differences among individuals.

Whether because of inflexibility or other reasons, there is evidence that a considerable number of young people in our high schools are finding their educational experience less than satisfactory. In a 1974 survey of high school students, 37% said that school is "boring" and 58% viewed their schooling as "routine" rather than "challenging."[4] Perhaps some of the more deprived of high school students today are the gifted. Fincher has argued that we have identified less than 5% of the gifted children in our schools, and that our approach to their education has been characterized by

. . . lack of funds, lack of leadership, lack of trained personnel, lack of public understanding, lack of priority, lack of legislation, appalling poor diagnosis of the very population it is supposed to serve, too much isolation, too little organization and a stubborn history of nonintervention and state autonomy in how federal funds should be used.[5]

It could be argued that the gifted can learn without the kind of help that is required by other students, so that the bulk of our time and money should be expended on the others. But Fincher points out that gifted children typically work beneath their abilities when they are in a conventional school atmosphere, and that many of them even drop out of school. Thus, the gifted may also find school to be more a matter of survival than of learning.

Of all high school students, the most deprived are those who are trying to learn in an atmosphere that may be called "ritualized deprivation." In such an atmosphere, the teacher performs in a substandard fashion. The building and facilities are substandard and contain little if anything to stimulate curiosity or motivate the intellect. There is a daily ritual—some of the motions of teaching and learning are present. But discipline may fail to the point that chaos appears to reign. And teachers may expect little more than failure from the bulk of the students. Students may perceive nothing but hostility and contempt from their teachers. Consequently, the learning ritual that occurs is so immersed in various kinds of deprivation that the student is more concerned to survive the process than to learn. The kind of school that has an atmosphere of ritualized deprivation is most likely to be found in the urban ghetto or other areas that are predominantly low-income.

In sum, schools in all kinds of communities have general atmospheres which result in many students focusing on survival rather than on learning. It may be a struggle for survival of the mind or survival of physical health. In any case, the schools have failed to create for some students, or for all, an atmosphere that facilitates learning.

## VIOLENCE IN THE SCHOOLS

In a 1974 poll, Gallup reported that the three most frequently named problems in the schools—named by students themselves—were discipline, racial problems, and drug use. A 1975 report of the Law Enforcement Administration of the Department of Justice said that crime in the public schools had reached "epidemic proportions." There were 70,000 serious assaults on teachers in 1973, which was a 77.4% increase over 1970. There was an 85.3% increase in the number of assaults on students during the same 3-year period. The same crimes which are found in the larger society are found in the schools, including extortion, gang warfare, rape, and murder. The student is the most common victim, with hundreds of thousands of students being assaulted each year.[6]

The problem of violence received increasing attention during the 1970s. An article in *Parade* magazine early in 1978 said that the nation's teachers "are taking a beating," with an estimated 70,000 public school teachers being assaulted in their classrooms during the year.[7] A few weeks earlier, *Time* magazine had an article on "The ABCs of School Violence," with the subtitle, "Classroom survival is the lesson of the day."[8] The articles indicate that violence is so common that students must attempt to learn in an atmosphere of constant fear. Both students and teachers must be concerned with survival—in this case, not the survival of interest and motivation but the survival of physical and emotional well-being.

Is there indeed such an atmosphere of fear? Has violence become so common that people actually fear for their safety in public schools? How typical is this problem? In 1977, Gallup surveyed youth and asked, among other things, "When you are at school, do you ever fear for your physical safety, or not?"[9] Nationally, 18% said that they did fear for their safety. The proportion who affirmed their fear did not vary much by area (rural, urban, suburban) or by region of the country. In addition, 4% said that they had been physically assaulted; 12% said money had been stolen from them, and 24% said that other property had been stolen. One freshman girl at a large high school in the Midwest expressed her reaction to the threat of violence: "This place is an absolute zoo. It's not even safe to walk in the corridors. I can't wait until school is over so I can get out of here and back to the safety of my home." Obviously, an atmosphere of violence that produces such a sense of threat is not conducive to learning.

## WHAT'S HAPPENING TO ACHIEVEMENT?

Considerable concern was expressed in the 1970s over declining scores on the Scholastic Aptitude Tests. The mean grade on the verbal portion of the test dropped from 476 in 1951-52 to 429 in 1976-77, while the mean grade on the mathematical part dropped from 494 to 471. Investigators found no single cause for this decline. A special panel appointed by the College Entrance Examination Board suggested that "an amalgam of social and educational changes—less emphasis on 'critical reading and careful writing' in America's high schools, too much television-watching, more one-parent families, and tumultuous political upheavals that formed a 'decade of distraction'—" combined to cause the deteriorating performance.[10] These factors were identified as "probable" causes, however, since the panel was necessarily engaging in some speculation.

In addition, the decline appears to reflect the changing composition of the student population taking the tests. The panel said that between two-thirds and three-fourths of the decline from 1963 to 1970 could be accounted for by the compositional change. In particular, increased numbers of minority group members and those from low-income families were taking the tests and attempting to get into college. Nearly half of all high-school graduates were going to college by 1970—almost double the proportion of the 1950s. Consequently, many more of the students who traditionally scored low on the tests are now taking them. These students do not totally explain the decline, however, and the factors mentioned above also appear to have had an effect.

In addition to declining test scores, concern was also expressed in the 1970s about the lack of basic skills on the part of high school graduates. Students with high–school diplomas, it was charged, could sometimes barely read and write. A Gallup poll in 1976 showed that 65 percent of the public favored the administration of a nation-wide, standard examination to students seeking a high–school diploma. Plainly, widespread dissatisfaction existed with the academic achievement of secondary education students. Some districts, therefore, considered a final examination that would demonstrate a student's basic skills before allowing the student to graduate. And a number of districts, under the mandate of the state legislature, began administering "literacy" and "basic skills" tests to determine whether students would receive a regular diploma or a certification of attendance. Although it is too soon to know the outcome, clearly a new determination arose in the late 1970s to insure that a high-school diploma would reflect at least minimal academic achievement.

## THE PUBLIC'S OPINION

The troubles sketched above were reflected in public opinion. In 1978, the 10th annual Gallup Poll on the public's attitudes toward public schools was conducted.[11] One question involved giving a letter grade to public schools, based on the quality of the schools. Fifteen percent of parents with children in public schools rated their schools "A," while a "B" was given by 36 percent, a "C" by 32 percent, a "D" by 10 percent, and a failing grade by 5 percent. Those most likely to give low grades were recent graduates (18 to 29 years of age), residents in the central cities (who gave the lowest ratings in the nation), and those who live in the West. Furthermore, the ratings had been steadily declining since 1974.

Why the lower ratings? What concerns the public about contemporary education? For one thing, a majority agreed that the declining test scores is a matter of concern. They believed that the scores show that the quality of education itself is declining. When the pollsters asked people to identify the major problems of the public schools, lack of discipline was named most frequently (by 25 percent of public school parents). Other problems named were those involving race (integration and busing), inadequate fiscal support, poor curriculum, drug use, quality of the teaching, lack of parental interest, the size of the school and/or its classes, school board policies, and lack of interest on the part of students.

In sum, whether we base our conclusions on conditions that exist in the schools or on public opinion about the state of education, we face a troubled situation. Every group involved in education—educators, students, parents of students, and the general public—has exhibited concern. It will not be easy to address the various concerns. As we shall discuss in the next section, the troubles of the schools are compounded by certain dilemmas.

## THE DILEMMAS OF CONTEMPORARY EDUCATION

There are any number of dilemmas involved in the current troubled state of education. For instance, serious fiscal problems plagued the schools in the 1970s. Many school districts were caught between declining tax bases and increasing inflation. By the fall of 1976, urban schools were showing various effects of the economic situation.[12] There were 5,000 fewer teachers in New York City than there were the previous fall. Some classes in Los Angeles had to be cancelled because of the lack of money for repairing leaking roofs. Many athletic programs were curtailed. Teachers went on strike in various places because of inadequate salary increases or none at all. In spite of such problems, the schools were expected to maintain high-quality education.

A different kind of dilemma is the continuing debate over "basics" versus innovation. The "back to the basics" people argue that our present troubles reflect the innovations of the 1960s. They believe that renewed emphasis on a three-Rs curriculum will bring quick and beneficial results. There is public support for this position, for in the 1976 Gallup poll mentioned above, 51% of the respondents agreed that more attention to the teaching of basic skills would improve the quality of public school education.

Along with the emphasis on basic skills, the public supports the role of the school in career preparation. When asked whether the high–school curriculum should give more emphasis or less emphasis to careers and career preparation, 80% said more emphasis should be given. On the other hand, the poll found "obvious confusion in the public's thinking about what constitutes career education and the kind of skills needed in today's society."[13]

The above discussion suggests what we believe to be a root dilemma in secondary education today—the contradictory demands of a variety of groups, each of which has some legitimacy in expressing its demands. If, for example, parents insist that the school should give more emphasis to career preparation, administrators must pay heed to the demand because they define the parents as a group that can legitimately try to influence the educational process. At the same time, if the current educational ideology stresses the importance of acquiring a broad base of knowledge and experiencing personal growth rather than merely preparing for a career, administrators must attend to that demand; the framers of the ideology are also a legitimate group in the educational process.

The problem of meeting contradictory demands is compounded by the fact that there are contradictions within as well as between groups. As the Gallup poll noted, the public wants more emphasis on career preparation, but there is disagreement within the public about the meaning of that preparation. Other groups also have internal contradictions. There may be a majority and a minority position on the board of education, and those in the minority may become a majority as a result of an election. There may be contrary educational ideologies held by teachers or by various administrators. All of these people may press legitimately for their point of view to prevail.

Because of the various troubles, the numerous contradictions that form the context of contemporary education, and the nature of contemporary society, the educator faces a demanding and perplexing set of problems. The educator's task is marked by ambiguity, by incompatible expectations on the part of various groups, by daily challenges and dilemmas, and by frustrations that are rooted in external factors over which the educator may have little or no control. The situation is well summed up in a series of questions framed by a committee of specialists in secondary education. The questions reflect "the several inescapably interrelated crucial issues in secondary education" today:[14]

1.  How can we maximize the development of the individual so that each individual may experience self-actualization?
2.  How can we help our students to accept and implement humane values so that the democratic ideal might be realized in the United States and throughout the world?

3. How can we provide our students with "the vision, knowledge, and competencies needed to cope with the social realities that threaten survival and vitiate the quality of life for mankind" both now and in the foreseeable future?
4. How can we help students make good use of the wisdom and insights gained by peoples of the past?
5. How can we utilize the facilities and resources we have in order to make the total environment a learning experience for young people?
6. How can we provide students with a curriculum that "simultaneously takes into account social realities, humane values, the needs of individual learners, and bodies of knowledge derived from disciplinary and inter-disciplinary studies?"
7. How can we discover and use the forms of organization that will maximize the quality of education?
8. How can we gather and make good use of the various instructional resources and processes so that they will create learning experiences for students?
9. How can we "best draw upon all affected groups, whether teachers, administrators, students, official bodies, interest groups, or individual citizens, in administering, supervising, and improving the educational enterprise?"

The above questions assume certain goals as legitimate and identify certain problems and tasks that will be involved in achieving those goals. The legitimate goals include the personal growth of students, the development of effective citizens, and the development of those competencies among youth that will enable them to function effectively and meaningfully in the modern world. Obviously, such goals cannot be achieved in the kind of atmosphere described earlier—an atmosphere in which there is more concern for survival than for learning, in which violence is a continual threat, and in which general achievement is declining.

What, then, is involved in achieving the goals? The questions suggest a number of problems and tasks. First, the curriculum of the school must be shaped in accord with the goals. Second, the school must be organized in a way that facilitates the achievement of the goals. And, finally, the organization must allow for the participation of all those groups legitimately concerned with and affected by the educational process.

We will show briefly below, and in detail through the remainder of the book, a model for secondary education that deals precisely with the above issues. First, however, we want to discuss the theoretical basis for the model. For the kind of high school we describe has a theoretical rationale as well as a track record of practical success.

## THE HUMAN ORGANIZATION

The first question framed by the committee of specialists, as noted above, dealt with the "fullest development of the individual's potentialities and experiences as a fully functioning, self-actualizing person." This goal reflects an approach based on humanistic social psychology. Our own approach, and that of the organizational theorists we shall discuss in this section, is also based on humanistic social psychology. In particular, we proceed from the assumption that a fundamental goal of social activity is the self-actualization of those individuals involved in the activity.

## THE SOCIAL PSYCHOLOGICAL BASIS

A number of theorists have argued that self-actualization is the goal of every individual. "The tendency to actualize its nature, to actualize 'itself,' is the basic drive, the only drive by which the life of the organism is determined."[15] "The overall and ultimate problem for each human being is his self-fulfillment and the living up to his potentialities."[16] "As nature abhors a vacuum so every organism abhors incompleteness."[17] The idea that every individual seeks to discover his or her own true nature and bring it into a state of wholeness or complete functioning is not new, of course. Such an idea was set forth in the ethical writings of Socrates, Plato, and Aristotle. Concern with the self-actualization of students is part of a respected and long-standing tradition of thought.

Various thinkers have expressed the idea of self-actualization in somewhat diverse ways. But as Maslow points out, there is a "solid core of agreement" in the varied approaches: "All definitions accept or imply (a) acceptance and expression of the inner core of self, i.e., actualization of these latent capacities, and potentialities, 'full functioning,' availability of the human and personal essence. (b) They all imply minimal presence of ill health, neurosis, psychosis, of loss or diminution of the basic human and personal capacities."[18] Furthermore, most theorists would accept the idea that self-actualization is more of a process than a state of being. Self-actualization involves ongoing growth as the individual confronts and succesfully deals with a series of tasks and challenges.

The growth that is an integral part of self-actualization is neither inevitable nor easy. Maslow talks about growth, or the lack of growth, as "the resultant of a dialectic between growth-fostering forces and growth-discouraging forces (regression, fear, pains of growth, ignorance, etc.)."[19] Those who are concerned about self-actualization in any specific situation, such as a high school, must be aware of those factors likely to facilitate and those likely to impede individual growth.

## ORGANIZATIONAL THEORY AND THE HUMAN ORGANIZATION

The name "human organization" was coined by Rensis Likert. Along with a number of other noted organizational theorists, such as Douglas McGregor and Chris Argyris, Likert may be placed in the more general category of human relations theorist. As pointed out by Haas and Drabek, there are seven central themes in the human relations perspective.[20]

First, workers are "viewed as complex social creatures with feelings, desires, and fears." Consequently, they behave in accord with factors other than the purely economic. People in organizations, even in industrial organizations, are motivated by ego needs, security needs, the desire to be creative, and the wish for new experiences as well as by economic incentives.

The second theme is that people obtain their basic satisfactions through participation in groups. Opportunities for group interaction of various kinds can be crucial in the outcome of organizational goals. Third, the formation of groups and the processes of interaction in groups can be manipulated to some extent. In particular, the human relations perspective emphasizes the importance of supervisors. The attitudes and motivation level of those in the organization are crucially related to the style of supervision. If a supervisor treats people in an instrumental fashion—as tools necessary to get a job done—the results may be counterproductive. If the supervisor treats others as "human beings" by being concerned with supportive and meaningful relationships among the workers, the results will be positive attitudes and a high level of motivation.

Fourth, people in organizations follow group norms, not necessarily the formal norms prescribed by the organization. The norms of peers invariably take precedence over the formal organizational norms if the two sets of norms are incompatible. Fifth, an effective organization must be a set of "interlocked functioning groups." All groups within the organization must be linked together in a communication network, and communication and influence must be able to flow "up" as well as "down" through the hierarchy of authority.

Sixth, the interlocking of groups enhances motivation because the individual senses that he or she is a participant in the overall organizational process. The individual has input into the organization; he or she is not merely on the receiving end of information and instructions. Finally, this kind of participative system is more effective than any other system of management.

Within this human relations framework, Likert has developed in considerable detail the characteristics of a human organization.[21] He asked a few hundred individuals to describe the highest- and lowest-producing departments in terms of the characteristics in Table 1. Invariably, low-producing departments tended to be described in terms of characteristics to the left (the System 1 end of the table) of those which described the high-producing departments. Thus, he concludes that System 4, which describes a "human" organization, is the most effective kind of management system. One can easily see that the characteristics of System 4 reflect the seven themes outlined above.

While not all of the variables in the table are directly applicable to the school situation, many of them are applicable and the general principles are valid for any kind of organization. In essence, a human organization is a participative organization in which there is emphasis on such things as supportive relationships, group loyalty, high goals, cooperation, open communication, a sense of confidence and trust among organizational members, participation by various groups in the decision-making process (including the setting of goals), and shared responsibility for maintaining an effective organization. This does *not* mean that there are no conflict or problems or struggles in the organization. Rather, the human organization is a different way of organizing for the achievement of goals, different from the traditional, authoritative type of organization.

In the human organization, there is a focus on people and their needs and not merely on organizational goals. In fact, goals or procedures or structures that impede the self-actualization of individuals are considered inappropriate in the human organization. Ideally, the organizational goals do not contradict the goals of individual members of the organization. We do not regard this ideal as fully attainable in any concrete organization. Nevertheless, we would argue that a school can be organized in a way that will facilitate the goals described above for the majority of students, staff, and parents of students.

**Table 1.**
Organizational and Performance Characteristics of Different Management Systems. From THE HUMAN ORGANIZATION by Rensis Likert. Copyright © 1967 by McGraw-Hill, Inc. Used with permission of McGraw-Hill Book Company

| Organizational Variable | Characteristics of Management Systems | | | |
|---|---|---|---|---|
| | System 1 | System 2 | System 3 | System 4 |
| 1. Leadership processes used | | | | |
| Extent to which superiors have confidence and trust in subordinates | Have no confidence and trust in subordinates | Have condescending confidence and trust, such as master has to servant | Substantial but not complete confidence and trust; still wishes to keep control of decisions | Complete confidence and trust in all matters |
| Extent to which superiors behave so that subordinates feel free to discuss important things about their jobs with their immediate superior | Subordinates do not feel at all free to discuss things about the job with their superior | Subordinates do not feel very free to discuss things about the job with their superior | Subordinates feel rather free to discuss things about the job with their superior | Subordinates feel completely free to discuss things about the job with their superior |

**Table 1.** *(cont.)*

Characteristics of Management Systems

| Organizational Variable | System 1 | System 2 | System 3 | System 4 |
|---|---|---|---|---|
| Extent to which immediate superior in solving job problems generally tries to get subordinates' ideas and opinions and make constructive use of them | Seldom gets ideas and opinions of subordinates in solving job problems | Sometimes gets ideas and opinions of subordinates in solving job problems | Usually gets ideas and opinions and usually tries to make constructive use of them | Always gets ideas and opinions and always tries to make constructive use of them |
| 2. Character of motivational forces | | | | |
| Manner in which motives are used | Fear, threats, punishment, and occasional rewards | Rewards and some actual or potential punishment | Rewards, occasional punishment, and some involvement | Economic rewards based on compensation system developed through participation; group participation and involvement in setting goals, improving methods, appraising progress toward goals, etc. |

| | | | |
|---|---|---|---|
| Amount of responsibility felt by each member of organization for achieving organization's goals | High levels of management feel responsibility; lower levels feel less; rank and file feel little and often welcome opportunity to behave in ways to defeat organization's goals | Managerial personnel usually feel responsibility; rank and file usually feel relatively little responsibility for achieving organization's goals | Substantial proportion of personnel, especially at high levels, feel responsibility and generally behave in ways to achieve the organization's goals | Personnel at all levels feel real responsibility for organization's goals and behave in ways to implement them |

3. Character of communication process

| | | | |
|---|---|---|---|
| Amount of interaction and communication aimed at achieving organization's objectives | Very little | Little | Quite a bit | Much with both individuals and groups |
| Direction of information flow | Downward | Mostly downward | Down and up | Down, up, and with peers |

**Table 1.** *(cont.)*

Characteristics of Management Systems

| *Organizational Variable* | *System 1* | *System 2* | *System 3* | *System 4* |
|---|---|---|---|---|
| Extent to which downward communications are accepted by subordinates | Viewed with great suspicion | May or may not be viewed with suspicion | Often accepted but at times viewed with suspicion; may or may not be openly questioned | Generally accepted, but if not, openly and candidly questioned |
| Accuracy of upward communication via line | Tends to be inaccurate | Information that boss wants to hear flows; other information is restricted and filtered | Information that boss wants to hear flows; other information may be limited or cautiously given | Accurate |
| Psychological closeness of superiors to subordinates (i.e., how well does superior know and understand problems faced by subordinates?) | Has no knowledge or understanding of problems of subordinates | Has some knowledge and understanding of problems of subordinates | Knows and understands problems of subordinates quite well | Knows and understands problems of subordinates very well |

| | System 1 | System 2 | System 3 | System 4 |
|---|---|---|---|---|
| **4. Character of interaction-influence process** | | | | |
| Amount and character of interaction | Little interaction and always with fear and distrust | Little interaction and usually with some condescension by superiors; fear and caution by subordinates | Moderate interaction, often with fair amount of confidence and trust | Extensive, friendly interaction with high degree of confidence and trust |
| Amount of cooperative teamwork present | None | Relatively little | A moderate amount | Very substantial amount throughout the organization |
| **5. Character of decision-making process** | | | | |
| At what level in organization are decisions formally made? | Bulk of decisions at top of organization | Policy at top, many decisions within prescribed framework made at lower levels | Broad policy and general decisions at top, more specific decisions at lower levels | Decision making widely done throughout organization, although well integrated through linking process provided by overlapping groups |

**Table 1.** *(cont.)*

| | | Characteristics of Management Systems | | |
| --- | --- | --- | --- | --- |
| *Organizational Variable* | *System 1* | *System 2* | *System 3* | *System 4* |
| To what extent are decision makers aware of problems, particularly those at lower levels in the organization? | Often are unaware or only partially aware | Aware of some, unaware of others | Moderately aware of problems | Generally quite well aware of problems |
| Extent to which technical and professional knowledge is used in decision making | Used only if possessed at higher levels | Much of what is available in higher and middle levels is used | Much of what is available in higher, middle, and lower levels is used | Most of what is available anywhere within the organization is used |
| To what extent are subordinates involved in decisions related to their work? | Not at all | Never involved in decisions; occasionally consulted | Usually are consulted but ordinarily not involved in the decision making | Are involved fully in all decisions related to their work |

| | | | |
|---|---|---|---|
| Are decisions made at the best level in the organization so far as the motivational consequences (i.e., does the decision-making process help to create the necessary motivations in those persons who have to carry out the decisions?) | Decision making contributes little or nothing to the motivation to implement the decision, usually yields adverse motivation | Decision making contributes relatively little motivation | Some contribution by decision making to motivation to implement | Substantial contribution by decision-making processes to motivation to implement |
| **6. Character of goal setting or ordering** | | | | |
| Manner in which usually done | Orders issued | Orders issued, opportunity to comment may or may not exist | Goals are set or orders issued after discussion with subordinate(s) of problems and planned action | Except in emergencies, goals are usually established by means of group participation |
| Are there forces to accept, resist, or reject goals? | Goals are overtly accepted but are covertly resisted strongly | Goals are overtly accepted but often covertly resisted to at least a moderate degree | Goals are overtly accepted but at times with some covert resistance | Goals are fully accepted both overtly and covertly |

**Table 1.** *(cont.)*

Characteristics of Management Systems

| Organizational Variable | System 1 | System 2 | System 3 | System 4 |
|---|---|---|---|---|
| **7. Character of control processes** | | | | |
| Extent to which the review and control functions are concentrated | Highly concentrated in top management | Relatively highly concentrated, with some delegated control to middle and lower levels | Moderate downward delegation of review and control processes; lower as well as higher levels feel responsible | Quite widespread responsibility for review and control, with lower units at times imposing more rigorous reviews and tighter controls than top management |
| Extent to which there is an informal organization present and supporting or opposing goals of formal organization | Informal organization present and opposing goals of formal organization | Informal organization usually present and partially resisting goals | Informal organization may be present and may either support or partially resist goals of formal organization | Informal and formal organization are one and the same; hence all social forces support efforts to achieve organization's goals |

Extent to which control data (e.g., accounting, productivity, cost, etc.) are used for self-guidance or group problem solving by managers and non-supervisory employees; or used by superiors in a punitive, policing manner

Used for policing and in punitive manner

Used for policing coupled with reward and punishment, sometimes punitively; used somewhat for guidance but in accord with orders

Largely used for policing with emphasis usually on reward but with some punishment; used for guidance in accord with orders; some use also for self-guidance

Used for self-guidance and for coordinated problem solving and guidance; not used punitively

Clearly, if the high school is to be a human organization, a greater amount of participation will be required by those groups that have traditionally had little or no involvement. Are the members of those groups prepared to be involved? There is evidence not only from particular schools, but also from surveys that suggests an affirmative answer to the question. The sixth annual survey of high school students reported that a considerable proportion would like some voice in important school decisions. Forty-seven percent of those surveyed said that they should be consulted about curriculum matters and 42% would like to be involved both in the development of curriculum and in the hiring and firing of teachers (63% said they have no voice in such matters now).[22] In the 1976 Gallup poll, 77% of the respondents said that it would be a good idea for the schools to offer courses for parents to help them learn how to help their children in school. A substantial number of people who have differing kinds of involvement in the educational process have indicated that they favor a more participative system of education. Exactly how can that be achieved? The next section gives a brief outline of the answer; the bulk of the remainder of the book will give details.

## THE HIGH SCHOOL AS A HUMAN ORGANIZATION

Many people would agree with the principles we have described above, but would argue that implementing these principles is a near-impossible task. As we have already pointed out, there are many barriers in the way of creating a school that fosters growth, competence, and effective citizenship. Many administrators and teachers would agree with the observations of one former teacher and principal, who argued that the primary responsibility for humanizing a school rests with the principal. In 25 years in secondary education, he said, he observed that most principals wanted to be "humane, fair, and just," but that the principal who wishes to implement those virtues "faces overwhelming odds in overcoming the barriers." Consider some of the problems: The school day, school year, and school schedule are locked in with the Carnegie Unit and college entrance requirements. School board policies are inflexible and inhumane. Patrons look askance at flexible and innovative programs. Teachers are caught up in the traditional model of the school. The principal's problems have been compounded by recent negotiations, as teachers and school districts narrow the options in scheduling, class load, fringe benefits, curriculum planning, and other professional responsibilities.[23]

The author goes on to say that there is a need for studies that support the humanization of schools. We believe that the present work will provide such a study. But turning a school into a human organization requires more than the efforts of the principal. Humane attitudes on the part of the principal and teachers are desirable, but not sufficient. The school must be structured along lines which are quite different from the traditional model.

In essence, a threefold design is necessary for creating a human organization in a high school. First, school policies and practices must be based on a communications system that allows both students and parents to share in the decision-making process. In particular, students and parents must share in those decisions which affect the educational program of the students. This sharing is achieved by means of the unique advisement system described in detail in Part I. Advisement becomes a participatory system rather than an authoritative dispensing of information.

Second, the school's curriculum must be organized to provide clearly defined options as well to offer those courses of study required by state law. It is true that the curriculum must be "closely related to the aims and purposes of secondary education, for it is through the learning experiences and activities that the purposes are attained."[24] But since one of the aims is self-actualization through participation, the interests and goals of parents and students help shape the curriculum. This is achieved through the responsive system detailed in Part II.

Third, the administrative role is based upon shared decision making, a commitment to students' personal growth, and the use of feedback in planning for the future. Administration must be viewed in terms of managing a human organization. The implications of this view are discussed in Part III.

The threefold design involves greater participation in the educational process by teachers, students, and parents than the more traditional models allow. The design also maximizes communication among the various involved groups. At the same time, it allows for the exercise of leadership by administrators. A participatory school is not one in which teachers, students, and parents have usurped all of the power once held by administrators. Rather, a participatory school is one in which all involved parties have responsibility, involvement, a real (rather than apparent) voice in the decision-making process, and, consequently, a personal investment in the outcome.

## CAN IT WORK?

The "human organization" concept sounds good on paper, but is it practical? We expect a good deal of skepticism on the part of those who first encounter the idea. We have, for example, been told by corporate managers that a participatory system in their setting would mean that they would go broke within a matter of weeks. Nevertheless, participatory management has been implemented with considerable success in a number of business and industrial settings.

But what about in education? We have evidence from a number of schools that have implemented various parts of the model described in this book that suggests both the practicality and the effectiveness of the human organization in education. For example, one high school, located in a Midwestern suburb, has largely implemented the three-fold design to be discussed in succeeding chapters. The school, which opened in 1970, is integrated (11 percent black in 1977–78) as a result of a court-ordered desegregation plan in 1976. The majority of the blacks are bussed in from a low socioeconomic community. There were a total of 2250 students in the school in 1977–78. This school, along with a number of others in the nation, stands in marked contrast to the troubled situations described earlier. Even in such matters as achievement scores, the school has not suffered the decline which is so pervasive.

With respect to creating an atmosphere in which participation, cooperation, respect, and high levels of motivation are present, a number of surveys of students and parents show considerable success. For example, a recent student satisfaction survey shows considerably more satisfaction with every aspect of the educational process than the average for the state (Table 2). The school received federal funding for implementing the advisement part of the model. In accord with the terms of the grant, a validation report was submitted in 1977. Included in the report were the results of a number of surveys of students and the following summary of those results:

> It is our assessment from the date collected and from our involvement in the program that many students perceive: 1) being personally known by the school, 2) having a degree of control over their environment (program planning), and 3) having personalized help in solving problems with which they are faced to be indicative of the types of involvement provided through a teacher/advisee program which students view as personally significant.[25]

Parents also perceive the school as achieving the goals of a human organization. A random sample of parents was surveyed in

**Table 2.**
Student Satisfaction Survey (in percentages)

| Item | Satisfied, No Change Needed | | Neutral | | Dissatisfied, Needs Improvement | | No Experience | |
|---|---|---|---|---|---|---|---|---|
| | Local | State | Local | State | Local | State | Local | State |
| Classroom Instruction | 73 | 57 | 19 | 26 | 8 | 17 | 0 | 1 |
| Number & variety of course offerings | 94 | 58 | 2 | 14 | 3 | 27 | 1 | 1 |
| Grading practices and policies | 63 | 49 | 26 | 27 | 11 | 23 | 0 | 1 |
| Number and kinds of tests given | 66 | 50 | 26 | 36 | 9 | 13 | 0 | 1 |
| Guidance services | 65 | 50 | 19 | 20 | 11 | 27 | 5 | 2 |
| School rules | 71 | 35 | 18 | 23 | 11 | 40 | 1 | 1 |
| Library | 72 | 53 | 14 | 22 | 13 | 23 | 2 | 2 |
| Labs | 64 | 39 | 20 | 25 | 5 | 25 | 10 | 11 |
| Special help (reading, math, etc.) | 43 | 27 | 17 | 21 | 17 | 25 | 23 | 26 |
| Provisions for outstanding students | 63 | 41 | 16 | 23 | 6 | 23 | 15 | 13 |
| Program planning | 64 | 36 | 16 | 26 | 12 | 30 | 8 | 7 |

1975. Among the responses were the following: 95% agreed that the courses offered in the school were relevant to the needs of their children; 80% said that their children looked forward to going to school each day; 90% said that their children were being taught according to their ability levels and interests; 95% agreed that "most teachers like children and take an interest in them;" 92% agreed that "principals try to treat all students fairly"; and 81% agreed that the school had provided them with an opportunity to discuss the educational plans of their children.

Finally, the effectiveness of the school is borne out by the report of the Visiting Committee of the North Central Association, which reviewed the school and its program in late 1975. The report concluded that "the school maintains a warm, positive, interpersonal atmo-sphere, which appears to motivate students to learn and teachers to enjoy their work . . . parents, students, and teachers alike hold positive attitudes toward the school. This point deserves stress, because it sug-gests an atmosphere not only conducive to learning, but one that stim-ulates students to achieve to the limits of their capacities."

This is not to say that schools that follow the model are free of problems or troubles. We are not trying to portray a utopian situation. On the other hand, those schools that attempt to create a human organization, to implement the model described in this book, tend to avoid some of the troubles that have plagued high schools throughout the nation. Students, staff, parents, and other groups involved in vari-ous ways with such schools indicate basic satisfaction. There tends to be a consensus that such schools are largely successful in providing an atmosphere that makes working and learning effective and enjoyable. In other words, a humane school is seen to support Likert's contention that a human organization will be much more effective than the tradi-tional authoritative organization. In the remainder of this book, we will show specifically how a high school may become a human orga-nization through the threefold design indicated above.

# Endnotes

[1]F. M. Hechinger, "Murder in Academe: The Demise of Education." *Saturday Review,* March 29, 1976, p. 11.

[2]*Time,* November 14, 1977, p. 62.

[3]Charles E. Silberman, *Crisis in the Classroom* (New York: Random House, 1970), p. 10.

[4]Reported in D. D. Miller, "What Do High School Students Think of Their Schools?" *Phi Delta Kappan* 57 (June, 1976): 700.

[5]J. Fincher, "Depriving the Best and the Brightest." *Human Behavior,* April, 1976, p. 19.

[6]Reported in *The Education Digest* 41 (September, 1976): 36–7.

[7]*Parade,* February 26, 1978, p. 6.

[8]*Time,* January 23, 1978, p. 33.

[9]This poll was reported in the *St. Louis Post-Dispatch,* December 21, 1977, p. 5F.

[10]C. M. Fields, "Why the Big Drop in S.A.T. Scores?" *The Chronicle of Higher Education* 15 (September 6, 1977): 1.

[11]Reported in *Phi Delta Kappan* 60 (September, 1978): 33–45.

[12]The facts in this paragraph are reported in the *St. Louis Post-Dispatch,* September 26, 1976, p. 1H.

[13]The Gallup Opinion Index, Report No. 135, p. 18.

[14]W. Van Til, "Crucial Issues in Secondary Education." *Theory Into Practice* 15 (June, 1976): 183–84.

[15]Kurt Goldstein, "The So-Called Drives," in C. Moustakas, ed., *The Self: Explorations in Personal Growth* (New York: Harper & Brothers, 1956), p. 16.

[16]A. H. Maslow, "Personality Problems and Personality Growth," in C. Moustakas, ed., *The Self,* p. 242.

[17]J. A. Hadfield, *Psychology and Morals* (New York: Robert M. McBride & Co., 1925), p. 82.

[18]Abraham Maslow, *Toward a Psychology of Being,* 2nd edition (New York: Van Nostrand Reinhold Co., 1968), p. 197.

[19]*Ibid.,* pp. 204–205.

[20]J. Eugene Haas and Thomas E. Drabek, *Complex Organizations: A Sociological Perspective* (New York: Macmillan, 1973), pp. 43–47.

[21]Rensis Likert, *The Human Organization: Its Management and Value* (New York: McGraw-Hill, 1967).

[22]D. D. Miller, "What Do High School Students Think of Their Schools?", p. 700.

[23]B. L. Abel, "Humanizing Secondary Schools: Words or Action." NASSP Bulletin 60 (October, 1976): 63–64.

[24]Rudyard K. Bent, Henry H. Kronenberg and Charles C. Boardman, *Principles of Secondary Education*, 6th edition (New York: McGraw-Hill, 1970), p. 208.

[25]Validation Report, Advisement Project, E.S.E.A. Title IV-C Program Grant #35–74–03–2, May 4, 1977, p. 30.

# Part

# 1

# ADVISEMENT:

## A
## PARTICIPATORY
## SYSTEM

# Chapter 1

# Goals and Tasks of Participatory Advisement

American education, according to sociologist Ralph Turner, has reflected the value we put on "contest mobility."[1] That is, Americans believe that we are all engaged in a kind of "sporting event in which many compete for a few recognized prizes." Furthermore, in any sporting event we admire the individual who starts off slowly but who comes on strong to win. The rules of the event insure the continuation of the game until everyone has had a full opportunity to compete for the prize. The prize is success, and education is believed to be the game in which all Americans are competing to attain the prize of success. No one should be deprived of the opportunity to compete, and the competition should remain open as long as possible to account for the "sleepers." As John Gardner put it: "We believe that the youngster should have many successive opportunities to discover himself. We postpone as long as possible any final closing of the door on the individual's chances."[2]

A number of events and developments in American society over the past decades intensified and/or reflected this norm of holding open the doors of opportunity to all for as long as possible. Because of these events and developments the function of the high school increasingly became one of holding out equality of opportunity for a longer and longer period. Students are retained in school for as long as possible so that both their own development and the well-being of society are maximized.

What were the events and developments involved in this renewed emphasis on equality of opportunity? For one thing, the Soviet launching of Sputnik resulted in a strong emphasis on training in science and math. America had to use all of its resources, including its human resources, in order to catch up with the Russian space achievements. Massive amounts of federal money were poured into education in an effort to meet the challenge. Second, the Civil Rights movement, school desegregation, and affirmative action programs pointed out inequities in the past and asserted the rights of minorities to equal educational opportunities. Third, the students' rights movement generated a somewhat different concern: equal opportunity means that students with diverse interests should have alternative curriculums available to them.

Fourth, technological developments seemed to open up the possibility of actually achieving the ideal of equal opportunity. Computerized instruction and other technologies seemed to make individualized instruction feasible. It appeared that the deficiencies involved in a single teacher attempting to meet the peculiar needs of each student could be overcome through technology. Finally, the recent emphasis on consumerism has affirmed that young people need to gain information, understanding and skills in various areas such as drugs, driving, sex, economics, careers, health, etc. And, of course, they need to be retained in the school until they have had the opportunity to participate in the courses in these areas.

The net effect of the above is an increasing proportion of the nation's teenagers remaining in school. In 1953-54, 59.5% of 17- and 18-year olds graduated from high school; by 1973-74, the figure had risen to about 74%.[3] There is a greater proportion of teenagers who remain in school, and there is at the same time an increased sense of the schools' responsibility to provide those students with an equal and meaningful educational experience. This means that the high school must respond to a greater range of interests, values, and expectations than ever before. The school's most difficult and most crucial task has become that of responding to each student on an individual basis, matching each student with an appropriate curriculum and a meaningful and useful set of experiences. "Equal opportunity" means that students must be treated as individuals, not as parts of a mass. In *Death of a Salesman*, Linda says of her broken and desperate husband, Willie,

"Attention must be paid to such a man." She expressed the essence of what America demands of its schools—no matter how difficult or easy to work with, how good or bad the individual is perceived to be, how competent or incompetent, attention must be paid to each individual and each individual's opportunities must be maximized. An educator expressed it this way:

> We will ceaselessly ask ourselves, "How does *this* youth need to develop to become more mature?" Neither a state's Department of Education nor a college's admission or departmental requirements nor a teacher's bias will be allowed to get in the way of his growth. We will provide greater diversity in learning modes and experiences in order to meet the needs of individual students.[4]

## RESPONDING TO THE CHALLENGES

### THE INITIAL RESPONSE—GUIDANCE COUNSELING

The establishment of the guidance counselor was one form of response to the challenges of equal opportunity and individualized learning. As Alexander, Saylor, and Williams put it: "One of the most marked contrasts between the high school of the 1970s and that of the 1930s or even 1940s or 1950s is in the provision of guidance and other special services found to varying extents by 1970 but rarely present in the earlier decades."[5] Guidance counseling is based on the beliefs that individuals differ and that we must work with people as individuals to help them develop themselves.[6] Typically, one counselor would work with three to four hundred students, and sometimes with as many as seven hundred, assisting them in selecting courses, in choosing college or a career, in solving problems, and in evaluating each student's progress.

Guidance counseling is rooted in the same assumptions that form the basis for the human organization. At first glance, then, the guidance counselor might seem to be a part of creating a human organization. In practice, however, the guidance role has not worked well. In fact, given the number of students for whom the counselor has been responsible, the role has been an impossible one to fulfill adequately. Furthermore, the use of counselors led to a narrowing of other roles. Teachers and administrators no longer felt responsible to do the sort of things counselors were supposed to do. With the growth of the comprehensive high school, roles became more specialized and individuals resisted any tasks which fell outside their specialties. Teachers, for instance, often came to view themselves as instructors only—any tasks other than instructional or those that contribute to effective instruction were resisted by the teacher. Ironically, therefore, students in some schools received less personal attention after counselors were brought in than they received previously.

Participatory advisement demands a reversal of the trend toward role specialization. In this system, teachers are more than instructors; they assume some of the tasks now thought to belong to counselors. Administrators and counselors also have broader roles in the system. Everyone in the school—administrators, counselors, and teachers —serves as an advisor. This broadening of roles may mean some initial resistance to the system. But once implemented, the system obviously represents a superior way of attaining the goals of equal educational opportunities and individualized learning. The goals and tasks of the guidance counselor are unrealistic and unattainable in the context of one counselor for every two hundred or more students. The same goals and tasks become practical in the system of participatory advisement. The advisor role involves all personnel in a common process. Their other functions, their more specialized tasks, are likely to be complementary rather than competitive because of their common efforts as advisors.

## PARTICIPATORY ADVISEMENT AS A RESPONSE

The system of participatory advisement is an effective and comprehensive response to the challenges of equal opportunity and individualized learning. For one thing, as noted above, it modifies the specializations which have developed among high-school personnel. Second, it brings all the staff, the students, and the parents into one common process—the advisement of each student in accord with his or her individual needs and preferences. Third, the school assumes some of the characteristics of a human organization as each student and parent relates to staff members on a personal basis and each also assumes some responsibility for planning an individualized educational program. Students and their parents have more information in this system—information about the school's expectations, the options available, and standards required by the school, the local board, and the state.

Fourth, participatory advisement provides systematic and regular contact between the staff on one hand and parents and students on the other. Student progress can be evaluated regularly, and changes may be made in accord with changing interests or needs. The staff is able to keep in touch with the feelings and concerns of students and their parents, a task which is impractical for the guidance counselor who is responsible for several hundred students.

Unlike the homeroom, which professed many of the same goals as those outlined above, participatory advisement brings advisors, students, and parents into a responsive, dynamic relationship. Home and school become a decision-making unit. The educational career of each student is not only individualized at its inception, but may be modified at any time. How is all of this accomplished? The next section details the various aspects of the system.

## THE TASKS OF PARTICIPATORY ADVISEMENT

Participatory advisement involves a considerable number of tasks, but these tasks fall logically into eight categories. Other categories than those described below could have been established. The eight we have selected, however, allow a careful analysis of the system, facilitate the planning of advisor training, and provide a useful scheme for evaluating the system. The eight categories are: program planning, developing awareness of school offerings, self-assessment, parent relations/conferences, career planning/preparation, feedback and evaluation, exploring school and community issues, and developing decision-making skills.

### PROGRAM PLANNING

Program planning is the central task of participatory advisement. Most other tasks support this one or are closely related to it. As an example, good program planning is based on accurate self assessment, depends upon the development of awareness of school offerings, and is essential to effective career planning.

It is important to keep in mind that program planning is not just registration for courses. The advisor's task is to match up effectively the individual student with the curriculum that meets his or her needs and goals. Thus, program planning involves a variety of specific tasks. It may include exploration and establishment of individual goals, the clarification of expectations, and the selection and sequencing of courses. There will be periodic assessment of progress, and changes in goals can result in alterations in the individual student's plan. The overall plan, if based on a realistic assessment of the student's goals and abilities, will provide an effective guide to course selection, making registration for specific periods of instruction a relatively simple matter, and tending to eliminate whimsical, thoughtless changes in schedules.

Much of the participatory advisement support materials relate to program planning. The materials include a working copy of student records (including grade reports and test scores); guides to course selection for either college or career plans; complete course catalogs for the school, with information on the nature and time of offering of each course; graduation standards; and requirements for college entrance or for various careers. The guidance center itself is also a major resource (as will be explained in chapters 3 and 4).

A tentative high–school program, with general goals and course sequencing, should be completed sometime during the freshman or sophomore year. The plan can, of course, be refined or modified during the junior and senior years to take account of the student's actual school experience, academic progress, and any changes in goals or expectations.


## DEVELOPING AWARENESS OF SCHOOL OFFERINGS

Each student and the student's parents need access to information about the school's overall curriculum and about the various options available to students. An important part of participatory advisement is helping students to become knowledgeable about all of the school's resources—personal counseling, career and college information, administrative services, honors and awards which may be attained, library and audiovisual services, and so forth. Students also need to understand how the school works, that is, the rules and regulations of the school, the recourse students have when they believe they have not been treated fairly, and students' responsibilities in using school resources.

It may seem obvious to say that student and parent awareness of the school's offerings should be developed, but unfortunately such awareness is too often taken for granted. The awareness must be deliberately cultivated. Simply making information "available" is not sufficient. The communication that pervades the human organization will include affirmative action with respect to information about school offerings—that is, there will be a definite dissemination of the information and not merely a gathering of the information in some central location for those who wish to get it.

Furthermore, when parents and students receive full information about offerings, they are more likely to develop positive attitudes toward the school. They will see the school as a resource rather than an impersonal bureaucracy which attempts to control and manipulate them. And they will see themselves as partially responsible for decisions about the students' educational careers.

### SELF-ASSESSMENT

Adolescents are at a critical developmental stage. They may be so caught up in daily experiences that a realistic self-assessment is improbable if not impossible without some help. In participatory advisement, there is a periodic questioning of students' feelings, behavior, and academic achievement that is useful not only in devising an educational career but also in learning self-assessment. Students may not have attempted to get in touch with their own feelings and aspirations until directly questioned about them. In expressing feelings, evaluating aspirations and achievements, and making decisions about their future course, students develop the belief that they can control many aspects of their lives.

In self-assessment, students are confronted with a number of tasks:

(1) identifying interests and possible career goals;
(2) recognizing academic and social strengths and weaknesses;
(3) identifying and developing those talents that can enhance social interaction and participation in various activities such as part-time jobs or extracurricular activities;
(4) learning to set goals and evaluate progress toward those goals.

The fourth task helps students to develop a hopeful attitude toward their lives. It helps students to gain some sense of control over their destiny. Those students who have low achievement motivation have a particular need to learn the skill of setting goals and evaluating progress. Some of these students may have had frustrating experiences in school and elsewhere or they may have failed at various tasks. Participatory advisement can help such students rekindle their hopes in the context of realistic goals.

A significant aspect of self assessment is the students' access to the complete school records and the students' sharing in the work of keeping the records up to date as they build it. In examining their records, all students can find some strengths upon which to build and some guidelines for setting goals. In other words, an open record is an important tool in aiding the student to begin the habit of effective self assessment.

### PARENT RELATIONS/CONFERENCES

There has been a tendency for school and home communication to occur primarily when report cards are issued or when negative reports must be made. There have also been some general meetings at schools where information is shared with parents but where there is little or no opportunity for personal interaction with the staff. The high-school PTA is perhaps the best example of the general meeting which is ostensibly set up for the benefit of parents but which offers little opportunity for teacher/parent interaction. The experience of working in a high school that is a human organization shows that parents are far more eager to discuss their child's progress, program, and future than attendance at PTA meetings might suggest. Parents do not support the PTA because that organization does not address their concerns.

In participatory advisement, every parent is invited to a number of personal conferences during the school year. Every parent has the opportunity to meet with a teacher—the child's advisor—and personally discuss the child's progress and plans. The advisor, the parents, and the student work together as a team. In some cases, the advisor may help with communication problems between teenagers and their parents. The student may feel alienated from the parents, or may simply not have developed the habit of free communication with the parents. Advisors have often heard parents exclaim such things as, "I didn't know you wanted to go to college." Even where there is good communication, the conference is important for gathering information and for solidifying plans.

The student meets with the advisor more frequently than the parents do. Those who are having difficulty communicating with their parents may learn to relate effectively with adults in a nonjudgmental situation and later apply what they have learned to communicate with their parents. Thus, one of the potential fringe benefits of the system is that a number of students begin a new, more effective relationship with parents.

### CAREER PLANNING/PREPARATION

As with the development of awareness of school offerings, this task involves a series of efforts to communicate information about careers directly to students and their parents. Files of information, speakers who represent various careers, analyses of career requirements, and some actual career experience (in a community-based learning program) are among the means which can be used to fulfill this task.

Career planning and preparation means that the students are taught to take a long-range view of their school work. They are helped to see some links between present and future activities. Their school work is not merely something to be endured, but an important aspect of a life process.

Furthermore, career planning and preparation helps students and parents become aware of the numerous options available. Most careers are probably "invisible" to students and parents alike, in the sense that most people do not know the nature of many careers, the requirements for careers, or even the existence of certain careers (there are over 30,000 occupations listed in the *Dictionary of Occupational Titles*). Advisors will not have the expertise of a vocational counselor, but they will provide some basic information on options, including the cost and amount of post-high school education which may be necessary.

## FEEDBACK AND EVALUATION

Regular and personal contact between the advisor and students and parents allows informal feedback and any criticism of the school's program or policies to surface early. Early detection, in turn, means that severe problems are less likely to develop and grievances are less likely to accumulate. One consequence of a system that provides feedback and evaluation, therefore, is the avoidance of certain problems which could become critical and traumatic.

A second consequence of feedback and evaluation is that data are gathered on various aspects of the school, and these data comprise a base for evaluating and planning the school's program and policies. Third, advisors become knowledgeable about all areas of the school's life. This eliminates their isolation and their confinement to a narrow role; they become a major factor in the improvement of the school.

These consequences occur because the task of feedback and evaluation involves a number of activities in which both students and parents tell the staff their reactions to the school's program and policies. Some of the activities are formal, such as the parent conferences or questionnaires. Some of them are informal, such as an advisor greeting an advisee in the hall and asking "how things are" with the advisee. A sensitive advisor can pick up signs of trouble early through such informal contacts, and can guide the student into preventive behavior.

## EXPLORING SCHOOL/COMMUNITY ISSUES

This task involves various activities which allow all members of the school to discuss and to be involved in the solution of problems or issues which affect the school and the community. Among these problems and issues are those specific to the school, such as excessive vandalism, drug abuse, attendance, and intergroup conflict. In the advisement process, students and parents are made aware of their own responsibility in dealing with issues and problems that concern the school. In one situation known to the authors, all advisors were instructed to discuss with their advisees a vandalism problem that had developed. Students helped develop ideas for dealing with the problem, and through their ideas and their assumption of responsibility there was a quick cessation of the problem.

Advisement can also help students learn to live in a pluralistic society. In our school, the advisement system was the major means of preparing students for court-ordered desegregation. Students became involved with their advisors in determining specific ways to help the new students who were being bussed in to feel welcome and comfortable.

Larger community issues can also be a part of the advisement process. Students are taught to cope with diverse values and viewpoints in a rational manner. For example, the advisor might gather a group of advisees, divide them up into smaller groups of five, and have them discuss topics such as vandalism, shoplifting, police-teen relations, or drug/alcohol abuse. The advisees then regroup and evaluate the discussions. The advisor guides the process so that it is handled in a rational, tolerant fashion.

## DEVELOPING DECISION-MAKING SKILLS

Participatory advisement is a decision-making process. In order to maximize the effectiveness of the process, the student not only shares in making decisions but also learns the skills used in making decisions. Learning the skills requires the student and the advisor to deliberately step back and examine the decisions that they have made, or to engage in a session that focuses on the decision-making process, or, preferably, to do both sorts of things.

A session on the decision-making process will provide the student with a model for making decisions. Students will learn that they must state the problem clearly, specify the alternative courses of action, try to identify possible consequences of each course of action, and choose the best of the alternatives in the light of the consequences and their own goals and capacities.

Deliberately stepping back from decisions can occur in a number of ways, including a nondirective reaction to a decision which has been made or is about to be made by the student. For instance, if the student says to the advisor, "I think I'll drop math," or "I might buy a car," or anything else that suggests a decision, the advisor can help the student focus on the decison-making process. The advisor achieves this by nondirective questions, such as: "what are your alternatives?" or "what are the pluses and minuses in that choice?" or "what do you think will happen if you do that?" The aim of such questions, of course, is to help the student acquire the skills of decision-making, so that the student asks himself or herself the questions when future situations demand a decision.

## PARTICIPATORY ADVISEMENT AND THE SCHOOL YEAR

Participatory advisement actually follows the ebb and flow of the school year. The emphasis which each of the above tasks receives varies with the student's grade level and readiness for various kinds of decisions. To be maximally effective, participatory advisement should be carried out in accord with an Advisement Calendar, which sequences tasks by grade level for each month of the school year. The Calendar is a detailed handbook, given to all advisors, that identifies the tasks considered most crucial at various points in the school year. The purpose of the Calendar is to set minimal standards by identifying a basic set of advisement tasks that must be fulfilled for the well-being of students and the smooth operation of the school. The pattern of emphasis will vary from school to school, depending in part upon the particular curriculum and programs of the school.

It is important to note here that the Calendar does not make the advisor-advisee relationship as formal and rigid as it might at first appear. Once an effective participatory advisement system is implemented, many advisors and their advisees will develop close working relationships and engage in a considerable amount of informal interaction. This informal interaction may take place both in the school and in the community. The positive nature of the advisor-advisee relationship produces a natural desire for communication.

Some of the activities suggested in the calendar are best done in group settings and some are best accomplished in an individual conference. The calendar itself does not separate tasks into the two types. This issue will be addressed in the chapter on implementation, which will also describe the kinds of materials needed to support participatory advisement. (The calendar should refer explicitly to a number of other documents or materials which are necessary to achieve the various tasks.)

The calendar that follows is part of one that has been used successfully, but it should be a guide and example, not an inflexible format. In essence, the calendar contains the areas to be explored each month for each grade level. The exploration is done by means of certain questions to be asked or certain topics to be pursued.

The handbook in which the calendar is contained should also contain a certain amount of resource material. The first half of the handbook, then, is the calendar and the second half includes helpful materials which are grouped according to the eight tasks described above. For example, the first area to be explored in the calendar below is the experiences of the student prior to coming to the high school (assuming a system in which there are junior high schools through the ninth grade). This review is a part of the student's self-assessment, and may be done either individually or in a group. The calendar refers the advisor to the page on which additional help is available. The advisor will find in the self-assessment section the goal for the activity, the size of the group which can be involved, the approximate time required, and some materials that can be used. In this case, the additional materials are a series of questions about various aspects of the pre-high school experiences, such as: "What school experiences did you have in junior high that made you feel good about yourself?"; "What kinds of out-of-class activities did you participate in?"; "What kind of person was the teacher you admired most?"; and so forth.

Not every item on the calendar will have additional materials. Not every item demands extra materials. Again, each school must develop the handbook in accord with its peculiar needs. The following calendar is for the 10th grade only and does not include any extra materials, but it should be useful for understanding the nature of the advisement calendar and for devising a calendar uniquely suited to a particular school.

# 10TH GRADE CALENDAR

August/September

### Self-Assessment Activities

Let's discuss the experiences you had in school before you came to high school.

Tell me how you feel about this school.

Do you think you will have to make some adjustments this year? What kind?

Tell me about any concerns you have about being successful either with teachers or with other students.

Is there any way that I can be of help to you right now?

### Awareness of School Offerings

I would like to meet with you before school starts. We will get acquainted, find your locker, see where you can find me, and locate all the special facilities (counseling center, nurse's office, library, etc.)

### Decision-Making Skills

Let's go over the various ways to choose courses.

We need to construct a system that you can use for making decisions and put a copy of that system in your file so that it can be used in the future.

### School/Community Issues

Let's explore the kinds of things upon which this school is based, such as personal relationships, the opportunity for you to make various choices, our system of advisement, some school policies, and how we will meet with your parents to help plan your school program.

### Feedback/Evaluation

How did your registration for high school go? Could you have used some help that you didn't get?

### Program Planning

Let's get your advisement folder up-to-date so that we can start keeping some records, filing some materials, and planning your program.

We need to go over the graduation requirements.

October

### Awareness of School Offerings

Let's look at the catalog of courses. Do you know how to use this catalog to select the courses you need and want?

How can other students, teachers, and your parents be of help to you in selecting your courses?

Did you know that there is a technical school available to you? Would you be interested in it?

### Feedback/Evaluation

Do you have a chance to decide the kind of activities you do in your classes?

We are all concerned about making newcomers feel welcome here. I'd like to hear about your experiences as a new student in this school.

### Parent Relations/Conferences

Let's plan the conference we will have with your parents.

### Program Planning

Let's make a tentative schedule for next semester. Before we finalize the schedule, you can consult with teachers and with your parents.

### Career Planning/Preparation

What are your hobbies and interests?

November

### Parent Relations/Conferences

How do you feel about the conference with your parents?

### Self-Assessment

Are you participating in any extra-curricular clubs or activities?

How would you feel about asking a teacher for extra help?

Now that you have your first report card, let's think about setting some realistic goals. To do that, we need to discuss how to go about setting up goals.

### Career Planning/Preparation

Some sophomores are already beginning to think about careers, about what they will do after high school. Let's look at the kinds of help available to you in making your own decisions when you are ready for them.

Decision-Making Skills

What do you think you might be doing three years from now?

When do you think you should make decisions about your future?

Program Planning

Do you understand all the information that is on your report card?

Have you completed your plans for registration for next semester?

## December

Feedback/Evaluation

Do you feel that you can freely express your opinions in this school?

Let's discuss the way to talk to teachers.

Program Planning

We need to record the credits you have earned.

You register for your courses far in advance of the new semester. Sometimes you may want to make changes in your schedule, so let's discuss the why and how of such changes.

Do you feel the need to make any changes in your next semester's schedule?

Self-Assessment

Let's discuss the grades you received last quarter, and how you are adjusting to high school.

Let's talk about those things that might affect the grades you get in school, such as how you use your time, your study habits, your attendance and attentiveness in class, how people learn, and so forth.

In the light of your experiences in school so far, what would you list as your strengths and weaknesses?

## January

Awareness of School Offerings

Do you know the various awards given at this school, such as the National Honor Society? Let's see if there are some awards that you would like to win.

Let's discuss the student organizations in which you might want to participate.

### Self-Assessment

What does the term "self-assessment" mean to you? Let's discuss its meaning and why we are going to use it a lot during our conferences.

You have already done some self-assessment, so let's make a list of any learning and other kinds of goals you have. We'll put them into your folder and look at them again in the future.

### Feedback/Evaluation

Do you have any opportunities for helping to decide what grade you should receive in any of your classes?

## February

### Awareness of School Offerings

Let's talk about some of the special courses and alternative programs at our school. We need to think about registering for next year, and I want to be sure you know about all the choices you have.

### Program Planning

Let's make a tentative plan for the rest of your time here. What subjects do you think you would like to take in your junior and senior years?

### Parent Relations/Conference

How do you feel about planning for another conference with your parents?

### Feedback/Evaluation

Are there any courses that you would like to see added to the catalog for next year? Are you interested in something that we don't offer now?

### Decision-Making Skills

You may want to decide at some time in the near future whether to look for a part-time job. If you do feel you would like to work part-time, I have some information about how to look for a job.

## March

### School/Community Issues

We have spent some time in self-assessment, but now we ought to go beyond that and think about the community and about what "communities" you belong to.

Program Planning

Let's record the credits you earned last quarter.

Self-Assessment

How do you feel about your progress so far? What do you think about your grades?

Do you think that we are ready for our last conference with your parents? Is there anything else we should do to prepare for the conference?

Feedback/Evaluation

What do you think about the materials you use in your classes? Are they interesting? Are they up-to-date? Do they put people down at all (particularly, minority groups)?

April

Self-Assessment

How do you feel now about yourself, other people, and your school? What have you learned about yourself and others?

Do you feel that you have changed any during your sophomore year? How?

Do you feel that you are prepared now to evaluate the learning and personal goals you set for yourself last January?

Let's review your scores on the Basic Skills Examination and see how they match your achievements in school.

Decision-Making Skills

Your biggest job this year has been adjusting to school and learning self-assessment. Next year, we are going to concentrate on making decisions, and our plans will depend upon your decisions. Let's make a list of the decisions you should make next year and put the list into your folder. Next fall, we'll look at it closely.

Feedback/Evaluation

You can be of help to other students in our group by sharing with us your evaluation of your classes this year.

May

Decision-Making Skills

Have you thought about plans for the summer? Do you feel an interest in or need for summer school?

Are you interested in a summer job? Remember that I have some helpful information available.

Self-Assessment

Do you think you will have any problems this summer?

Program Planning

Let's look at your third quarter grades and record them.

Feedback/Evaluation

What bugs you the most about this school?

If you could do it, what would you change in your school?

Please complete the formal sophomore evaluation of the school.


## ADDITIONAL HANDBOOK MATERIALS: AN EXAMPLE

As pointed out above, the handbook contains not only the calendar, with monthly emphases for each grade level, but also some additional materials to be used by the advisors. We noted briefly one example of the kinds of materials to be placed into the handbook. Here we will give another—complete—example. The November calendar included an item under self-assessment about setting realistic goals. The calendar refers the advisor at that point to a later page in the handbook that contains materials for teaching students how to establish realistic goals. The task for the advisor and advisee or advisees is to learn to set goals, and the materials in the handbook suggest the following:


## GOAL SETTING FOR ADVISEES

The goal of this activity is for the advisor to learn and then teach a process of goal setting. This activity may be done with individuals or with small groups. It will require about 15 minutes, and should follow the format below.

1. *Describe a Successful Person.*
Who do you know in this area that is successful? Why is that person successful? Isn't it something that he or she does? Brainstorm for a few minutes and write down the things that would describe someone successful at achieving *your* goals. What would he or she say and do?

Write down everything that comes to your mind. For example, the successful person would—

> get better grades.
> enjoy classes more.
> learn more.
> be absent less.
> spend more time studying.

In brainstorming, you always come up with more items than you can use. Select the ones that seem especially important to you and write each one down on a separate sheet of paper.

2. *Specify.*
Some of your items are probably vague. So try to write down for each of them some more specific details about what a person does to be successful. Be as specific as you can. Exactly what does the successful person say or do? For example:

| | |
|---|---|
| Better grades | Enjoy classes more |
| Raise grades from C's to B's | Participate in class discussions |
| Get a B in math | Respond when the teacher asks a question |
| Make a grade of 80 or more on the next math test | Bring my math book home and read over each day's assignment more carefully than I have been doing |

3. *Judge and Select.*
From your final lists, select one that you feel is important and write it out as a complete statement of intent. Also, write down what you might have to do before you can achieve your goal. For example: I will bring my math book home and read over each day's assignment more carefully than I have been doing. Before I can achieve that, I might have to watch less television at night, pay more attention in math class, and be willing to ask for special help if I still have trouble understanding.

4. *Use the Hey, Jack Test.*
You want to make sure that you stated your goal in a way that you know exactly what you need to do. So use the "Hey, Jack" test. Complete this sentence by inserting the statement of your goal in it: Hey, Jack, let me show you how I can _____. If "Jack" still doesn't know

exactly what you are going to do, you need to be more specific. For example: Hey, Jack, let me show you how I can make better grades; I'm going to bring my math book home and read over each day's assignment more carefully than I have been doing. (Jack knows exactly what you will do and why you want to do it.) Another example: Hey, Jack, let me show you how I can make better grades; I'm going to try harder. (That's great, says Jack, but exactly what will you do? How will you try harder?)

## SUMMARY

Various events and developments, combined with the ideal of equality of opportunity, have resulted in an increasing proportion of the nation's teenagers remaining in school for longer periods of time. It is the demanding task of the comprehensive high school to provide a meaningful educational experience for each of these students. An initial response to the challenges of equal opportunity and individualized learning was the establishment of the guidance counselor. A more effective and comprehensive response is the system of participatory advisement.

An effective participatory advisement system demands attention to eight kinds of tasks: program planning, developing awareness of school offerings, self-assessment, parent relations/conferences, career planning/preparation, feedback and evaluation, exploring school and community issues, and developing decision-making skills. Fulfilling these tasks can best be achieved by use of an Advisement Calendar, which sequences tasks by grade level for each month of the school year. The calendar is included in a handbook that also contains monthly emphases for each grade level and other materials useful to advisors.

# Endnotes

[1] Ralph H. Turner, "Modes of Social Ascent Through Education," in R. Bendix and S. M. Lipset, eds., *Class, Status, and Power,* 2nd edition (New York: The Free Press, 1966), pp. 449–58.

[2] John W. Gardner, *Excellence* (New York: Harper & Row, 1961), p. 69.

[3] U.S. Department of Commerce, *Social Indicators 1976* (Washington, D.C.: U.S. Government Printing Office, 1977), p. 304.

[4] Douglas H. Heath, *Humanizing Schools: New Directions, New Decisions* (New York: Hayden Book Company, Inc., 1971), p. 161.

[5] William Alexander, J. Galen Saylor and Emmett L. Williams, *The High School: Today and Tomorrow* (New York: Holt, Rinehart and Winston, Inc., 1971), p. 221.

[6] Rudyard K. Bent, Henry H. Kroneberg and Charles C. Boardman, *Principles of Secondary Education,* 6th edition (New York: McGraw-Hill 1970), p. 380.

# Chapter 2

# Implementing Participatory Advisement

There is an old story about a Scottish theologian who declared, "God grant that I may always be right, for I never change." The tale illustrates the common belief that people invariably resist change. As Walter Bagehot expressed it, "One of the greatest pains to a human nature is the pain of a new idea."[1] More recent observers have called social change such things as an "ordeal," a "crisis," and a "foreign and unwanted agent."[2]

There is, of course, ample evidence to support the argument that people resist change. We now regard the automobile as virtually indispensable to our way of life, but when automobiles first appeared in a small Missouri town they were resented as ostentatious, as impractical, as extravagant, as immoral "for people to own and run," as dangerous to people who drove them and to people and beasts obliged to meet them on the roads, as "just a passing fad," and as a threat to the value of horses and the market for grain sold as horse feed.[3]

Nevertheless, the idea that people *inherently* resist change is a fiction. It should not be forgotten that in every instance where some group of people is resisting change there is another group promoting that change. Furthermore, there is some evidence that people tend to

52

be dissatisfied when there is too much stability, that is, too little change, in their social environments.[4] Given the proper conditions, people not only accept but find satisfaction in change.

The above perspective on change is important as a basis for dealing with the problem of implementing a participatory advisement system. There may be resistance to the system, but not because there is something about humans that inherently resists change. What is needed is a proper perspective on change, an understanding of organizational change in general and educational change in particular, and a practical program of implementation. We have already established our perspective. In the remainder of the chapter, we will discuss the problems of organizational change and examine in some detail a program of implementation.

## ORGANIZATIONAL CHANGE

Implementing a participatory advisement system (or, for that matter, any new program) is a complex and challenging undertaking which will require considerable planning and an understanding of the change process. Organizational change has certain characteristics which are independent of the particular kind of organization involved; therefore, while the information below is derived from studies of industries, hospitals, and social service agencies as well as from schools, it is all applicable to the educational organization.

## CHANGE AS A MULTISTAGE PROCESS

Planned change in an organization is a process that has a number of stages. There are somewhat differing demands and problems that will be encountered at each stage. Successful implementation of a new program requires a sensitivity to the unique aspects of each stage as well as to the demands and problems common to the stages.

Various researchers have offered a number of models of organizational change. The model that appears most useful to us, that of Zaltman, Duncan, and Holbek,[5] posits two major stages and five substages in the process of organizational innovation (Figure 2.1). Some would add other stages such as evaluation and/or renewal. We regard renewal, however, as either an ongoing task in the final substage of maintaining implementation (or routinization) or a new process of change involving all of the stages and substages. Similarly, evaluation is an ongoing task at every phase of the change. We could well write the word "evaluation" next to each stage and substage to highlight its

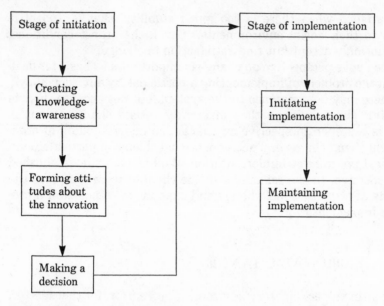

**Figure 2.1**
The Zaltman, Duncan and Holbek Model of the Innovation Process in Organizations. From Gerald Zaltman, Robert Duncan, and Jonny Holbek, *Innovations & Organizations* (New York: John Wiley & Sons, 1973), pp. 58–70. Reprinted by permission of John Wiley & Sons, Inc.

critical importance. In spite of the significance of evaluation, it is often neglected in the process of educational innovation. In his comprehensive review of innovations in education, Matthew Miles noted that "a near-axiomatic statement is this: Educational innovations are almost *never* evaluated on a systematic basis."[6] The reason for the lack of evaluation, he says, is that the innovators *know* that the changes they advocate are the best possible ones under the circumstances. Evaluation, they feel, is really superfluous. An unfortunate consequence of the neglect of evaluation is that some potentially useful innovations have been abandoned before they were given a fair and reasonable trial, while some poor innovations have been adopted and have persisted for decades.

Briefly, the innovation process involves the following stages and substages. First, the initation stage includes all activities up to the point of implementing the innovation. The first substage, "knowledge-awareness," reminds us that members of the organization who will be affected by the innovation need to become aware of its potential usefulness. Awareness may come about in various ways, but in a human organization that awareness does not come *after* the decision to adopt the innovation has been formalized. Of course, not every member of the organization needs to be aware of the innovation at this initial point. Those people in the organization who would be particularly influential in successfully implementing an innovation, however, should acquire their knowledge in the initial substage.

The second substage involves the formation of attitudes about the innovation. Rational consideration of a proposed innovation (and a relatively smooth implementation of an innovation) will be facilitated by such attitudes as openness, flexibility, optimism, and the willingness to make a commitment to success. We will show below some of the steps that can maximize such attitudes among the school's staff.

The third substage under initiation includes evaluating information about the innovation and making a decision to accept or reject. This substage requires maximum information if the decision is to be a rational one, and effective channels of communication if the organization is to be participatory.

If the decision is to accept, we enter the implementation stage. In the initial substage, there is the first attempt to make use of the innovation. In many cases, this implementation will be on a trial basis, and only a portion of the organization will be involved. In other cases, the innovation demands involvement of the total organization, though it still may be attempted on a trial basis. The second substage, that of maintaining implementation (routinization), warns that the necessity of meeting demands, facing problems, and making decisions will continue after the innovation has been adopted.

## INITIATING CHANGE

The above discussion of the stages of change implies that someone or some group is actively attempting to introduce an innovation. Who is it that sets in motion the stage of initiation? Answers will vary depending upon the kind of organization, the setting, the nature of the innovation, and other factors. But in the case of educational organizations, administrators play a crucial role.

In a study of people involved in a national program to train teachers for low-income schools (the Teacher Corps program), Corwin found that administrators were very important in the successful implementation of innovations in schools.[7] Schools were more likely to change when the higher administrators introduced the innovation and pressed for its acceptance. This does not mean that administrators bring about the change by fiat. It does mean that the administrators must be committed, knowledgeable, and enthusiastic about the potential benefits of the innovation.

We use the term "administrators" somewhat loosely here, to indicate not only administrators of the local school, but also those in the superintendent's office and those who are members of the school board. All of these groups are important bases of support for innovations. Indeed, it is this structure of education that underlies the fact that educational change "typically generates from outside rather than from within."[8] It is not incompetence or apathy or weakness that accounts for educators proclaiming the virtues of change even while failing to bring it about in their own organizations. Rather, educators work within the context of a set of roles and an institutional system that minimizes incentives to innovation:

> Schools are social agencies, created and maintained to achieve social purposes. What such purposes are, and the priorities assigned to each, are defined by majority opinion. In practice, representatives selected by the majority (school board and trustee members) interpret constituency goals and attitudes into educational objectives, programs, and in many situations, even instructional procedures. Educational personnel are employed to follow the prescriptions.[9]

Some of the initial work of innovating, therefore, may have to be done among the groups who have responsibility in the administration of the school's programs and policies. The innovation may first have to be sold to the administrators, a task that may require the use of external resources (accounts of the success of the innovation in other schools, the use of consultants, and so forth). External resources can be most helpful and may, in fact, be necessary throughout the change process. Among the schools he studied, Corwin found that external resources—cooperative university personnel, high regard for those resources, and the perceived quality of the relationship between the schools and the universities—were among the most important factors in explaining the differing rates of innovation.[10]

In sum, although anyone or any group may become aware of an innovation and suggest its consideration, the commitment of administrators must be secured very early in the change process. External resources may be important in gaining such commitment and will be useful to administrators throughout the stages of initiation and implementation.

## THE NATURE OF RESISTANCE

It is unlikely that an innovation can be introduced into an organization without resistance appearing among some members. It is important to understand the sources of that resistance. We have already dismissed the notion that it is human nature to resist change. If it were human nature to resist change, very little change would occur. Yet it is commonly agreed that we live in an era of rapid change, and that there have been a considerable number of changes in the field of education (including new types of buildings, curricular changes, and the introduction of new methods such as team teaching and programmed instruction). Obviously, there are a lot of people who are promoting and implementing change.

At the same time, there are obviously many examples of resistance to change. If it is not human nature to resist change, what is it? We can also dismiss the notion that it is particular categories of people—males, females, older members, or less educated members—who will be the source of resistance. A study of 20 schools in the San Francisco Bay area concluded that such individual characteristics as sex, age, satisfaction with career, and education were not useful as predictors of leaders in organizational change.[11]

What, then, is the nature of resistance? There are some individuals like the committee member who said, "As long as I'm a member, there'll be no unanimous decisions." But generally we will find reasonable bases for resistance—reasonable, that is, when we understand the way in which those who resist perceive the situation. The only effective way to cope with resistance is to understand the reasonable bases upon which it rests.

There are a variety of reasons why people resist change.[12] Generally, people will resist change perceived to be:

(1)  an economic threat or liability;
(2)  ambiguous or obscure in terms of the meaning of the changes for the structure and functioning of the organization;
(3)  imposed upon them;
(4)  too risky, in the sense that the potential negative consequences far outweigh the potential benefits;
(5)  of too little benefit to go through the inconvenience of discarding the old ways for the new;
(6)  a threat to existing interpersonal relationships;
(7)  a threat to self-concepts;
(8)  incongruous with existing values and/or ideologies;
(9)  a threat to individual status and power.

Consider the following example from a business setting.[13]

In 1968, the management of a national concern introduced an employee motivation program into its warehouse operations. An outside evaluation a few months later concluded that the motivation program failed to produce the anticipated results. Furthermore, the evaluation contradicted an earlier assessment by the plant manager. The manager was given the report and asked for additional information in order to resolve the contradictions. But the manager replied that no more information would be given and insisted that no one else see the report. The program continued, even though the evaluation indicated that it was ineffective.

According to the evaluation, changes needed to be made in the program. The plant manager resisted any such changes because he "was ideologically committed to the underlying principles of the motivation program and was active in introducing it into the plant's operations."[14] The manager's resistance grew directly out of his psychological investment in the program.

An example of resistance in an educational setting involves a new principal in a high school who decided to introduce a more centralized guidance program.[15] Since the faculty had the reputation of being guidance oriented, the principal expected the change (which he defined as desirable) would be easily implemented. In essence, the change meant that a number of activities—handling certain problems of students and advising students on colleges and academic programs—were removed from teachers' responsibility and placed under administrative control. Although newer teachers approved the change, the bulk of the more experienced teachers disliked the new system and made as little use of it as possible.

There were a number of reasons why the more experienced teachers resisted the change, one of the most important being that the teacher's classroom role was changed by the new system. The old role reflected a belief that a good teacher can handle his or her own problems. The values of independent and self-dependent action by the teacher were violated under the new arrangement. Furthermore, some alterations in patterns of interpersonal relationships were demanded by the new system.

In other words, the teachers resisted for a number of the reasons we have listed above. Even though they were committed to the notion of guidance, and even though the principal believed that the new system would enhance the effectiveness of guidance, the program was resisted because it contradicted certain values and ideologies, threatened existing interpersonal relationships, and posed some threat to the self-concept of the experienced teachers.

Similarly, resistance to a participatory advisement system can be expected for various reasons. Initially, counselors may see the system as a threat to their status and power; teachers may see the system as too risky, as involving a considerable amount of extra work with questionable benefits, and so on. The point is that those who want to implement the change must deal with resistance realistically. That means that they must see the real bases upon which resistance is built, and not dismiss the resisters as a group of unthinking recalcitrants.

One other point about resistance must be made—the kind of resistance encountered will vary with each stage or substage of the innovation process. Zaltman, Duncan, and Holbek provide some detail on the kinds of resistance which tend to appear throughout the process and the kinds that tend to appear in particular phases.[16] For example, they note a case of passive resistance at the implementation stage that resulted from an attempt by administrators to bypass participation in the initiation stage. In this case, a number of school principals ordered simulation games for use in classes. The games were either neglected or used halfheartedly. The teachers said they tried to use the games, but found them ineffectual. Many of the principals decided to abandon the innovative method. The passive resistance of the teachers effectively stopped the innovation. And the resistance was rooted, in part, in the failure to include the teachers in the decision-making process.

## THE HUMAN APPROACH

The characteristics of the human organization which we detailed in the introduction are associated not only with higher productivity but also with successful change efforts. A few examples will illustrate this assertion. First, in a survey of industrial and business organizations, Greiner found a number of similarities among those that successfully implemented planned change.[17] He notes that different approaches can be used to introduce change into the organization—the unilateral, the shared, and the delegated approaches. The unilateral is change by the exercise of authority, the kind attempted by the principals in the case of simulation games noted above. The delegated approach involves the giving of most responsibility for the change to subordinates; it can amount to the virtual abrogation of leadership. The shared approach, which emphasizes group decision making and problem solving, is the approach that characterizes human organizations. It is also the approach, Greiner found, that was used by those organizations that were most successful in introducing change.

In addition to the sharing of power and responsibility, other characteristics of the human organization are the building of confidence and trust and the setting of high goals to which members commit themselves. The importance of such qualities for successful change is illustrated in an experiment reported by King that was conducted in four manufacturing plants.[18] Certain problems had arisen in the plants which could have been ameliorated by changing the work patterns of the employees. Two such changes were proposed—job enlargement and job rotation. In two plants, the managers were told that the changes would increase productivity. In the other two plants, managers were told that the aim was to improve employee relations. During the experimental period, output increased at the two plants where the managers expected higher productivity, demonstrating, says King, that expectations were more important in the outcomes than the innovation. That is, the innovation per se did not bring about the desired results; only when the innovation was implemented in the context of certain anticipations was the change successful. Thus, the creation of high goals and the building of confidence in the achievement of those goals are seen to be crucial aspects of successful change.

We have also emphasized the importance of communication in the human organization. A study by Gross, Giacquinta and Bernstein of unsuccessful innovation at the elementary school level underscores the importance of bilateral communication.[19] The administrator, according to the researchers, made two fundamental mistakes. First, there was no attempt to anticipate and discuss the problems that teachers would encounter when they tried to implement the innovation. Second, there was no system of feedback so that problems could be monitored during implementation and dealt with through shared discussion and decision making. As a result, the innovation was not successfully implemented even though the teachers had been favorable toward it initially.

There is one additional observation that is quite important. We have stressed the point that there is a sharing of power and responsibility in the human organization. "Sharing" does not, of course, imply that all members have equal power and responsibility, but that all have *some* share. The amount of power exercised by any particular role within a human organization can vary from one organization to another and from one situation to another. It is important to recognize this factor because a good deal of research shows that there are different requirements for the exercise of authority at the different stages of the change process. In essence, the initiation stage is more successful when there is maximum sharing of power, responsibility, and information, while the implementation stage demands a greater exercise of administrative authority and control for success.[20] The human approach to change involves flexibility, not rigidity, in organizational roles.

CONCLUSION: PRINCIPLES OF CHANGE

The above discussion implies a number of basic principles that must be followed in any effort at organizational change. We can summarize these in terms of four key words: participation, definition, identification, and expectations. Each word symbolizes an important principle of change.

*Participation* stresses the fact that people who are affected by the change should participate in the decision-making process. Such participation is important not only to maximize the well-being of those people but also to maximize their commitment to the change. Classic social psychological studies by Kurt Lewin showed that people are much more likely to change their behavior when they participate in the decision-making process related to the change.[21] Similarly, studies of classroom innovations have shown that teachers who participated in planning the change are much more likely to accept the innovation than those who did not participate.[22]

*Definition* refers to the fact that the change must be defined as desirable from the point of view of those affected by the change. This fact demands that we attend to the various bases for resistance, try to anticipate the kinds of resistance that will develop, and address concerns early in the process of change. An administrator will have to show, for example, that the change is congruent with the values and interests of all parties, that it is not too risky or costly, and so forth. Each group must see that the change is valuable for *them* as well as for the school as a whole and for other groups in the school. Teachers will be interested in a change that benefits students, but at some point they must also see that it benefits them as well.

*Identification* means that key people must be identified, people who will be particularly important if the change is to succeed. Studies of the diffusion and adoption of innovations show the importance of "change agents" and "opinion leaders." The change agent is the individual or individuals attempting to bring about the change. Administrators will normally be the change agents in schools. To be effective, they must be committed, knowledgeable, and enthusiastic about the innovation and its benefits. The opinion leader is the person whose opinion is valued by his or her peers and who, therefore, will be influential in getting people to adopt or reject the innovation. Interpersonal influence is very important in the fate of any innovation. In one case, among the reasons that new audio-visual methods were rejected by a number of teachers in some elementary schools were: friends didn't use them; the principal didn't seem to really care if they were used; and other teachers had made negative remarks about them.[23] Interpersonal channels of influence are an essential tool for change. Opinion leaders need to be identified and sold on the innovation.

*Expectations,* finally, refers to the fact that the attitudes of change agents are of prime importance. An expert in business organizations puts it this way:

> Another attitude that gets staff men into trouble is the *expectation* that all the people involved will resist the change. It is curious but true that the staff man who goes into his job with the conviction that people are going to resist any idea he presents with blind stubbornness is likely to find them responding just the way he thinks they will. The process is clear: whenever he treats the people who are supposed to buy his ideas as if they were bullheaded, he changes the way they are used to being treated; and they *will* be bullheaded in resisting *that* change![24]

Those who expect cooperation, understanding, and success are more likely to get it. We do not mean to be Pollyannas at this point. It is true that any effort at change is likely to involve difficulties, and the change agent must expect to confront obstacles, but the agent must also expect to overcome those obstacles and, ultimately, to be successful. And in the course of attaining that success, the agent should expect people to be generally open, understanding, and willing to cooperate. To go at the business of change as though people were, by nature, going to resist and criticize at every point is to weigh the odds in favor of failure.

## INITIATING PARTICIPATORY ADVISEMENT

In the remainder of this chapter, we will use some of the above insights to discuss the initiation and implementation of participatory advisement. We will also show the practicality of the system by providing details of various tasks involved in initiation and implementation. One of the first tasks is the gathering of information that will be necessary for creating knowledge-awareness, developing positive attitudes, and providing a sound basis for rational evaluation.

### GATHERING INFORMATION

Participatory advisement is a challenging innovation because it requires that all individuals in the high school alter their roles to some degree. New relationships must be developed within the staff and among the staff, students, and parents. Generally, teachers and administrators have had little if any specific preparation for many of the important advisement responsibilities. In such a situation, we would expect a certain amount of doubt and anxiety to arise. The task of gathering information must be designed to address the doubts and anxieties of those who will be affected by the proposed innovation. In essence, the information should identify problematic areas, show how they can be resolved by the new system, and point out the practicality and the benefits of the new system.

To facilitate the gathering of information, a broad, representative committee should be established. The committee will collect and analyze information and report its findings to the faculty and interested parents and students. Included in the important information gathered by the committee are needs and problems perceived by all the relevant groups—administrators, teachers, students, and parents. The committee can also identify what it believes to be appropriate goals in the problem areas. The committee may report, for example, that only 40% of the students at the school feel that they get insufficient help in selecting courses and planning for a career, whereas the committee believes that at least 85% ought to feel that they receive sufficient help in these areas.

Administrators play an important role in any change effort. Consequently, both prior to and during the committee's work administrators should talk with individuals and small groups informally. These informal talks provide administrators with the opportunity to express concern about the needs and aspirations of teachers and to express a conviction that the school can improve. For instance, small groups of faculty members could be invited to an informal meeting to talk about the "ideal school." Such gatherings manifest the sharing of power and responsibility; they maximize participation in the change process.

## THE SOURCES OF INFORMATION

A certain amount of information may already be available. The school may have previously conducted a survey of teacher, student, or parent attitudes. The ACT college aptitude examination reports student satisfaction with eleven aspects of school life and compares local results with state and national scores.

Most of the information will probably have to be collected by conducting surveys. The value of the surveys will be maximized if careful consideration is given beforehand to the kind of information desired. In turn, the kind of information desired may be determined by having the committee formulate a set of statements or questions that reflect important issues, problems, goals, and concerns. The committee would want, among other things, information to answer the following questions:

1.  What access do students have to information about themselves, their records, their options in the educational process?
2.  What help is given students in planning for career and educational choices?
3.  How is the curriculum changed and who can and should influence such changes?
4.  What is the state of interpersonal relationships in the school in terms of how much understanding, caring, and helping occurs?
5.  What percentage of students and parents use various counseling services and how are counselors viewed by students and parents?
6.  What kind of relationships do parents tend to have with the school?
7.  What kind of contacts do parents have with the school throughout the year?
8.  Who are the primary decision-makers in the school, and who participates in various kinds of decisions?
9.  What mechanisms exist for regular evaluation of the school program and climate?

It is important to keep in mind that such questions must be answered in terms of the perceptions of all involved groups while being attentive to any objective measures that might apply. As an example, the committee might be able to specify the process by which curriculum changes are made, a process that includes the potential for student initiation of some changes. But this is not to say that students do initiate any changes, and if, in fact, 90% of the students believe they have no voice in shaping the curriculum, a problem exists because the perceptions contradict the actual policy (or the actual policy is subverted by the behavior of the staff). Problem areas frequently involve conflicting perceptions of the situation or ignorance of the perceptions of others. We need information on the perceptions of all concerned groups, therefore, in order make a rational decision about an innovation and to implement that innovation if it is adopted.

The surveys need not be complicated, but they should be preceded by careful thought and planning. The questionnaires used in the surveys should secure the desired information without burdening the respondents with unnecessary or irrelevant questions. Generally, the most useful and simplest questionnaire is one that uses a series of statements with Likert-type responses (the responses range from strongly agree to strongly disagree). The following are some statements that should be useful to most schools (in this task, as in all tasks, each school needs to act in accord with its own particular situation, which will include both typical and unique elements).

From a student questionnaire:

1. The teachers in this school like me.
2. The principals of this school are helpful to students.
3. I know what the teachers want me to do.
4. The assignments given in my class are dumb.
5. Our teachers like to help us.
6. Someone in this school knows me well and would help me with a problem.
7. Parents take a real interest in their children's school work.
8. I get enough help picking the courses that are right for me.
9. Our teachers really care about the students.

From a parent questionnaire:

1. Parent-student-advisor meetings are useful and productive.
2. This school helps parents understand how their children are doing.
3. Teachers are concerned about their students.
4. This school gives attention to the individual differences and the needs of my child.
5. My child's curriculum is not well planned.
6. My child is positive about school.

From a teacher questionnaire:

1. Students' attitudes and values should not be a major concern of teachers.
2. The faculty here quite often exchange ideas on curriculum and method.
3. The community served by this school is truly interested in the school system.
4. Student behavior is acquired in the home and there is little the teacher can do to alter it.
5. Communication between teachers and administrators is well developed and well maintained.
6. Students receive adequate help in setting up a useful curriculum.

Both before and after the questionnaires are used, it will be helpful to discuss the items with parents, students, and a few faculty members who are not on the committee. No matter how carefully a questionnaire is constructed, the various statements will have somewhat different meanings to different individuals. Before administering the survey, therefore, the committee should pretest the questionnaire on a few members of each of the recipient groups. After the survey is complete and the results tabulated, the committee may find it helpful to discuss the meaning of the results with members of the groups. Such consultation with representatives of the various groups of respondents will facilitate a valid analysis.

## FORMING ATTITUDES AND MAKING A DECISION

The key to the quality of any school program and to the successful implementation of change is the attitude of the faculty. If positive attitudes toward the innovation are to develop among the faculty, there must be open communication and participation in the decision-making process. Certain kinds of resistance are likely to emerge that can be dealt with at this early phase of the innovation process. For instance, some teachers will see the participatory advisement system as incongruous with their ideology. Academically oriented teachers, in particular, may view the system as an intrusion upon their proper roles. As one teacher expressed it: "Anything that takes away from the time I have for teaching is unacceptable." Such objections, which usually stem from a genuine commitment to the teaching role, need to be dealt with openly in the early phases of change.

One process that has been used successfully to deal with conflicting points of view and build consensus is "We Agree," which was developed by the Institute for the Development of Educational Activities. The object of the "We Agree" process is to develop a set of long-range goals or beliefs that every member of a group accepts. The process searches for the highest level of agreement among group members. If one person in a group cannot commit himself or herself at some level to a statement of belief or a goal, the statement is disregarded.

The "We Agree" process is relatively easy to use (although the carrying out of the process may involve considerable debate), and consists of the following steps:

1. Divide the faculty into groups of six to eight. Include representatives from parents, students, and the administration in the groups.
2. Select from the faculty certain individuals to serve as group leaders and train them in their roles as leaders.
3. Establish a time, ideally a full day (or a series of meetings after school or a number of half-days) when the entire faculty can participate. Explain the "We Agree" process to the faculty before beginning.

4. Each small group begins by getting members acquainted with each other, building trust among them.
5. Each person in the group submits statements expressing his or her idea of an ideal school. The entire group must agree on each statement. This means that the statements should express principles rather than specifics. For example, a group might state, "Students should have some choice in their program," rather than, "Students should have free choice in one half of their courses."
6. Each group submits its list to a small group of three or four people who will consolidate all the lists into one master list of principles.
7. The composite list of "We Agree" statements is given to each group for approval. If a statement is not acceptable, the group may reach consensus by qualifying the statement until the highest level of agreement is reached. While a group might not accept the principle that all students should have some choice in their program, they may accept a modification that says, "Students who have reached appropriate levels of maturity should have some choice of courses."
8. The results of all the groups are sent again to the small group for consolidation.
9. The final consolidation is presented to the total faculty for acceptance. This master list should be printed, distributed, and used as a reference for later discussion and decision making.

There are a number of other steps which can be taken to prepare the staff for making a decision about whether to adopt the advisement system. We have already noted, in addition to the "We Agree" process, the sharing of information gathered in the surveys, informal discussion groups, and the overt, positive support of administrators. Further information may be gathered by visiting schools where an effective advisement system is in operation. Such visits are most useful when the visiting team is composed of a teacher, administrator, board of education member, parent, and counselor. All viewpoints will thus be represented and will share in the evaluation.

Finally, a report to the faculty should be prepared, including recommendations for action. The report should achieve a number of objectives. First, it should answer immediate concerns and anxieties of the faculty. Second, it should deal with any perceived roadblocks to implementation. Third, it should clearly state the decisions that need to be made and show how the faculty will participate in them. Finally, it should present the system as practical and as appropriate to meet the needs and achieve the goals of the particular school.

Obviously, the report anticipates and deals with objections and problems. Some of these will have already been voiced through surveys and discussion groups; some will arise during the course of implementation. Anticipating problems during implementation can be facilitated by careful consideration of decisions that need to be made prior to and during the implementation stage. We will detail these in the next section. Here we want to recognize the fact that some staffs may decide that the system is not adaptable to their situation or that other changes need to be made prior to the adoption of participatory advisement. Nevertheless, we are convinced that the system will greatly benefit any school, and that given proper preparation and strong administrative support, most schools will decide to accept the innovation. In any case, we will assume that a decision to adopt has been made. We are now ready for the stage of implementation.

## IMPLEMENTING PARTICIPATORY ADVISEMENT

Some researchers on organizational change have considered their analysis complete at the point of the decision to accept or reject an innovation. But a decision to adopt does not insure successful implementation. We have already noted cases where innovations failed during the implementation stage. It takes more than good intentions to implement change successfully. The philosopher Kierkegaard tells of a friendly fireman in a small town who was well loved by the residents. When a large fire broke out one day, the townspeople gathered at the scene, each shooting small streams of water from a water pistol at the fire. They explained that out of their love for the fireman they had each come to do their small part. The fireman sent them away, telling them that they were no help at all, for the situation demanded more than well-meaning people each doing their own little part. The good intentions that reputedly pave the road to hell also adorn the roads to ineptitude and failure. Successful implementation of innovations demands careful planning and hard work. The planning and work revolve about a number of decisions that must be made about people, time, space, and resources.

## DECISIONS ABOUT PEOPLE

WHO WILL BE ADVISORS?    It is possible to use all professional people in the school, or selected individuals or groups, or individuals who volunteer. In a participatory advisement system, all professional staff members serve as advisors. This distributes the advisement load equitably and secures the commitment of the entire staff to the success of the program. Furthermore, there are a number of other benefits:

1. All members of the staff share a common role and experience in addition to their specialized roles.
2. All staff members, students, and parents have the opportunity to relate to each other on a personal basis. In participatory advisement, everyone has someone who knows him or her personally.
3. To function as an advisor demands a knowledge of the school's total program and its effectiveness with individuals. When staff members acquire such knowledge, they are better able to participate in evaluation and share in decision-making processes with administrators.
4. Factors such as academic specialization that tend to isolate teachers from each other are mitigated somewhat. In fact, the specialization of each teacher becomes a valuable resource to other teachers in their role as advisors, thereby increasing staff interdependence.
5. Personal growth occurs through the development of advisement skills. The advisement role prevents people from functioning narrowly as administrators, teachers, or counselors and transforms them into those who must function in the broader and more powerful role of educator.

In addition to being deprived of the above benefits, the school that uses only a portion of the faculty as advisors will run the risk of experiencing some diviseness, a loss of morale, and, eventually, a retreat into the traditional pattern of narrow roles. No advisement task is beyond the capability of a trained, professional educator as long as the necessary time, resources, and support are provided. To establish a participatory advisement system, therefore, it should be clear from the outset that total staff participation is the goal.

WHO ARE THE ADVISEES?   Obviously, all students are advisees. During the first phase of implementation, however, there are other options. Some schools may elect to begin with one or two grade levels (this is a way of instituting an innovation on a trial basis). If this method is used, the faculty can also be phased into the system. Some faculty members would function immediately as advisors. The rest would be "stand-by" advisors, who would help develop needed materials and support services until all students become advisees. If the decision is to make all students advisees immediately, there is the option of initially assigning advisees to advisors by grade level. Multi-grade assignments would be made only after the advisors have had the opportunity to focus on a particular grade. Regardless of the options selected, the goal is to provide each student and his or her parents with a continuing relationship with one advisor (or perhaps more if reassignment is necessary or requested) throughout the school years. This insures continuity in program planning, the exploration of career and college options, and communication with parents.

Although it is possible to phase in the system, there are some distinct advantages to including all staff members and all students from the outset. First, total implementation insures that all persons and groups share responsibility for the successful operation of the system. Second, administrative procedures are simplified by having the entire school participate. Third, students in the upper grades can be useful in evaluating the program, identifying helpful activities, and aiding in the production of materials. Seniors, for example, may be acutely aware of mistakes they have made or of help that would have been timely.

HOW ARE ADVISEES ASSIGNED?   Ideally, students and parents should be able to choose the advisor, selecting a faculty member that they feel will understand them best and give them the help they need. Practically, this is not possible, though the goal of having an understanding and helpful advisor is possible. The following procedure is relatively easy to administer and will insure an equitable distribution while allowing for a certain number of requested assignments.

Prior to entering high school, the student and the parents are asked to name a person or a number of persons they would prefer. If they do not know anyone by name, or if the person they designate is not available, they will be assigned an advisor. To aid in such an assignment, the student and parents should indicate any criteria which they regard as important—sex, age, academic or outside interests of the advisor. After the system is operating for a few years, a greater number of students and parents will request advisors by name. In relatively stable communities, an advisor might find himself or herself getting advisees who are the younger brothers and sisters of former advisees. Parents in such instances will have a continuing personal and secure relationship with the school that can be very meaningful.

After students complete a semester or a year, they and their parents should have the opportunity to request a change in advisor assignment. This will, of course, increase the administrative workload, but it will also increase the chances that all students and parents will establish an effective relationship with the school. Forms, such as that shown in Figure 2.2, can be used not only to facilitate the administrative task but also to remind staff and students of the necessary limitations involved in making a change of advisor.

## ADVISOR CHANGE

Student_____ Student Number_____

Grade_____

A student may change advisors a maximum of one time a year. There are two times during the school year when this can take place:

(1) between December 1 and Christmas vacation
(2) between May 1 and the end of the school year.

Changing advisors at any other time must be approved by an administrator.

Use the following procedure to change advisors:

*Step 1*
  1. Select a staff member with whom you would like to work as an advisor.
  2. Talk with the person and obtain approval. No advisor can admit more than 22.

_____
Signature of teacher

*Step 2*
Obtain approval of present advisor.

_____
Signature of advisor

*Step 3*
  1. After getting the above signatures, give this form to the registrar so that records can be changed. The change is not made until this step is completed.
  2. Ask your present advisor to send your advisor folder to your new advisor.

**Figure 2.2**
Sample Change-of-Advisor Form

The above procedure would allow most students, at least in their last two or three years, to have the advisor of their choice. In some instances, advisors may request that a student be reassigned. These instances will probably be rare, but advisors should not continue a relationship if it does not seem productive or if it has become a source of frustration.

WHO COORDINATES AND PROVIDES LEADERSHIP FOR THE PARTICIPATORY ADVISEMENT SYSTEM ON AN ONGOING BASIS?   Certainly, the principal should be an advisor and at the same time act as a primary facilitator of the program. In addition, the principal should have a representative group of teachers and counselors who will comprise an advisement leadership group. This group can meet regularly in order to identify any problems that arise, develop ways of coping with those problems, identify needed support services and materials, find ways of positively reinforcing advisors, and give direction to evaluation efforts.

A number of important consequences will flow from the work of the advisement leadership group. For one thing, the group can keep vested interests of particular roles from competing with advisement or subverting the goals of the advisement system. Second, the group will help the particular functions of administrators, counselors, and teachers to develop in complementary rather than antagonistic ways. Third, the group will make available a broad range of viewpoints and resources for resolving problems as they arise.

The existence of the group does not relieve the principal of primary responsibility for the system. The organizational structure of the high school means that the principal's role has a significant impact on the functioning of the rest of the staff. The principal might consider making a special effort to encourage advisors by giving them positive feedback whenever possible. Any kind of positive information that comes from students or other staff members should be passed on to the individual. The feedback may be brief, such as: "Your advisee, Mary, told me in the lunchroom today that you have really helped her make up her mind about trying for nursing school"; or "You must be doing some good work with Joe; he told me that he made the honor roll for the first time"; or "Your advisee, John, was given detention today for skipping classes. But he told me you had talked with him about his attendance and he seemed to be worried that you would be disappointed. I think he really cares about your opinion of him." Even a little such feedback will foster enthusiasm, and enthusiasm will enhance the sense of a personal relationship between advisor and advisee.

WHAT WILL COUNSELORS DO?    Initially, it may appear that the advisement system undercuts the work of counselors. The system will have a significant impact on counselors and the services they provide, but it will enhance rather than detract from their role. Because the possibilities for counselors are so significant, the entire next chapter will discuss their role. We will show that the advisement system frees counselors to focus on preventive rather than crisis-oriented counseling programs. In other words, counselors will have time to do some things for which they were trained but have not had time to do in most high schools.

## DECISIONS ABOUT TIME

What are the temporal implications of participatory advisements for the typical school day? The traditional high school provided time for group activities, primarily through "home room" plans. Most home room programs have come and gone, primarily because they were viewed as mere conveniences, or because they did not have well-defined activities planned, or because they tended to be one-way systems of communication. The home room was often used to make administrative announcements, to give standardized tests provided by counselors, and to conduct elections for student government. But the home room did not provide for student and parent participation in decision making, program planning, or school evaluation. Home rooms have not been, for the most part, participatory either in design or in practice.

The traditional home room and group advisory programs in high schools may have been more effective and lasting had the activities for them been organized around the participatory advisement concept. Certainly, many of the activities outlined in the previous chapter can be conducted in group settings. An advisor can even find time on occasion for short individual conferences in the group situation.

Nevertheless, the group approach cannot fulfill the goals of participatory advisement—to focus on the individual and provide time for both individual conferences and group activities. The personal relationship that develops in the individual conference brings a human touch into the system that is lacking in the group approach.

Given the value of the individual focus, however, the question of the temporal practicality of the system remains. Is participatory advisement feasible in terms of the daily schedule? The following plan has been used in several high schools and can be modified to suit any particular school setting. The plan allots each advisor two hours each week for conducting individual conferences. It is based upon the traditional six period per day class schedule.

First, the faculty is organized into 15 advisement teams, each team consisting of members from various subject areas.[25] Counselors and administrators also belong to various teams. Second, three teams are assigned to each day of the week. For example, Monday would be advisement day for teams A, B, and C; Tuesday would be advisement day for teams D, E, and F; and so on. With 15 teams, there will be advisement going on each period of each day. Third, the advisement periods for each team are rotated, so that a particular team is advising during the same two periods only once each three weeks, as shown in Figure 2.3.

---

### ADVISEMENT CONFERENCE SCHEDULE

Monday—Team A: Smith, Dalton, Green, Williams, Edson, Reilly

| Date | | Periods | Date | | Periods |
|------|---|---------|------|---|---------|
| Sept. | 15 | 1–2 | Feb. | 2 | 5–6 |
| | 22 | 3–4 | | 9 | 1–2 |
| | 29 | 5–6 | | 16 | 3–4 |
| Oct. | 6 | 1–2 | | 23 | 5–6 |
| | 13 | 3–4 | Mar. | 2 | 1–2 |
| | 20 | 5–6 | | 9 | 3–4 |
| | 27 | 1–2 | | 16 | 5–6 |
| Nov. | 3 | 3–4 | | 23 | 1–2 |
| | 10 | 5–6 | | 30 | 3–4 |
| | 17 | 1–2 | Apr. | 6 | 5–6 |
| Dec. | 1 | 3–4 | | 20 | 1–2 |
| | 8 | 5–6 | | 27 | 3–4 |
| | 15 | 1–2 | May | 4 | 5–6 |
| | 22 | 3–4 | | 11 | 1–2 |
| Jan. | 5 | 5–6 | | 18 | 3–4 |
| | 12 | 1–2 | | 25 | 5–6 |
| | 19 | 3–4 | | | |

---

Figure 2.3
Sample Advisement Schedule for a Team

The above plan has some distinct advantages for the advisement process. Advisors belong to a team. Team members, especially when they represent different subject areas or different kinds of expertise, can help each other. New teachers, for example, would have support from veteran advisors until they became confident in the various advisement tasks. Furthermore, assuming that the team meets for conferences in a common place, the members can plan some joint activities for advisees and possibly for themselves. For instance, a team may schedule time for a counselor to help team members interpret test scores more effectively or to explain how to use career information files.

What has happened to a teacher's classes during those periods when he or she is scheduled for advisement? The problem is not as great as it might at first appear. Consider a high school with an enrollment of 1400, a total staff of 75 (including administrators and counselors), and 15 advisement teams. Each advisement team would have five members. During any given hour, then, only five advisors would be in conferences. Of those five, one would likely be an administrator, librarian, counselor, or departmental chairperson who would have no assigned classes or possibly a teacher whose planning period corresponds with the advisement period. Out of five advisors there may be three or perhaps four classes that would require supervision while the teacher has conferences. Schools have used a variety of means to deal with this problem.

One solution is to develop a student commons program, which allows students to report to other supervised areas of the building for study or socializing when a teacher is advising (once every three weeks). The students may go to the library to work on assignments or read, to the cafeteria, or to another classroom (with that teacher's permission). Such a program assumes that the high school student is a young adult who is prepared to assume some responsibility and who can make decisions affecting the use of, on the average, two hours of time each week. It will be recalled that in a human organization each member senses and accepts his or her own responsibility to achieve the organization's goals, and that the human organization strives for considerable self-guidance on the part of members rather than control by authority. Many people, of course, do not accept the notion that high-school students can adequately handle such responsibility. But the plan has worked in those schools where parents and authorities have accepted the idea, and where students have participated in its planning and have assumed a large share of responsibility for its successful operation.

An alternative solution is to have students report to a study hall or supervised area where attendance is taken. This plan requires up-to-date class lists for those assigned to monitor the study halls or other areas. If available supervisory personnel are already used to monitor the typical study hall, students assigned to regular study periods can be assigned to study at the back on ongoing classes, thereby releasing supervisors for the advisement program. This plan for providing daily study periods for some students is often better than the large, traditional study hall, particularly if the students are assigned with care to appropriate classes for study. A student who was having difficulty with algebra, for instance, might benefit by being assigned to study in another algebra class.

A third solution to the problem is to have supervisory personnel report to the classroom to conduct study activity while the teacher is in advisement. Finally, if a school is implementing the system on a trial basis or attempting to implement it by stages, the supervisory solutions may be used until the advisement seems to be running smoothly. Then the commons program, which is more congruent with the idea of a human organization, can be phased in.

In any case, the alternatives demand close analysis by the school in the light of that school's particular setting. Problems of acceptability, cost, and personnel allocations and assignment must be resolved in particular settings. There is, incidentally, a variation of the plan that reduces by one-half the number of students who would be released to a commons program or who would require more structured supervision. The variation involves one-hour conference time each week. The faculty is divided into 30 teams, with 6 teams functioning each day of the week.

In addition to the individual conferences, it is often desirable to schedule some group advisory sessions. Certainly, some of the tasks in the participatory advisement system are more efficiently and effectively done in groups. Schools can schedule group advisement sessions on a regular basis or simply announce group sessions as the need arises. The principal and the advisement team leaders can work together to determine how many group sessions are needed and when to schedule them. Group sessions are easy to schedule since they are all held simultaneously. Care needs to be taken, however, to insure that every advisor has a reasonable space to conduct his or her session.

In addition to the question of the daily schedule, decisions must be made about the actual schedule of implementation and about inservice activities for personnel. These decisions will vary from school to school. As far as implementing the system is concerned, a school should plan on a full year of preparation. A typical implementation schedule is shown in Figure 2.4.

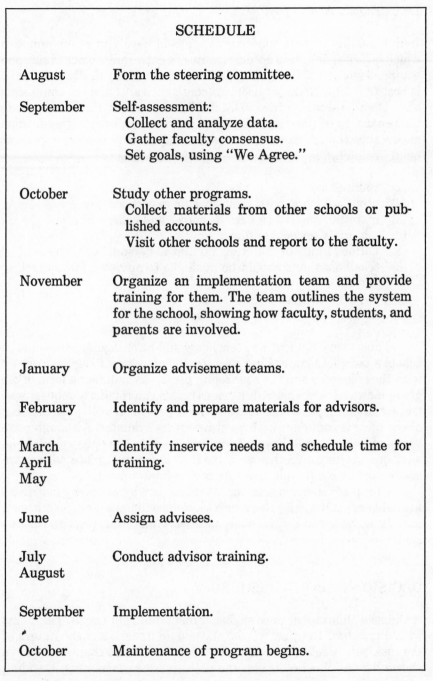

SCHEDULE

August          Form the steering committee.

September       Self-assessment:
                    Collect and analyze data.
                    Gather faculty consensus.
                    Set goals, using "We Agree."

October         Study other programs.
                    Collect materials from other schools or pub-
                    lished accounts.
                    Visit other schools and report to the faculty.

November        Organize an implementation team and provide
                training for them. The team outlines the system
                for the school, showing how faculty, students, and
                parents are involved.

January         Organize advisement teams.

February        Identify and prepare materials for advisors.

March           Identify inservice needs and schedule time for
April           training.
May

June            Assign advisees.

July            Conduct advisor training.
August

September       Implementation.

October         Maintenance of program begins.

**Figure 2.4**
A Schedule for Implementing Participatory Advisement

## DECISIONS ABOUT SPACE

Individual advisement conferences are held ideally in a common area which is large enough to accommodate the entire advisement team and equipped with all of the appropriate materials. If physically possible, it is best to integrate the advisement conference area and the counseling area. If not, it would suffice to locate the advisement conference area in the proximity of the counseling area. Allocating space in this fashion means that the advisor and the advisee have many resources close at hand, including:

(1)  counselors;
(2)  other advisors, with their specific expertise;
(3)  materials related to various career and college options;
(4)  materials for course planning;
(5)  various kinds of materials related to personal concerns;
(6)  telephones (one should be available to advisors for contacting parents);
(7)  posted announcements;
(8)  testing opportunities and information.

Thus, every student and teacher would have regular access to the school's complete counseling resources. This kind of regular contact with the resources and the counseling personnel is in fact a form of ongoing inservice training. Advisement teams can regularly request special assistance from counselors and other personnel until each member of the team is confident with most resources available. Although advisors and advisees will have informal contacts in the halls or cafeteria, advisors working together as a team in a common place with counselors creates a dynamic and supportive environment.

Group advisement sessions, of course, are by necessity held in all available areas. Usually the group sessions will have a single purpose, and the advisor can be given any necessary materials prior to the session.

## DECISIONS ABOUT RESOURCES

A Chinese philosopher once said that one should not try to open clams with a crowbar. In other words, one should understand the nature of the task before selecting one's resources. In the last chapter, we have shown how a school identifies the objectives of advisement. Deciding on objectives, and developing a calendar or handbook for advisors, clearly determines the nature of the task and thereby the resources which will be needed.

First, resources are needed for training advisors. The school district may have personnel available or may need help from schools that have successfully implemented the system. If a school has adopted reasonably comprehensive objectives for advisement, the initial training (or the training for new teachers coming into an established system) should include sessions on understanding the advisor's role, the program planning process, the parent conference, the nature of student records, the school's curriculum, and graduation requirements. Additional training can be given on an ongoing basis in special sessions or in the context of the advisement team, for advisors should gain skills in such areas as interpersonal communication, conflict resolution, decision making, the building of trust, and techniques of positive reinforcement.

The training sessions need not be long or complex, but at a minimum, each session should be based upon a clearly stated rationale, should have explicit and specific objectives, and should follow a well-planned method of presentation. Since new teachers who come into the school in subsequent years will have to have some training, the materials used by those conducting the sessions can be mimeographed or printed and kept for future use. Examples of the kind of materials useful for someone conducting sessions on the advisor's role and program planning are shown in Figure 2.5.

A number of resources will be required for the work of the advisors, and these will have to be prepared prior to the implementation of the system. We have already indicated that advisors will need a calendar or handbook to use as a guide for advisement activity from month to month. What other materials should advisors have? The answer may vary somewhat from one school to another, but the following should prove helpful.

First, each advisor should have student advisement folders, which are essentially copies of the students' permanent records plus such working advisement documents as long-range planning forms. Second, each advisor can use a course catalog that has systematic information about courses, graduation requirements, and college admission requirements. Third, the teams will each need a leader, and each leader should have a guide that clearly outlines the leader's responsibility. Fourth, there are numerous optional materials that can be developed as support for the advisor in various activities defined by the advisement calendar. Such materials would help the advisor by facilitating record keeping, providing directions on conducting some activities, and organizing useful information.

## TRAINING SESSION: THE ADVISOR'S ROLE

### Rationale

There are many reasons why an advisement system is necessary in our schools. First, it helps to keep our schools personal and humanistic in the face of many forces that tend to lead them to become large, impersonal institutions, unaware and uncaring for the individuals they serve. Second, as our schools try to meet the diversified needs of today's youth by providing many different types of learning programs, the student and his or her parents need more direct assistance in planning school goals. Third, advisement can give students the encouragement and feedback they need to become more self-actualizing individuals who recognize their own self-worth. To bring about these three goals, a student chooses a teacher to be his or her advisor. In the advisor role, the teacher must function differently than in the classroom. Some new skills, new attitudes and new knowledge are needed. How different is this new role? What is an advisor expected to do? This session will provide answers to some of the participants' personal questions.

### Objectives

The participant will learn to describe to a parent the ways in which an advisor is responsible for the following:

(1) program planning
(2) school offerings awareness
(3) self-assessment
(4) parent relations/conference
(5) school/community issues
(6) feedback/evaluation
(7) decision-making skills
(8) career planning/preparation.

### Method of Presentation

This is basically a question and answer session. A brief presentation of what an advisor does should be a good starting point since some participants may not be familiar with the role. If no questions are volunteered, the instructor may ask such things as: What is your biggest concern? What aspect of advisement do you think you will like best? What benefits do you see to advisement? How do you think students will react to advisement?

*(cont.)*

## TRAINING SESSION: PROGRAM PLANNING

### Rationale

Since the practical aspects of program planning (schedules, times, procedures) will vary from school to school, this session will focus on some of the problems advisors may encounter. For some of these problems, there may be no single solution, but discussing the problems will help the advisor deal with them when they arise.

### Objectives

The advisor will list in order the steps an advisor and student go through in program planning. Also, given a sample student record and several self-assessment instruments, the advisors will role-play both the advisor and the student in the program planning process.

### Method of Presentation

The instructor should explain the above rationale to the group, assuring them that when the time comes, they will be able to take care of the procedures for the individual school. However, there are common issues to long-range planning. The issues below should be distributed or written on the board. The instructor should describe the problem briefly. In small groups, the participants should choose two of the problems to consider in their group. Their results should be turned in to the instructor. Time could be allowed at the end of the session for the groups to share their results. The problems are:

1. Develop the criteria for judging a long-range program—e.g., does it match up with students' goals?
2. Develop a format (worksheets) for long-range planning. Should there be a common one in the district?
3. Analyze the role of parents in program planning. Define what involvement now is and what it should be ideally.
4. Draw up a list of specific resources to use for long-range planning—e.g., the course catalog, career goals, college catalog, etc.
5. Determine the steps a student should go through to make a long-range plan.
6. Determine how permanent a long-range plan should be. What are the criteria used in deciding whether a plan should be changed? How much should a student be held to his or her plan?

*(cont.)*

7. What type of conflicts are likely to arise and how should advisors deal with them? (For instance, parents may insist on a course that the advisor and advisee do not like, or there may be a disparity between a student's ability and selection of courses, or the courses may not relate to a stated career goal, and so forth.)

**Figure 2.5**
Sample Sessions for Training Advisors

We have already given examples of optional materials in the last chapter (goal setting for advisees). Two additional examples are shown in Figure 2.6. The figure illustrates both the variety of resource materials which should be made available to advisors and a format that will facilitate the use of the materials. A basic package of such materials should be available at the outset of the system. Additional materials can be developed by teachers, departmental chairpeople, counselors, and administrators as the need for them is identified by advisors.

## MIDPOINT INTERVIEW

*To the advisor:* Here are some questions to consider to help an advisee summarize how he or she is progressing in present classes. The objective should be to help the student pinpoint any problems and then help plan what to do about those problems. The student may need to talk to a teacher, or rearrange priorities for study time, or get special help such as tutoring. In some cases, the student may want his or her advisor to talk to a teacher or to parents.

Goal: A casual discussion early in the course period can help advisor and advisee prevent or resolve difficulties.

Group size: Individual
Time required: Flexible
Materials: None

1. How are things going for you in your classes?
2. Is any particular class causing you some concern?
3. Are you fairly pleased with your grades so far?
4. Is there any interesting activity or project that you are doing?
5. Which class do you like best?

*(cont.)*

6. If you had it to do over again, what changes would you make in your schedule?
7. Is the reading in any course difficult for you? If so, have you talked to the teacher about it?
8. Are you reading anything interesting?
9. Is there anything you wish your teachers understood that they don't yet know about you?

## WHERE DO I STAND ON GRADUATION REQUIREMENTS?

*To the advisor:*   This activity is most helpful when the advisee is encouraged to figure his or her own credits with your help. It leads to the advisee's greater understanding of future school planning needs.

Goal: This activity will help the student assess progress toward graduation.

Group size: Any size
Time required: 15 minutes
Materials: "Where do I Stand on Graduation Requirements?" sheet

| *Required Credits* | *Credits Earned* | *Credits for Courses in Which Enrolled* | *Remaining Credits Needed* |
|---|---|---|---|
| 1. 3 Social Studies (including 1 unit of American Hist) | _____ | _____ | _____ |
| 2. 3 Communications | _____ | _____ | _____ |
| 3. 1 Math | _____ | _____ | _____ |
| 4. 1 Science | _____ | _____ | _____ |
| 5. 1 Fine Arts | _____ | _____ | _____ |
| 6. 1 Practical Art | _____ | _____ | _____ |
| 7. 1½ Physical Education | _____ | _____ | _____ |

**Figure 2.6**
Sample Materials for Use by Advisors in their Conferences

The last kind of resource that needs to be developed relates to evaluation of the system. How will participatory advisement be evaluated? In addition to the informal evaluations which will be obtained throughout the year, some formal collection of data from all participants should be planned. The formal collection would secure the attitudes of students and faculty about the school's climate and attitudes of students, parents, and advisors about various facets—including the effectiveness—of the advisement system. Participatory advisement involves participation in the fullest sense of the word, since all concerned groups share in the planning, the implementation, the operation, and the evaluation of the system.

## SUMMARY

Implementing participatory advisement demands an understanding of the change process in organizations. The Zaltman, Duncan, and Holbek model of change posits a two-stage process: a stage of initiation, with substages of creating knowledge-awareness, forming attitudes about the innovation, and making a decision; and a stage of implementation, with substages of initiating implementation and maintaining implementation. Evaluation must be carried on at all points of the process. The early commitment of administrators is crucial for educational change.

People do not inherently resist all change, but most change efforts encounter some resistance. The only effective way to cope with resistance is to understand the reasonable bases upon which it normally exists. The characteristics of a human organization which were detailed in the introductory chapter can be applied to efforts at change in the school. The basic principles of change can be summarized in four key words: participation, definition, identification, and expectations.

The process and principles of change apply to the creation of a system of participatory advisement. Initially, there must be a gathering of information. Attitudes must be shaped and a collective decision must be made to proceed with the innovation. During implementation, a number of key decisions must be made about people, time, space, and resources. All concerned groups should share in the planning, implementation, operation, and evaluation of the system.

# Endnotes

[1]Quoted in Morris Ginsberg, *The Psychology of Society* (London: University Paperbacks, 1964), p. 96.

[2]Robert H. Lauer, *Perspectives on Social Change*, 2nd edition (Boston: Allyn & Bacon, 1977), p. 9.

[3]James West, *Plainville, U.S.A.* (New York: Columbia University Press, 1945), p. 17.

[4]Lauer, *op. cit.*, pp. 13–14.

[5]Gerald Zaltman, Robert Duncan, and Jonny Holbek, *Innovations & Organizations* (New York: John Wiley, 1973), pp. 58–70.

[6]Matthew B. Miles, "Innovation in Education: Some Generalizations," in Matthew B. Miles, ed., *Innovation in Education* (New York: Teachers College, Columbia University, 1964), p. 657.

[7]Ronald Corwin, "Strategies for Organizational Innovation: An Empirical Comparison." *American Sociological Review* 37 (August, 1972): 441–54.

[8]Lindley J. Stiles and Beecham Robinson, "Change in Education," in Gerald Zaltman, *Processes and Phenomena of Social Change* (New York: John Wiley, 1973), p. 257.

[9]*Ibid.*, p. 258.

[10]Corwin, *op. cit.*, p. 447.

[11]J. Victor Baldridge and Robert A. Burnham, "Organizational Innovation: Individual, Organizational, and Environmental Impacts." *Administrative Science Quarterly* 20 (June, 1975): 165–76.

[12]See Leonard R. Sayles and George Strauss, *Human Behavior in Organizations* (Englewood Cliffs: Prentice-Hall, 1966), pp. 303f. and Lauer, *op. cit.*, pp. 10–11.

[13]Reginald Carter, "Clients' Resistance to Negative Findings and the Latent Conservative Function of Evaluation Studies." *The American Sociologist* 6 (May, 1971): 118–24.

[14]*Ibid.*, p. 119.

[15]M. S. Atwood, "Small-scale Administrative Change: Resistance to the Introduction of a High School Guidance Program," in Matthew B. Miles, ed., *op. cit.*, pp. 49–77.

[16]Zaltman, Duncan, and Holbek, *op. cit.*, pp. 85–94.

[17]Larry E. Greiner, "Patterns of Organizational Change." *Harvard Business Review* 45 (May-June, 1967): 119–30.

[18]Albert S. King, "Expectation Effects in Organizational Change." *Administrative Science Quarterly* 19 (June, 1974): 221–30.

[19]Neal Gross, Joseph B. Giacquinta and Marilyn Bernstein, *Implementing Organizational Innovations: A Sociological Analysis of Planned Educational Change* (New York: Basic Books, 1971).

[20]Zaltman, Duncan, and Holbek, *op. cit.*, pp. 154–55.

[21]Kurt Lewin, "Group Decision and Social Change," in Eleanor E. Maccoby, Theodore M. Newcomb, and Eugene L. Hartley, eds., *Readings in Social Psychology* (New York: Holt, Rinehart and Winston, 1958), pp. 197–211.

[22]Robert S. Fox and Ronald Lippitt, "The Innovation of Classroom Mental Health Practices," in Matthew B. Miles, ed., *op. cit.*, pp. 271–97.

[23]Gerhard Eichholz and Everett M. Rogers, "Resistance to the Adoption of Audio-visual Aids by Elementary School Teachers: Contrasts and Similarities to Agricultural Innovation," in Matthew B. Miles, ed., *op. cit.*, pp. 307–308.

[24]Paul R. Lawrence, "How to Deal with Resistance to Change," in Gene W. Dalton, Paul R. Lawrence, and Larry E. Greiner, eds., *Organizational Change and Development* (Homewood, Ill.: The Dorsey Press, 1970), p. 193.

[25]The plan can work rather easily with any number that is a multiple of five (so that an equal number of teams are advising each day). It can also be modified to suit the schedule of schools that have something other than the traditional six-period day.

# Chapter 3

# The Role of Counselors

"Counseling as an activity cannot and will not be neglected."[1]

"The overall finding from a large New York study (1971) examining public schools was that 'guidance counseling as currently performed is substantially ineffective.' The jobs of 800 counselors were dissolved."[2]

As illustrated by the above two quotations, the history of guidance and counseling is marked by conflict between those who are zealous advocates and those who are unremitting critics of the work of school counselors. Advocates often admit that counselors do not function in accord with the ideal, offer various explanations for the disparity between the ideal and the real, and suggest ways of making counseling more effective. Critics often agree with the analyses of advocates, but may draw a different conclusion—that counseling is, at worst, a waste of resources or, at best, an expendable activity. Although our description of participatory advisement includes various tasks which have been done by counselors in typical schools, we do not view counselors as expendable. In fact, we would argue that the work of counselors in the human organization becomes more important and more congruent with the counseling ideal.

In order to provide the background for our argument, we will begin by looking briefly at the historical development of guidance and counseling and at certain developments in the nature of high schools. We will then examine counselor training and the ideal role of the counselor (ideal as defined by those in the profession). We will contrast the ideal with the actual role, and show the various factors that account for the discrepancy between the ideal and the real. Finally, we will describe the work of the counselor in a human organization, and discuss how that work becomes more important and more closely approximates the tasks for which counselors are trained.

## THE BACKGROUND—HISTORICAL DEVELOPMENTS

The guidance movement began shortly after the turn of the century as an effort to provide effective vocational guidance. Increasing numbers of young people were going to high school. Occupations were becoming more complex and specialized. Psychology was emerging as an important science. With the conjunction of these various developments, "it was inevitable that actions would be taken to help youth to choose, prepare for, enter, and be successful in an occupation."[3] That occupational choice had become a matter of concern and, indeed, a problem to many is evidenced by a number of books that began to appear as early as the 1880s. Books with titles such as "What Shall Our Boys Do for a Living?" and "Careers for the Coming Men" offered various kinds of advice, and one author advocated a new profession—"vocophy"—to help young men select their careers.[4]

Some work in vocational guidance was initiated in San Francisco in 1895 at the California School of Mechanical Arts.[5] A more influential effort, however, was that of Frank Parsons, who founded the Vocation Bureau of Boston in 1908. Parsons became noted as the founder of vocational guidance. The Bureau was initially a private agency. Later, it became a part of Harvard University. Parsons and his coworkers emphasized the success that would follow upon an individual finding the occupation for which he was most qualified. But "the real innovation by the Bureau was to establish a professional role—counseling—whose incumbents could, because of their training in and knowledge of individual assessment and occupational information, aid the process of occupational choice."[6]

By about 1910, vocational guidance counselors began working in some community organizations and a few high schools. By 1916, about 1,000 counselors were employed by the nation's schools. Once begun, the movement spread fairly rapidly. But even as the movement was expanding, the schools were changing. As we shall discuss further, the high school was becoming "comprehensive," with the purpose of fulfilling the needs of all students, and increasing numbers of students began to look toward college. Gradually, the concern with students' vocational futures gave way to an interest in educational futures (college). Vocational counselors began to do educational guidance as well as vocational counseling.

By the 1940s, however, the stage of vocational and educational counseling was giving way to a second stage of "meeting individual needs." Counselors increasingly viewed themselves as therapists, as those who were providing a service to individuals rather than as those who were implementing a school program. While this broader notion of guidance had been considered by some of the earlier counselors, it was given considerable impetus by the mental health movement. The social-emotional adjustment of students became a prime concern, and Carl Rogers was the guiding light. Many, perhaps the bulk of, counselors were trained in Rogerian techniques. They perceived their proper role in terms of nondirective counseling. Ideally, the counselor was one who would provide each student with an understanding and supportive relationship so that each could mobilize his or her own resources. Students thus served would be able to resolve their problems and grow into mature people.

In the 1960s, counseling entered the third stage of "transitional professionalism." Medical therapeutic models became popular and professional guidelines were developed by the American School Counselors Association. Finally, in the 1970s the stage of "situational diagnosis" emerged.[7] This stage has been characterized by disenchantment with models based on psychopathology, and by experimentation with various other therapeutic techniques such as transactional analysis and behavioral modification. Counselors have also become increasingly aware of the limitations of individual therapy and of the need for identifying and manipulating the social or environmental factors involved in individual problems.

Thus, guidance/counseling has been a dynamic field. Significant changes in the counselor's role and in counseling techniques have occurred during the century. At the same time, there have been significant developments in the high school in which counseling occurs.

## THE CHANGING HIGH SCHOOL

After the Civil War, American secondary schools rapidly expanded from organizations offering a classical liberal education for a small number of affluent males to training organizations that provided capable workers for the expanding industrial economy. Guidance became a part of the secondary school system in order to facilitate the development of effective workers. Later on, while the emphasis of guidance was shifting from vocations to higher education and self-realization, the primary function of the high school was changing from vocational preparation to college preparation. Increasingly, the high school was seen as a step on the educational ladder rather than as a door to the job market.

Educational aspirations, educational attainment, and employers' expectations for educational levels of their employees all tended to rise together. After the Second World War, a high school education became the goal, even the right, of everyone. The determination to provide all Americans with a high-school diploma was reflected in programs aimed at dropout prevention in the 1950s and 1960s.

Eventually, the comprehensive public high school came into being, "a school for everyone." The comprehensive high school has a program that fits the needs of all students. Guidance and supervision are fully developed in order to insure that every student will attain his or her maximum potential. With the expanded mission of educating the entire populace, the comprehensive high school had to work with more heterogeneous student bodies, more varied and complex curriculums, and the expectation of success on the part of every student and parent. Whatever the talents, ability, or inclination of the child to learn might be, the high school is expected to work with that child until the diploma is achieved.

The modern comprehensive high school confronts the staff with problems and challenges that would not have arisen in previous generations. The staff must work with students of widely divergent abilities and interests and help them all to succeed. Extracurricular activities and opportunities must be planned and supervised (a task that has been intensified in recent years by the efforts of females to have programs equal to those of males). Court-ordered desegregation may suddenly thrust students of divergent cultural and economic backgrounds together, increasing problems of control and communication. And perhaps the most severe challenge of all is the expectation that the school will be concerned about, and responsive to, a wide variety of student problems and concerns, such as:

1.  Sexuality. To what extent should, or must, the staff provide sex education?
2.  Racial attitudes. How can the staff counter racial prejudices which have been formed and which continue to be sustained in the family?
3.  Smoking. Should it be completely disallowed, or would it be better if the school provided a particular area in which smoking is permitted?

4.  Alcohol and drug use and abuse. How can deleterious attitudes and behavior which are sustained by peer-group pressure be changed?
5.  Driver safety.
6.  Behavior disorders, which may raise the problem of individual versus group well-being. (Can you allow a disturbed student to remain in school even though expulsion or suspension may be detrimental to that student?)
7.  Academic problems resulting from such things as broken homes or child abuse. How can the staff motivate a student, or even expect a student to be motivated, who is emotionally shattered by a problem home?

Because the comprehensive high school is expected to be responsive to such problems and concerns, the staff has become increasingly specialized. As counselors have been added to schools to deal with many of the concerns listed above, teachers and administrators have tended to perceive their roles more narrowly. Teachers have insisted that they be held accountable only for teaching their subject specialty. In many cases, teachers expect someone else to be held accountable for such matters as discipline, the school environment, the personal problems of students, and communications with parents. In some cases, teachers have been known to resist such tasks as taking attendance, supervising students in areas outside the classroom, and handling routine administrative matters in "home rooms."

Administrators have also tended to define themselves as specialists. The administrator has become less of an instructional leader and more of a disciplinarian and a manager of the physical setting (books, buildings). The role of manager is accepted by teachers, and some of the more academic teachers may view administrators with a certain disdain. As typically happens in settings where specialists work together, the staff of the high school is composed of groups of people with various kinds of expertise and each group believes that all policies and practices should be set up to facilitate that particular group's special functions.

The counselor has become the person in the middle, a marginal member of the school team who is expected to fill in the gaps left by teachers and administrators. Starting from their own positions as specialists, teachers and administrators have often attempted to define the counselor's role to suit their own vested interests or to protect their own narrowly defined spheres of activity. As we shall see below, the role which has been defined for counselors has not been in accord with their own preferences. Counselors have had to struggle to avoid becoming mere pawns of administrators. They have had to resist the notion held by teachers that they are totally accountable for social and psychological problems in the school. Often, tension has developed among administrators, teachers, and counselors, with each group blaming the others for inadequate fulfillment of responsibility (which has most often meant, "you have not measured up to our expectations for what you ought to be doing").

In essence, then, the comprehensive high school has tended to become a tripartite system, with teachers viewing themselves as academicians, administrators defining themselves as managers, and counselors perceiving themselves as human relations specialists. This compartmentalization of responsibility has led to confusion and sometimes to conflict. There is a lack of mutual understanding among the groups. There is actually a lingering suspicion in some faculties that counselors do not do anything. Teachers and administrators both may be keenly aware of the fact that counselors are the last to arrive and the first to leave. Worse, the counselors leave without papers to grade, lessons to plan, or athletic events to supervise. In such a situation, it is not surprising that counselors have been called upon to demonstrate their value or necessity. "Why do we need counselors?" has been asked by numerous teachers and administrators. At first glance, the participatory advisement system appears to make the question even more urgent. Before showing how counselors have important functions in the human organization, however, we need to look at the ideal role for which they have been trained.

## WHAT COUNSELORS ARE TRAINED TO BE

Hermann Hesse wrote of one of his characters: "Harry consists of a hundred or a thousand selves, not of two. His life oscillates, as everyone's does, not merely between two poles, such as the body and the spirit, the saint and the sinner, but between thousands and thousands."[8] When we ask what the counselor is trained to be, we must realize that, like Harry, the counselor may be a hundred or a thousand different selves. As our historical overview showed, the counselor was trained to be a quite different person at different points in time. Furthermore, at any particular time, counselors will be trained in the context of diverse theoretical orientations and, once trained, will function in differing contexts of expectations.

In spite of the differences, there is some consensus about the high-school counselor's role. The role is multi-faceted, as we shall detail below. Following our discussion of the functions of the counselor, we will briefly look at the various theories of counseling which have been advocated.

## THE COUNSELOR'S IDEAL ROLE

What should counselors ideally be doing in the high school? Based upon studies conducted by the American School Counselor Association (which included surveys of counselors from every state in the union), H. L. Isaksen identified ten functions of the counselor.[9] The ideal role we are discussing, then, is not our own creation. We are presenting the role as developed more or less consensually by counselors themselves.

First, the counselor should be involved in planning and implementing guidance and the curriculum. The counselor will work at this task in the light of student needs.

Second, the counselor will help students understand themselves as individuals in particular social and psychological environments, accept themselves for what they are, gain decision-making skills, and resolve their personal problems.

Third, the counselor will play a key role in student evaluation. The counselor will be responsible for the gathering and proper use of data about students and will interpret those data to students, parents, teachers, and any other professionally concerned individual. The evaluation process will enable the counselor to identify any special abilities or needs among students.

Fourth, the counselor will gather information related to school offerings, higher education opportunities, and careers. This information is shared with students and their parents.

Fifth, the counselor utilizes services available in the community as the need arises. The services may be those which the counselor is unable to provide. In order to utilize them, the counselor must be aware of them, must maintain contact with various community agencies, and must help students and parents take advantage of them. The counselor at times may also need to work for the development of services which are not available but which are important for certain student needs.

Sixth, the counselor works with students, teachers, and administrators to provide an adequate placement service for students. This task includes the proper grouping and scheduling of students, advising students in their course of study, and helping students as they move from one school level to another or from school to a job.

Seventh, the counselor offers help to parents in a number of ways. The counselor can confer with parents about the progress (academic, social, or psychological) of their children. Parents may need certain information about their children which can be provided by the counselor within the limits of confidentiality. Parents, like their children, may need information about higher educational or career opportunities, or about community services available to them and their children. Parents may also need to have a realistic appraisal of a child's potential. Some parents underrate their children and fail to encourage them sufficiently. Others overrate their children, and pressure them to attain unrealistic goals.

Eighth, the counselor acts as a consultant for teachers and administrators in matters of guidance. The counselor may need to convey certain information to other members of the staff, or help staff members identify particular needs and problems. The counselor also provides resources for in-service training and for teachers who want to provide guidance experiences in the classroom.

Ninth, the counselor plays a key part in researching the needs of students and the responsiveness of the school program to those needs. This task may demand that graduates and dropouts be contacted. It will also require an examination and analysis of various records (such as comparing aptitudes and achievement), and an evaluation of various programs, including the counseling and guidance services of the school.

Tenth, the counselor has a public relations function. Effective public relations are maintained by such activities as participation in community gatherings and programs, and by sharing information with local mass media.

The above ten functions are, for the most part, student-centered. Directly or indirectly, the functions are aimed at the needs of students, and their purpose is to enable all students to achieve self–actualization. To fulfill these varied functions, the counselor will be given specialized training within a particular theoretical context. There is, however, no single theoretical context used by all counselors. Let us examine the various theories which may be used, keeping in mind that, whatever the theory, all counselors have the goal of maximizing student well-being (where well-being may include adjustment, coping, acceptance, satisfaction, growth, etc.).

## THEORIES OF COUNSELING

Theories are important in a number of respects. First, theories are, in simplest terms, explanations. As such, they provide us with a way of understanding something. Part of that understanding comes from the assumptions about human nature and human personality contained in most theories about human behavior.

Second, theories provide us with directives about behavior. That is, once a theory explains for us why people behave as they do it also indicates to us—implicitly or explicitly—how to deal with people and with situations. Since different theories have somewhat different understandings of human nature and behavior, they also prescribe somewhat different techniques for helping people. All counselors have the paramount goal of helping students, but their training has led them to use differing methods to attain that goal.

Third, theories lead us to ignore or dismiss certain things. In directing us to understand something in a certain way and to look for certain aspects of a phenomenon, a theory necessarily directs our attention away from other things. Theories blind as well as illuminate. The blinding function occurs in the natural as well as the social sciences. Clearly, for example, medieval scientists were blinded to reality in a way that inhibited scientific progress as long as they accepted the Aristotelian theory that reality is composed of the four elements of fire, air, earth, and water. Similarly, the contemporary counselor who is trained in the Rogerian tradition may not perceive a student's need for simple advice, or the counselor trained in behaviorism may ignore a student's need to gain insight into his or her own feelings. As long as a particular theory is followed, we understand and act in particular ways, which necessarily means that we do not understand and act in other ways which are possible.

Since theories direct toward certain things and away from other things, shouldn't we try to find the correct theory so that the blinding effect no longer has undesirable consequences? As it turns out, studies on the therapeutic process show that the various techniques all have about the same success (and failure) rate.[10] Thus, if a counselor employs any one of the approaches discussed below, he or she is likely to have as much success as a counselor who employs any other of the approaches. From our point of view, the important thing to keep in mind is that all of the approaches have the goal of helping students, but that each approach will lead a counselor to employ different techniques, to make different kinds of recommendations to teachers and administrators about policies and practices, and to perceive problems in different ways.

### CLIENT-CENTERED THERAPY

Probably the majority of counselors have been trained in accord with principles developed by Carl Rogers.[11] Within this perspective,

... the counselor's basic task is to help the counselee be what he can be, so that as an individual person he can never be "captured" by the forces demanding conformity that surround him, so that his manhood is not fully predicated on the whims and subtle conditioning of the society in which he lives. Thus, a basic and crucial aspect of the counseling encounter is (or *ought* to be) the gradual achievement of a sense of personal liberation.[12]

In the Rogerian school, people are assumed to be rational and realistic, and to have a basic drive toward self-actualization. The therapeutic relationship results in the release of the individual's resources, for all individuals have the resources within themselves for resolving problems and experiencing growth. The individual is able to mobilize his or her resources because of the relationship created by the counselor—warm, positive, empathic, supportive. Originally, Rogers emphasized the non-participation or non-directiveness of the counselor. The relationship was one of non-interference on the part of the counselor. Later, the emphasis became one of creating a non-threatening climate that will be conducive to the counselee's growth.

How does the counselor create this growth-conducive relationship? Basically, there are certain qualities which must be possessed by, or developed by, the counselor and brought to the relationship. First, the counselor must be accepting. Literally, the counselor prizes the counselee as a person, fully accepting the counselee without any conditions. The counselor makes no judgments or evaluations. This does not mean that all behavior is condoned, but that whatever the behavior or problems of the counselee, the counselor feels and communicates a genuine caring. Second, the counselor is consistent in his or her words and behavior. Nonverbal gestures do not contradict the verbal assurance of caring.

Third, the counselor must be able to empathize with the counselee, to accurately understand the counselee's feelings and reasoning. Fourth, the counselor should be able to communicate the above qualities to the counselee. When these qualities are present and perceived by the counselee, the non-threatening, supportive relationship necessary for insight and growth has been created.

## DEVELOPMENTAL COUNSELING

Developmental counseling is a relatively new perspective that uses insights from a number of different disciplines and a variety of theories. Like client-centered therapy, it aims at maximizing human freedom and human effectiveness. A number of assumptions about human nature and human behavior underlie the work of developmental counselors. Dinkmeyer and Caldwell list, among others, the following:

1. Behavior patterns are dynamic, reflecting certain stages of development and changing as the child grows.
2. Individuals attempt to actualize themselves.
3. Individuals differ considerably in their pattern and rate of development.

4. All behavior is purposive, reflecting the needs and goals of the individual.
5. The individual's behavior is rooted in that individual's perception of his or her needs.
6. The psychological development of individuals is continuous and patterned.
7. Adult behavior reflects patterns developed between the ages of six and ten.
8. The extent to which developmental tasks are learned is a useful indicator of individual growth.
9. Individuals grow towards "responsible personal autonomy."
10. Individuals must have insight into themselves before they can become self-directed and responsible.[13]

To help counselees become more free, responsible, effective individuals, counselors use a number of techniques. It is particularly important that the counselor be a good listener and that goals be formed mutually by counselor and counselee. Beyond that, the counselor may use various techniques and may structure the interview in various ways. Among the useful techniques are appraising (helping counselees engage in self-appraisal); providing information; encouraging; planning that derives from insights gained in the counseling process; and reinforcing any strong points or successes of counselees. Developmental counseling is flexible and eclectic, allowing and even encouraging each counselor to develop his or her own personal philosophy and theory of counseling to attain the desired goals of counselee freedom and effectiveness.

## EXISTENTIAL THERAPY

Rollo May is the representative theorist in this approach. The well-known capsule summary of existentialism, "existence is prior to essence," emphasizes the concern of all existentialists with the facts of existence over the more abstract question of human nature. One of the primary goals of existential therapy is to help the counselee become more aware of his or her existence, that is, of his or her situation as a creature who lives in the world and who must make choices and accept the responsibility for those choices. Existentialists also have the goals of helping counselees become more free and responsible individuals and more effective in interpersonal relationships.

Rollo May said that the existential approach offers an understanding of humans and their experiences rather than a specific set of techniques. Nevertheless, there are certain techniques which have been used by existential therapists. A particular therapist is likely to use a variety of techniques, even with the same counselee. Existentialists are flexible; they "sharply question the use of techniques simply because of custom."[14]

One technique is "presence." "The word 'presence' means that the relationship of the patient and the therapist is taken as a real one. The therapist does not merely reflect but understands and experiences the patient."[15] This is similar to the Rogerian notion of empathy. In addition, existential therapists attempt to discover and remove any kind of behavior that suppresses or removes presence. A third aspect of existential techniques involves the counselee's experience of his or her own existence—the counselee must perceive that existence as real, which means becoming aware of his or her potential and acting upon the basis of that awareness. Finally, the existential therapist stresses the notion of commitment on the part of the counselee. The individual must make choices. The commitment to proceed with the business of responsible choosing brings insight to the counselee. Thus, the counselee is ready to function effectively in his or her world.

## BEHAVIORAL COUNSELING

Behaviorism, associated above all with the name of B. F. Skinner, offers the technique of behavior modification as a form of therapy. Unlike the other approaches discussed, behaviorism rejects personality and various cognitive processes as important to understanding human behavior:

> Each youth and adult is identified by behaviors that occur again and again. In common parlance these behaviors constitute a person's personality. Guidance team members typically are not interested in producing some global description of an individual, therefore they are not interested in a construct labeled "personality." They are interested in specific patterns of behavior and in the specific patterns of stimuli that maintain those behaviors.[16]

In behaviorism, humans are ethically neutral creatures who behave in accord with learned patterns. What is learned can be unlearned, and new patterns can be learned. But again, it is *behavior* that needs to be learned or unlearned that is the concern of the therapist. An individual in an existential crisis, such as one wrestling with the question, "Who am I?", will not be helped by behavioral counseling. Counseling is a learning process in which the counselee is helped to formulate goals and behavioral techniques for attaining those goals.

Behavior counselors use a variety of techniques, including positive reinforcement (technically, anything following a particular response that increases the chances of that response recurring) and aversive control (something unpleasant that reduces the chances of a particular response recurring). There are variations of the basic techniques. For instance, positive reinforcement may take the form of money, praise, tokens which can be exchanged for valued goods, or anything else of value to the counselee. Of course, one counselee's meat is another counselee's poison. Or as Byrne put it, "an Arabic youth's behavior will be reinforced by eating sheep eyes, an aversive food for Westerners."[17]

Although the techniques of behavioral counseling are quite different from the other theories we have discussed, the goals are often the same. After all, people generally value such things as individual autonomy and responsibility and interpersonal skills. And of course counseling goals are set by the educational context as well as by the theoretical orientation of the counselor. Thus, like other counselors, behaviorists will attempt to help their counselees become more responsible and effective individuals who more nearly realize their own potential.

## SUMMARY

There are other theories of counseling. For instance, there is rational-emotive counseling, developed by Albert Ellis. In this approach, the counselor is much more active:

> The counselor forcefully confronts the client with those irrational beliefs which are at the root of his disturbance and teaches him more rational ways of thinking and behaving. The goals of rational-emotive counseling are clearly both attitudinal and behavioral.[18]

Our purpose here is to show the common elements of the various approaches rather than to provide a detailed description and analysis. In particular, we wanted to show how certain themes or goals tended to characterize all theories, even though techniques of achieving those goals differed. In essence, the counselor is an individual who is trained to use various techniques to help others become more free, responsible, effective humans, thereby realizing their own potential. Ultimately, the ten functions listed in the last section all enable the counselor to fulfill this basic purpose. But has the purpose been fulfilled? What is the actual as opposed to the ideal role of school counselors?

## WHAT COUNSELORS ARE

What do counselors actually do in high schools? The typical role which we describe below contains some functions which are congruent with the ideal and some which contradict it. The contradictions are sufficiently important and time-consuming that many counselors despair of ever fulfilling what they regard as their proper functions. The typical, actual role has four facets—the counselor tends to function as an administrative assistant, a student advocate, a trouble-shooter, and a therapist.

## THE COUNSELOR AS
## ADMINISTRATIVE ASSISTANT

The American School Counselors Association has recommended that there should be one counselor for each 250 students. In practice, there is more likely to be one counselor for every 400 students and in some schools the ratio may go as high as one to 800. The counselor is expected to relate personally to all these students, helping them plan their programs, meet graduation requirements, and plan for higher education or a career. With the typical counselor–student ratio, this becomes a matter of mere scheduling rather than personalized program planning. The task requires counselors to spend an inordinate amount of time in record keeping.

Furthermore, with the number of counselees involved, there is a natural tendency to treat individual students as members of groups and to act toward individuals on the basis of what is good for the mythical average student. "You have a high test score, Janet. You should select strictly college prep courses." "George, you're a sophomore, so you must take these courses." Such advice may be appropriate for some and inappropriate for others. It requires time to identify significant individual differences which may transcend grade level, age, and other criteria which are used to categorize individuals, and counselors do not have the necessary time when they are working with hundreds of students. As a consequence of time demands, counselors tend to be forced into the impersonal, bureaucratic role. Ironically, they must give so much time to the task of schedules that they have little time left to use their other skills.

The problem is compounded when counselors are assigned the task of managing the scheduling itself. That is, in some schools counselors must design the master schedule, oversee the printing and distribution of student schedules, make schedule changes, and keep class size balanced throughout the school.

Testing—both individual testing and group testing for purposes of college applications and school evaluation—is another task of counselors. It is important to the fulfillment of the ideal role, but it is also another administrative straw on a breaking back. Moreover, when counselors administer tests for the purpose of evaluating the school they may find themselves in conflict with teachers and administrators, particularly if the counselors are the bearers of bad news. In one high school, the English department developed a bitter relationship with the counselors because the latter publicized in the community student deficiencies in language skills. The students were persistently scoring at a low level in grammar, usage, and written expression, suggesting that changes needed to be made in the English curriculum and teaching methods.

The administrative assistant role of the counselor, then, not only consumes a great amount of time, but tends to lead the counselor to behave in ways (like a bureaucrat) that contradict his or her training and to thrust the counselor into situations (like that of conflict with certain teachers) that consume even more time and energy while blunting effectiveness.

## COUNSELORS AS STUDENT ADVOCATES

During the turbulent 1960s and early 1970s, many counselors began to define themselves as student advocates. Students during the period affirmed the idea of student rights. Those rights had to be gained in the context of oppressive institutions, which automatically meant that students had aligned themselves against the staff, the keepers of the institutions. Not all staff members defended the institutions; however, some counselors sided with the students, which created tension and conflict between the counselors and other members of the staff.

Counselors could easily defend their roles as student advocates. By training, after all, they have special insight into the adolescent and a concern for the whole person that may not be shared by teachers and administrators. Indeed, where schools have become excessively bureaucratic (that is, authoritarian, inflexible, and impersonal), students may need advocates who will work with them to create a more humane organization. When counselors feel the need to be student advocates, there may be an enormous amount of alienation and antagonism in the school.

Undoubtedly, many counselors fulfilled the role of advocate effectively. One typical strategy of the counselor as student advocate is the attempt to humanize the teaching staff. The counselor may establish small groups of teachers and administrators and discuss such things as interpersonal communication, understanding adolescents and their life styles, and the effective use of student records. In many instances, counselors have had an impact upon teachers and teaching methods. They have helped teachers exercise more understanding and compassion in the classroom, particularly in those schools where administrators give teacher–student relations a high priority and value a "counseling oriented" classroom.

On the other hand, the role has also created problems for counselors. We have already noted the possibility of conflict with other staff members. In addition, it is in the role of student advocate that the counselor has often developed an aversion toward any form of student discipline. One of the livelier issues in counseling today is whether the disciplinary process should be part of the functioning of counselors.

## COUNSELORS AS TROUBLE-SHOOTERS

Trouble-shooting is a crisis-oriented approach. In many schools, the counselor is boxed into this role; students are expected to fit into school policies and practices, and counselors are expected to deal with those who do not fit in. In such a school, the emphasis is on adjustment. Such matters as the schedule, various school regulations, and normal operating procedures are the "givens." Students are expected to adjust to the givens. Little or no flexibility may exist in the policies or program to account for individual interests and needs. The counselor in this situation applies "human relations" bandages to cover up the cuts and scratches created by various problems. The counselor attempts to get students to adjust, even though the counselor or an outside observer might identify the situation rather than the students as the real problem. The counselor who fails in this task will hear complaints from teachers: "I sent Harry to Mr. Jackson and nothing happened. Harry has been sent back to class but hasn't changed a bit."

The counselor in this situation is fighting a losing battle in more than one sense. It is a losing battle because it betrays the purpose for which counselors are trained, namely, to focus on the needs and well-being of the individual. Counselors who function primarily as trouble-shooters are fulfilling institutional rather than individual needs. The counselor may actually be teaching students to think and behave in ways that are detrimental to the students' growth. But it is also a losing battle if the counselor remains sensitive to the unique needs of individual students. If the counselor articulates the need for greater flexibility or for organizational change in the name of student well-being, that counselor may suddenly find himself or herself with the label of troublemaker. Teachers or administrators may argue that such a counselor has abandoned the proper role of trouble-shooter and assumed the improper role of student advocate.

In other words, where the counselor is expected to function as a trouble-shooter, he or she is in a classic "damned-if-you-do and damned-if-you-don't" situation. To function as expected is to betray one's training and goals. To function otherwise is to intensify discontent, maintain tension, create conflict, and perhaps risk one's job.

Some schools have committed themselves rather heavily to a crisis-oriented approach by developing the "open counseling lounge." The idea of the lounge is that counselors will be very accessible. Any student who needs help can come into the lounge and meet with a counselor in a warm and relaxing atmosphere. But there are a number of problems with the lounge idea. In the first place, if the attitude that counselors are basically trouble-shooters is not changed, counseling in the lounge will present the same dilemmas we noted above. Greater accessibility does not mean more effective counseling. Second, there is often no systematic way to get students to make contact with counselors. Greater accessibility does not necessarily mean greater usage. The students who most need the services may never attempt to secure them. Many students with problems will deliberately avoid counselors. Furthermore, there may be a stigma attached to visiting the lounge—"what's the matter with you that you're seeing the counselors?" Finally, putting counselors into a comfortable lounge may increase the suspicion and/or envy of other staff members toward the counselors. As we have noted before, the effectiveness of counselors is blunted when other staff members define them as marginal to the basic purpose of the school or view them as a pampered adjunct of questionable utility.

## COUNSELORS AS THERAPISTS AND FACILITATORS

By virtue of their training and interests, many counselors view their work as therapists and facilitators as primary. Therapy in a high-school setting refers to a relatively intense and long-term counseling relationship which is oriented to resolving specific problems. It does not imply psychoanalytic or psychiatric treatment, although a counselor may refer students and parents to appropriate community agencies for such services. We use the term "facilitators" to include the important function of helping people engage in self-actualization. The deeply troubled individual is not the only concern of the counselor. In fact, some theories of counseling stress the importance of a different kind of work. Developmental counseling "represents a shift from crisis counseling toward a preventive and positive approach toward helping pupils . . . developmental counseling is concerned with developmental-educative and preventive goals rather than remediative-adjustive and therapeutic outcomes."[19] Both the troubled and the untroubled are the concern of the counselor. The former may benefit by the counselor's work as a therapist, while the latter may benefit by the counselor's work as a facilitator of personal growth.

In traditional school settings, the legitimate counseling needs of students—whether for therapy or facilitation—have been given low priority because of the time required. It is physically impossible for one counselor to be responsible for anywhere from 400 to 800 students. "Responsible" means that the counselor will regularly show personal concern for each student, help each student make adequate self-assessment and plans for college or career, maintain regular contact with each student's parents, assist each student with those decisions which naturally occur in adolescence and in the educational process, and give the necessary help so that students will experience personal growth and those with personal problems or crises will have a therapeutic relationship.

Moreover, counselors are likely to be unequal partners in the high school. Teachers and administrators are the primary staff members, for the basic mission of the school is academic. Thus, the personal growth and development of students that often appears in school rhetoric is in fact given low priority when resources are committed. The net result is that all students have legitimate counseling needs which are unmet.

## FORCES THAT SHAPE THE ROLE

We have already noted some of the forces that have shaped the actual role of counselors—their marginal position in the staff, the impossibility of fulfilling the various functions given the number of students for which they are responsible, and the nature of their work assignments in various schools. For the most part, the forces that shape the counselor's actual role may be reduced to one basic factor—the varying expectations of what Merton called the role-set. Merton pointed out that any particular status in society involves a set of associated roles. The role-set is the "complement of role relationships which persons have by virtue of occupying a particular social status."[20] The role of any particular member of the set is shaped by other members. For instance, Merton says, the status of medical student involves not only the role of student vis-a-vis teachers, but a variety of other roles that relate to that status—other students, nurses, physicians, other medical personnel, and so forth. The extent to which any particular role is shaped and controlled by others in the set depends, in part, upon the distribution of power (recall that counselors are often relatively powerless members of the staff).

Among the significant roles in the role-set of the counselor are students, teachers, administrators, and parents. We must understand the actual role of the counselor, therefore, in terms of the expectations and opinions of people in those roles. A study by Shertzer and Stone in the 1960s focused on that very question: what are the perceptions of counselors held by students, teachers, administrators, and parents?[21] The researchers' conclusions make it understandable that the actual role of counselors would diverge from the ideal.

How do students view counselors? In general, they do not define counselors as effective sources of help other than for making decisions about educational or vocational matters. Students believe that counselors should be available to those who have serious problems; at the same time, they indicate that they themselves would not utilize the services of a counselor. In some cases, counselors may be seen in even less helpful terms. On the basis of questionnaires administered to seniors in nine schools, Knox and his associates concluded that counselors are defined as helpful more for decisions about educational matters than for either vocational or personal adjustment concerns.[22] Obviously, there is considerable disparity between student perceptions and counselors' self-perceptions. And obviously counselors cannot fulfill their ideals if students do not define them as useful sources of help.

How do teachers view counselors? Teachers tend to be more negative in their assessment than students. The stereotype of the counselor that emerges from teachers' attitudes is that of an individual who uses jargon to defend or coddle students who really need discipline, and who is at best of questionable value and at worst a nuisance or even an unnecessary evil. What about administrators? The administrator may view the counselor as a useful assistant in terms of such administrative tasks as scheduling, but in terms of a therapist or facilitator the administrator is likely to define the counselor as ineffective and incompetent. Finally, the little research that has been done on parents' expectations (as opposed to that reporting counselors' perceptions of parents' expectations) suggests that they too see the counselor as more helpful with educational and vocational problems than with personal, emotional, or family difficulties.

It is not surprising, then, that the actual role of counselors diverges from their ideal role. It should be emphasized here that the problem is not simply one of lack of understanding or communication. That is, we cannot simply educate teachers, administrators, students, and parents about counseling functions and expect that the problem will be resolved. Our point here is underscored by a study of high-school principals in Utah.[23] The principals were sent a role questionnaire about counselors. The questionnaire was also filled in by six counselor educators from various sections of the country. A factor analysis yielded six areas of counselor responsibilities as perceived by the principals: discipline, clerical activities, personal-emotional counseling, confidentiality with the principal, confidentiality with laymen, and counselor versatility (which referred to a variety of miscellaneous duties often expected of counselors). The counselor educators agreed perfectly in their responses, so their answers were used to define the ideal role. There was a significant difference between the ideal role and the principals' responses in all six areas.[24] More important for our purposes here, principals with 13 or more hours of counselor training and experience disagreed with the ideal role as much as those with only one to five hours of training, and on the clerical factor the principals with little training agreed more closely with the ideal role than those with the 13 or more hours. The answer to the counselor's dilemma will not be found in counselor education for administrators.

What then is the answer to the problem of counselors? To phrase the question in soap-opera language, can a trained counselor find happiness in an American high school? We believe that the answer is yes, but only if we recognize that the problem is inextricably rooted in the structure of the school. Participatory advisement is a restructuring that will make the counselor's role more meaningful and fulfilling.

## THE COUNSELOR IN A PARTICIPATORY ADVISEMENT SYSTEM

Initially, counselors may feel that their roles are threatened by participatory advisement. Some of the ten functions of the ideal role which we listed above are assumed by all advisors in the system. Nevertheless, the role of counselors is enhanced, and it is important to stress this fact early in the process of implementing the system. Counselors will no longer be marginal members of the staff, but vital resources.

The system will create new demands on counselors, bringing them into a more dynamic, interdependent relationship with teachers, students, and parents. In fact, the system demands of counselors those things which they do best—communicating, helping, planning, evaluating.

In participatory advisement, the emphasis is on preventive counseling. The counselor's task will not be to adjust students to the system on a crisis-oriented basis, but to actively initiate and develop means of meeting the personal, developmental needs of all adolescents. Counselors will provide services directly to advisors as well as to students and parents. And counselors will be involved in instruction as "teachers" of psychology. The exact functions will vary somewhat from one school to another, but the following are the most important aspects of the counselor's role in participatory advisement.

## THE COUNSELOR AS MODEL ADVISOR

Counselors, unlike many teachers and administrators, are not anxious about advising skills. By virtue of their training and experience, they are already competent and confident advisors. As a regular member of an advisement team, the counselor will be a model to other team members. This means that the counselor will teach and demonstrate the following:

(1) communication skills, particularly the skill of listening;
(2) how to plan and conduct conferences with parents;
(3) how to interpret and use the scores on various tests;
(4) ways of helping students solve various problems;
(5) how to assess students' strengths and weaknesses;
(6) ways to secure and share information on careers and higher education.

Counselors will be vitally important in helping other staff members deal with their anxieties about advisement skills and also improve their skills.

As one who teaches as well as demonstrates, the counselor can conduct specific training sessions on advisement skills. Such sessions will certainly be important during the implementation phase and may be helpful on an ongoing basis. At a minimum, each advisement team should periodically assess the skills of members and request special training sessions from counselors as needed.

In many schools, it may be important not to put the total burden of training on counselors. As noted above, some teachers do not have the highest professional regard for counselors, and may resent having counselors "tell them how to do it." This resentment can be minimized by using those teachers and administrators on the staff who are highly competent in particular advisement skills. Such staff members should be particularly useful during implementation. Outside consultants may also be important during the implementation phase.

Counselors, of course, will also function as advisors. By experiencing the advisement role themselves, they will be more sensitive to the frustrations and limitations involved. They will be able, therefore, to identify areas where advisors need support, or more resources, or encouragement.

## COUNSELORS AS SUPPORT PERSONNEL

Various advisors will have differing strengths and weaknesses. Any particular advisor will occasionally encounter a student with needs or problems which are beyond the advisor's capacity for helping. A particular advisor may feel uncomfortable talking about drug use, or sexual concerns, or psychological problems. An advisor may simply not have sufficient time to spend with a student who has a serious problem. The student may need the longer-term more intense counseling that can only be given by the counselor, or the student may need professional help which is not available at the school. In all such cases, the advisor should make a prompt referral to the counselor. The counselor is always available as support for the advisor—support both in the sense of being available for individual and/or crisis counseling and in the sense of being available for those cases where advisors may feel some discomfort or inadequacy.

Here again we must face the problem that many teachers and administrators are unconvinced of the counselor's ability to deal with such problems. One way to help overcome the negative views of other staff members is for counselors to establish a referral system. The system would require good communication. First, counselors would maintain communication with advisors, encouraging and even soliciting referrals and helping advisors feel comfortable about making referrals. Second, counselors need to maintain communication with administrators and advisement teams to identify students with special needs. Third, counselors should maintain regular communication with students by explaining their services in classes, and with parents by mailings that describe available services. Fourth, after conducting individual and group counseling with students, useful (non-confidential) feedback should be given to teachers, administrators, advisors and parents so that the total interaction with a given student is reasonably consistent and coherent. The feedback will also underscore the value of counseling and encourage subsequent referrals.

## COUNSELORS AS DELIBERATE PSYCHOLOGICAL EDUCATORS

Mosher and Sprinthall developed at Harvard University a model for psychological education which provides a means for promoting personal development.[25] The model stresses the need for preventive counseling. The "teaching" done in Deliberate Psychological Education combines a practicum experience and a seminar, avoiding the more passive classroom approach which relies mainly on telling and maximizes student dependence on teachers. This curriculum alternative will be described in more detail in Chapter 5.

One way to implement the model is to place students in a service or educational agency for direct experience for a portion of the school day and provide a weekly seminar on related curriculum. For example, students could be placed in a day care center and offered a curriculum on child care. They could be placed in a residential center for the aged and offered a curriculum on the psychology of aging. They could be employed in a peer counseling experience and given a curriculum on counseling strategy. In any case, counselors conduct the weekly seminars and coordinate the placement of students with agency supervisors. The coordination with agency personnel includes a mutual development of objectives and a description of student opportunities and responsibilities at the agency. Student placement will also require communication with advisors and parents.

While this program has academic objectives, some of the primary objectives are related to the personal growth and development of the adolescent. Issues relating to adolescents' personal development emerge and can be dealt with in the context of the life cycle. The experience brings adolescents into contact with people at different stages of development and ties that contact into the literature and discussions in the seminar.

Deliberate Psychological Education is not, of course, an integral part of the participatory advisement system. But it is a practical option in the context of the restructuring for participatory advisement and is a useful complement to the system. Teachers become advisors and counselors become teachers. The expansion of roles means that all staff members focus on developmental needs of all students in a systematic manner. Moreover, the overlap of traditional functions strengthens the interdependent relationship between teachers and counselors.

## COUNSELORS AS INFORMATION AND PROGRAM SPECIALISTS

Many of the guidance and counseling functions in the typical school must be reexamined under participatory advisement. What are the counselor's responsibilities for such matters as college admissions assistance, career preparation, job placement, human relations, special services such as tutoring, and individual and group testing? Each area must be analyzed and broken down into a series of activities for the school year, and responsibility must be assigned for each activity.

Making decisions about the above areas can be facilitated by asking a number of questions about each:

1.  What kind of information can be distributed to advisors for effective use?
2.  What kind of information should be available for advisors and students to use in the counseling center?
3.  What kind of information do parents need in print, in conferences, or in special group sessions?
4.  What direct services, such as programs, counseling, or literature, can we make available to students?
5.  Which services need publicity? How can they best be publicized?
6.  What procedures will be needed to insure effective liaison and referral to alternative schools and other agencies?

Once the questions are answered and the needed activities identified, specific responsibilities are assigned to various counselors. The assigned responsibilities should be published and explained to advisors, students, and parents. All counselors, of course, will share in personal and group counseling activities and, if the school uses it, in Deliberate Psychological Education. Beyond that, however, each will be a specialist in certain areas.

For example, let us assume a high school of 1500 and five counselors. The distributon of specialist functions might take the following form:

(1) Counselor A:
  Personal/group counseling
  Deliberate Psychological Education
  ACT-SAT-PSAT testing
  Home tutoring service
  College information
  Coordinator of counseling services
(2) Counselor B:
  Personal/group counseling
  Deliberate Psychological Education
  Financial aid and scholarships
  Advanced Placement Test coordinator
  CLEP testing information
  Guidance news editor
(3) Counselor C:
  Personal/group counseling
  Deliberate Psychological Education
  Coordinator of D. P. E. placements
  Liaison for high school equivalency program
  Social concerns (drugs, pregnancy, etc.)
(4) Counselor D:
  Personal/group counseling
  Deliberate Psychological Education
  Coordinator testing-achievement for 10th and 11th grades
  Liaison for educational alternatives (technical high school,
  alternative high school, dual enrollment with local colleges)
(5) Counselor E:
  Personal/group counseling
  Deliberate Psychological Education
  Career information
  State-wide basic competency testing
  Liaison with military representatives
  Job placement services
  CETA-job training program

Each of the above functions, of course, involves a series of activities. The distribution of functions will depend not only upon the training and interests of the counselors but also upon the amount of time required. For example, counselor E above is responsible for career information. Figure 3.1 shows a sample career information program. The program was developed through the process described above of analyzing the various areas and identifying necessary activities.

## CAREER INFORMATION PROGRAM

1. *Guest speaker program:* Objective is to provide students with opportunities to meet representatives of various careers. Activities include:
   a. Solicit from students by questionnaire their career interests or preferences.
   b. Invite guest speakers on the basis of preferences, giving students who expressed the preference a special invitation to attend. All other students will be invited by broadcast announcement. Speakers from various careers come weekly throughout the school year.
   c. Sponsor a career fair one night each year for students in all grades. All district schools could be organized to participate.

2. *Career information:* Objective is to help students use appropriate career information in preparing for career entry or further education. Activities include:
   a. Arrange career materials so that students and advisors have easy access, and provide advisors with assistance in teaching students to use open career files.
   b. Identify career information and activities which relate to various courses of study and encourage teachers to use them in classes. Meet with department chairpeople to coordinate this task.
   c. Make a list of speakers available to teachers of appropriate subjects and encourage teachers to solicit career speakers.
   d. Identify basic skills required in various careers and list related courses in the school's curriculum. Make this available to students and advisors.

3. *Career inventories—individual assessment:* Objective is to assist students in assessing their career interests and aptitudes. Activities include:
   a. Publicize availability of individual career inventories or aptitude tests. Some may be a regular part of the testing program and some may be optional.
   b. Provide short training sessions for advisors on interpretation and appropriate use of career inventories and aptitude tests.

*(cont.)*

4. *Community relations:* Objective is to coordinate with the community to create positive relations and avoid confusion. Activities include:
   a. Organize a volunteer committee of adults from different careers to help evaluate school programs and offerings each year.
   b. Organize a coordinating committee within school to assist administration in coordinating contacts with the community. Meet once or twice yearly with school personnel who: solicit jobs for work/study students; locate placements for students in community-based learning programs; use guest speakers or technical assistance. The committee will be responsible for avoiding multiple contacts, sharing resources, and keeping accurate records of community resources used.

**Figure 3.1**
Sample Career Information Program

We would make two final observations about the distribution of specialist functions. First, to the extent possible, the distribution should result in groups of related functions. In the sample given above each counselor shares in the testing program, usually assuming responsibility for tests related to the other assigned functions. Second, the liaison functions given in the sample mean that the counselor will screen any student who requests, or who is recommended for, some educational alternative. The counselor is responsible to see that the student's needs will be served by the alternative and to assist in the enrollment or transfer procedure.

## THE COUNSELOR'S WORK LOAD

In a participatory advisement system, as we have shown, the counseling program is organized so that services are explicitly defined for all school personnel, students, and parents. The counseling services are carefully planned to support and complement advisement relationships. Counselors spend the greater part of their time and energy in preventive counseling strategies, deliberately emphasizing the personal growth and developmental needs of students. The resulting change in the typical role is illustrated in Figure 3.2. Note that over

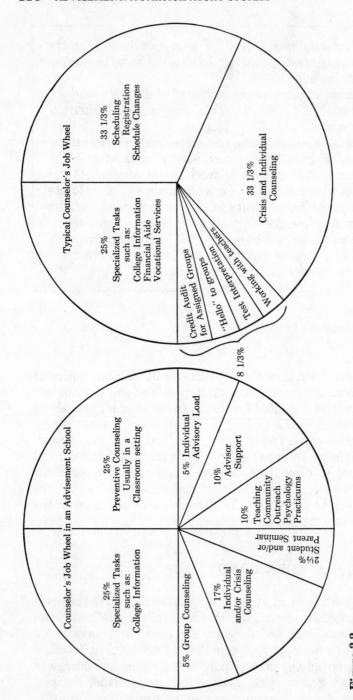

**Figure 3.2**
The Counselor's Work Load in a Traditional and Participatory Advisement System

two-thirds of a counselor's time in a traditional school can be consumed by scheduling and crisis counseling. In the participatory advisement system, on the other hand, the counselor becomes more deeply involved in those kinds of activities for which he or she is trained.

## SUMMARY

The guidance movement developed around the turn of the century, initially to provide effective vocational guidance. Vocational guidance counselors soon began to do educational guidance as increasing numbers of students prepared for college. By the 1940s, the stage of vocational and educational guidance was giving way to the stage of meeting individual needs through a therapeutic relationship. This stage, in turn, gave way to a stage of transitional professionalism and finally to the most recent stage of "situational diagnosis." The changing field of guidance and counseling reflects changes occurring in American society and American schools.

Although the role of the counselor has changed over time, there is some consensus about the contemporary high-school counselor's role. Counselors themselves tend to agree on a number of basic functions of the role. In order to fulfill these functions, counselors have been trained by diverse theories, though most have probably been trained in the Rogerian school.

In contrast to their training and ideal role, counselors typically function in high schools as administrative assistants, student advocates, troubleshooters, and therapists. Their actual role has been shaped by various forces and groups. In a participatory advisement system, the counselor's role takes on a new dimension. The emphasis is on preventive counseling. The counselor becomes a model advisor, a part of the support personnel, a deliberate psychological educator, and an information and program specialist. The counselor's work load in a participatory advisement system shifts from a heavy emphasis on scheduling and crisis counseling to those kinds of activities for which the counselor is uniquely trained.

# Endnotes

[1] Duane Brown and David J. Srebalus, *Selected Readings in Contemporary Guidance* (Dubuque, Iowa: Wm. C. Brown Company, 1973), p. xii.

[2] Marjorie K. Bradley, "Counseling Past and Present: Is There a Future?" *Personnel and Guidance Journal* 57 (September, 1978):43.

[3] Richard Hill Byrne, *Guidance: A Behavioral Approach* (Englewood Cliffs: Prentice-Hall, Inc., 1977), p. 8.

[4] David J. Armor, *The American School Counselor* (New York: Russell Sage Foundation, 1969), pp. 27–28.

[5] Frank W. Miller, *Guidance: Principles and Services* (Columbus, Ohio: Charles E. Merrill Books, Inc., 1961), p. 27.

[6] Armor, *op. cit.*, p. 31.

[7] The first three stages were identified by A. Stiller, ed., *School Counseling: View from Within* (Washington, D.C.:APGA, 1967). The fourth is described by Bradley, *op. cit.*, p. 42.

[8] Hermann Hesse, *Steppenwolf* (New York: Bantam Books, 1963), p. 66.

[9] The ten functions as described by Isaksen are given in W. Phillips, "Guidance Services: Range and Scope," *The High School Journal* 54 (1971):243–50.

[10] Stuart A. Pizer and Jeffrey R. Travers, *Psychology and Social Change* (New York: McGraw-Hill, 1975), pp. 12–13.

[11] In discussing the various theories of counseling, we are following Louis M. Cunningham and Herman J. Peters, *Counseling Theories* (Columbus, Ohio: Charles E. Merrill, 1973), pp. 25ff.

[12] R. J. Rousseve, "The Role of the Counselor in a Free Society," in Duane Brown and David J. Srebalus, *op. cit.*, p. 11.

[13] Don Dinkmeyer and Edson Caldwell, *Developmental Counseling and Guidance: A Comprehensive School Approach* (New York: McGraw-Hill, 1970), pp. 88–92.

[14] Cunningham and Peters, *op. cit.*, p. 70.

[15] *Ibid.*, p. 71.

[16] Byrne, *op. cit.*, pp. 117–18.

[17] *Ibid.*, p. 128.

[18] Cunningham and Peters, *op. cit.*, p. 120.

[19] *Ibid.*, p. 56.

[20] Robert K. Merton, *Social Theory and Social Structure*, revised and enlarged edition (New York: The Free Press, 1957), p. 369.

THE ROLE OF COUNSELORS 117

[21]Bruce Shertzer and Shelley C. Stone, "The School Counselor and His Publics: A Problem in Role Definition," *Personnel and Guidance Journal* 41 (April, 1963):687–93. This study is a summary of the findings of various other pieces of research.

[22]William E. Knox, David J. Pratto and Cheryl Mann Callahan, "Domains of Decision-making and School Counselor Use Among High-School Seniors," *Sociology of Education* 47 (no. 4, 1974):466–90.

[23]Darrell H. Hart and Donald J. Prince, "Role Conflict for School Counselors: Training versus Job Demands," *Personnel and Guidance Journal* 48 (January, 1970): 374–80.

[24]The principals were divided into groups. Three of the groups had no counseling experience, but were divided according to whether they had no counselor education, 1–5 quarter hours, or 13 or more quarter hours of counselor education. The fourth group had 13 or more quarter hours of education and four or more years of counseling experience. The one exception to the significant differences was that only the group without any counselor education or experience differed significantly from the ideal on the discipline factor. The other three groups agreed with the ideal—namely, that counselors should not be responsible for discipline.

[25]Ralph L. Mosher and Norman A. Sprinthall, "Psychological Education: A Means to Promote Personal Development during Adolescence," *The Counseling Psychologist* 2 (no. 4, 1971): 3–82.

# Part

## 2

# THE CURRICULUM:

## A RESPONSIVE SYSTEM

# Chapter 4

# Designing a Responsive Curriculum

In a small Missouri town around 1940, the school superintendent stated that his aim was to give the people "exactly the kind of a school that they want." According to the adults of the community, the basic purposes of school were

(1) "to learn children readin', writin', and 'rithmetic and maybe a little joggerfy";
(2) "to give our children the same kind of education and the same chance that children have anywhere";
(3) "to keep children out of the way and out of trouble until they get old enough to know how to act";
(4) "to keep children from growing up as wild and ignorant as the animals."[1]

If the superintendent had indeed given the people exactly what they expected, he would have had a challenging task of curriculum design.

While we would not agree with the superintendent that the school should simply give people exactly what they want, ignoring educational principles and the insights of the school's staff, we do feel that he was partially right—the expectations of the clientele must be a factor in designing the curriculum. The curriculum should be reasonably responsive to the needs of individuals and also to the larger goals of the school and the society.

In this chapter, we will look at some recent ideas about the curriculum in a comprehensive high school. We will then examine some elements involved in designing a curriculum that will maximize flexibility and provide students with optimum choices. Finally, we will briefly discuss the importance of ongoing evaluation and the means of bringing about changes in the curriculum.

## THE CURRICULUM IN THE COMPREHENSIVE HIGH SCHOOL

From World War I through World War II, considerable controversy raged over the appropriate emphasis for a high-school curriculum —whether the curriculum should offer the student a good liberal education or mold the student into an effective social-vocational creature. In senior high schools, the curriculum tended to reflect the social-vocational emphasis. Students were segregated according to their social-vocational aims—some were planning on college, while others were preparing to enter the business world, to engage in industrial or manual arts, or to pursue farming. "The high school and its curriculum underwent an extraordinary degree of democratization during this period, but in many respects it was so organized that it increasingly operated to support social stratification and the status quo."[2]

After World War II, educators responded to the situation created by the cold war by stressing a "discipline-centered" curriculum. That is, the curriculum was organized around the varied academic disciplines. Academic specialists taught within the narrow confines of their particular knowledge in an effort to produce the "highly trained leaders, scientists, and technicians" who could "meet the challenge" of international communism.[3] Eventually, the cold war lost some of its intensity, and Americans became increasingly aware of a host of internal problems (racism, poverty, environmental problems, and so forth). During the 1960s the discipline-centered curriculum was attacked on the grounds that it was irrelevant or immoral or unrelated to the realities of social life or that it produced experts but not necessarily good citizens or humane individuals.

"Once again the struggle between liberal and vocational education was joined" and "out of this syndrome of reaction was born (or reborn) the humanistic movement in curriculum."[4] The humanistic movement emphasizes the development of the individual, the relevance of learning, the various dimensions of learning (learning is more than a cognitive process), and the interpersonal relationships in the learning situation.

With this brief historical overview as a background, we will now look at some of the ideas of one of the most influential figures in American education, James Bryant Conant. We will then briefly discuss an important representative of the humanistic perspective, J. Lloyd Trump, and a significant document on reforming secondary education, the RISE report. These three viewpoints all emphasize the importance of keeping individual differences in mind as the curriculum is developed. A curriculum can only be *responsive*, of course, as individual differences are recognized and taken into account. But there are, as we shall note, some formal and informal constraints on any effort at individualizing the curriculum.


## THE INFLUENCE OF CONANT

Probably no single person has had more to say about, or had more influence on, the comprehensive high school and its curriculum than James Bryant Conant. In a publication of the National Association of Secondary School Principals, Passow offers a concise summary of Conant's major recommendations for the secondary school curriculum over the last three decades.[5]

According to Conant, the changes which occurred between 1905 and 1930 involved a "revolutionary transformation" of the American high school. By the latter date, the comprehensive high school could be found throughout the nation. Students in the eleventh and twelfth grades spent as much as half of their time on courses aimed at developing marketable skills, preparing themselves for various kinds of jobs. At the same time, of course, they had had minimum exposure to those elements of the good liberal education which had been deemed so important at the turn of the century.[6]

In Conant's view, the development of the comprehensive high school was a triumph of democracy. He argued that the comprehensive high school was a uniquely American phenomenon that would develop a competent citizenry for our pluralistic, democratic society. To achieve this aim, students from diverse backgrounds would have certain common experiences in the school. It is valuable for all students to have some exposure to the social sciences, the natural sciences, literature, and the arts. But if all should be exposed to a common core, an important question arises: "Can a school at one and the same time provide a good general education for *all* the pupils as future citizens of a democracy, provide elective programs for the majority to develop useful skills, and educate adequately those with a talent for handling advanced academic subjects—particularly foreign languages and mathematics?"[7]

To answer the question, Conant undertook his now famous study of 103 schools. Out of this study he developed his criteria for the ideal comprehensive high school. The comprehensiveness of a high school was to be evaluated in terms of fifteen points which were grouped into four categories. The four categories can be phrased as questions:[8]

1. How adequate is the general education for all students?
2. How adequate are nonacademic elective programs?
3. What kind of arrangements are made for gifted or highly talented students?
4. What other features does the school possess that enhance the educational experience?

These questions were to be answered by looking at particular aspects of a school. The adequacy of the general education was to be evaluated by offerings in composition, English and American literature, social studies, and by ability grouping in required courses. The adequacy of nonacademic elective programs was to be judged in terms of such things as vocational and commercial programs, opportunities for supervised work experience, and help for slow readers. Evaluation of special arrangements for gifted students was made in terms of such things as particular provisions and individualized instruction programs for such students rather than standardized courses of study. Finally, the school was evaluated in terms of such other features as guidance, student morale, and the nature of student interaction.

Obviously, several of Conant's recommendations dealt directly and specifically with curriculum. He urged that all students have access to an individualized program and that such labeled curricula as "college prep" or "vocational" be eliminated. All students would, of course, be expected to take those courses necessary for a "general education." All students would be well grounded in English and social studies, and would have at least a minimal amount of math and science. But beyond that, Conant argued, there should be flexibility and guidance in order to accommodate individual needs.

The graduation requirements Conant recommended for all students correspond very largely to those found today in most schools. Though Conant was criticized for his adherence to the "Carnegie unit" measure, that too is still the norm among the nation's schools.

Conant foresaw the public reaction that would take place as schools diversified their offerings in an attempt to provide individualized instruction. He said that the time might arrive (as it has) when there would be so much diversity in a high school's curriculum that people would demand a return to more order.

By 1967, in the face of continuing criticisms of the secondary schools and in spite of the shortcomings which he himself identified in the schools, Conant remained committed to the comprehensive high school and felt that its continued development and improvement was vitally important to the nation. He opposed, for instance, separate vocation schools on the grounds that all kinds of work are worthwhile in American society. To keep students together in the same school would stress the equality of status of diverse kinds of work and the equality of opportunity that characterizes American society. In other words, there are social as well as educational purposes in the comprehensive high school. Without question, then, "public schools should operate within an *elective* and not a *selective* framework."[9]

Criticism of the comprehensive high school increased during the turbulent 1960s. As a consequence, broad national reviews of the high school and of adolescents generally, were conducted by a series of commissions and panels, including the National Commission on the Reform of Secondary Education, the National Panel on High School and Adolescent Education, and the Panel on Youth of the President's Science Advisory Commission. Although the studies that were undertaken by these groups looked at the same areas and problems that Conant had focused on, and although they often leveled similar criticisms at the schools, they made contrary recommendations about how to deal with the problems. In spite of the sharp differences among the studies and between them and Conant's earlier recommendations, there was consensus at one point—it was strongly recommended that the variety of options and alternatives open to the students should be dramatically increased.[10] Of particular significance was the emphasis placed on learning options that occur in the community and that relate to career or real-work situations and experiences.

What is the net result of all the studies? Years after the reports, the comprehensive high school remains essentially unchanged in many communities. It appears that the comprehensive high school will continue to be the major means of delivering educational services and programs to most of American youth.

## THE IDEAS OF TRUMP

"Sometimes," wrote Whitehead, "the period of change is an age of hope, sometimes it is an age of despair. When mankind has slipped its cables, sometimes it is bent on the discovery of a New World, and sometimes it is haunted by the dim sound of the breakers dashing on the rocks ahead."[11] The changing America of the 1960s was an age of both hope and despair. The hope was expressed in the passionate call for human freedom; the despair was manifest in the numerous innovations in education which attempted to articulate freedom in schools but which foundered on the rocks of failure.

The failure of the innovations should not obscure the importance of the ideas which impelled them. To quote Whitehead again: "Great ideas enter into reality with evil associates and with disgusting alliances. But the greatness remains; nerving the race in its slow ascent."[12] We must judge ideas on their own merit, and the idea of human freedom is certainly meritorious for Americans.

J. Lloyd Trump was influential throughout the 1950s, 1960s, and into the 1970s in espousing individual freedom and growth through the organization and curriculum of the high school. As we have argued, the fact that many of the innovations which attempted to implement the ideals were failures should not blind us to the validity of the ideas. The human organization is one in which individual freedom and growth are maximized. Trump tried to show how a more flexible, humane, individualized program could contribute to the ideals of freedom and growth. The "Trump plan" became known throughout the country. Many schools adopted certain aspects of the plan, such as differentiated staffing, modular scheduling, and independent study.

Over an eight-year period, Trump and his ideas gave direction to the Model Schools Project, called *Schools of Tomorrow*.[13] Trump advocated the development of organizations and curricula which would provide a "school for everyone":

> A *school for everyone* is a concept, a locale, and a program that responds actively to the diagnosed needs of each person. What does a school look like when personalization is a basic goal? . . . Personalization in a school is directly proportional to the number of opportunities for choices that the program provides under systematic guidance and supervision.[14]

In an individualized program, each student would be able to complete certain uniform requirements and would also be able to take special interest courses "at a pace that is appropriate for him or her. The conventional idea that all students should complete courses or units of work in the same amount of time is unrealistic."[15] Individualization does not mean, however, that the student works alone. Rather, each student would work at times with others who are at the same stage of development in a particular subject.

In order to work, Trump argued, individualization would require each student to have a teacher–adviser, who would continually monitor the student's progress and help the student pursue a course of study which is optimal for that student's development. Such individualized help cannot possibly be provided by a counselor who is responsible for 300 or more students. We have, of course, earlier argued the same point, and have shown a system—participatory advisement—that effectively implements such individualized education.

## INDIVIDUALIZED EDUCATION

Clearly, the comprehensive high school envisioned by Conant and especially by Trump is a place where the individual differences of students are of primary importance. As Trump put it, we need to break up the masses of students and make certain that each student "is known completely and continuously by someone who has the time and the authority to take constructive action."[16] The ideal of individualized education was also reflected in the RISE Report (Report of the California Commission for Reform of Intermediate and Secondary Education) of 1975. The report eloquently restated the belief that secondary schools can be reformed into effective, responsive systems, systems which begin with the "recognition and acceptance of each student or learner as its primary client, the most important individual to be served."[17]

Many of the recommendations of the RISE Report deal with curriculum design. A design is advocated which allows wide variety of choices, many of which involve the use of resources outside the traditional school setting. The report recommends that in addition to the more traditional programs, students have such options as work-study programs, occupational training programs, and special interest centers. Moreover, students should have the opportunity for "firsthand learning experiences" in various community locations such as business and industry, or public service agencies, or cultural centers. There should also be considerable flexibility in the time used for learning. That is, education should not be thought of as something that takes place only during school hours.

> School attendance requirements should allow a learner to leave the school system temporarily with the approval of the learner's parents and the school. These furloughs should be of flexible duration, of educational value to the learner, and consistent with the learner's educational needs and objectives.[18]

In all the report's recommendations for expanding choices, creating options, and responding to the individual needs of students, there is implicit the idea that schools will also create a communication system that enables the staff to plan effective programs on a personal basis with each student and his or her parents.

Recent criticism of the schools, particularly that involving declining test scores, claims that schools have in some cases offered the increased number of options without creating the means for helping each student make appropriate choices. Given an effective system of advisement and counseling, a responsive and responsible curriculum is both possible and desirable. In other words, we view the participatory advisement system as an essential base from which to design a responsive curriculum.

We should note that there are both formal constraints and personal factors involved in individualizing education. The formal constraints are those which may be imposed by state and local boards of education or by legislatures. Formal constraints include such things as graduation requirements, which normally demand certain specific courses (health, civics, and so forth), specific numbers of credits in particular subjects, and certain minimum competencies that have been added in a number of states. Nevertheless, a high degree of flexibility is usually allowed in meeting these imposed requirements. Formal constraints are essentially minimum standards and are not sufficient descriptions of the needs of individual students. For instance, a serious college preparatory program would far exceed the minimum graduation requirements.

The formal constraints set forth certain boundaries, then. The personal factors, on the other hand, help to establish the nature of the program which is developed within the boundaries. Personal factors include varied student goals (college or career), individual interests, individual abilities and talents, and individual motivation.

The point is that individualization does not mean chaos. A responsive curriculum is orderly and logically organized. The curriculum does not contain simply a vast hodgepodge of courses and programs, but a set of courses and programs that reflect state and local requirements, the individual goals and needs of students, and the staff's definition of a sound education. Let us see now what is involved in the design of such a curriculum.

## CURRICULUM DESIGN FOR OPTIMUM CHOICE AND FLEXIBILITY

We have already indicated that a responsive curriculum is not chaotic. There is order and logic in the responsive curriculum. Furthermore, the responsive curriculum is not merely a response to specific student requests. Students need rules and guidance as well as freedom. Karl Menninger illustrated this point when he told of the small girl in a progressive school who asked, "Do I *have* to do as I please today?"[19] The curriculum should be responsible as well as responsive. We aim at *optimum*, not absolute, choice and flexibility. Before looking specifically at what is involved in the design of such a curriculum, it will be helpful to discuss briefly the traditional design.

## THE TRADITIONAL CURRICULUM AND ITS PROBLEMS

The traditional secondary curriculum offers year-long and semester courses of study, courses that are usually designed for specific grade levels and ages. Some individualization can be achieved in such a context by the ability-grouping of students and by individualizing instruction within classrooms. In the traditional setting, students are offered an increasing number of electives in the higher grade levels.

Students are usually scheduled into their courses at the beginning of the year and are expected to remain in the program as scheduled. Changing a student's program is frequently difficult. The student's actual progress and motivation in the class are generally considered insufficient reasons for making program changes.

Students are placed in much of their program as a result of their group membership—grade, age, sex, and ability label. The curriculum is organized around group needs rather than individual needs. There is usually not a sufficient communication system for dealing with the great variety of existing individual needs.

The number of options and the amount of flexibility that can be built into a curriculum in the traditional setting will vary from school to school. But the options and flexibility will have a group focus, and the school is seriously limited by the lack of a system for the articulation of individual needs and goals.

Dissatisfaction with the lack of individualized education has resulted in a number of suggestions for change. One recent, and meritorious, idea has come out of the Institute for the Development of Educational Activities and the Wisconsin Center for Educational Research and Development. These organizations have developed models for secondary education that involve organization of the comprehensive school into "learning communities" or "instructional/advisement units." In this plan, a set of teacher/advisors and students (about 150 to 250) has a high degree of autonomy to determine the curriculum for themselves as a group and as individual learners. The determination is based on diagnosed needs and interests as well as daily/weekly feedback and evaluation of progress. Except for highly specialized learning objectives, which the student would be forced to explore with teachers or resources outside his or her "learning community," objectives and learning experiences are planned by the student, the advisor, and the other teachers in the student's "community." Pre-planned courses of study might exist in a learning community but the concept implies that curriculum can also develop somewhat spontaneously—teachers, advisors, and students share the responsibility for planning, organizing, and carrying out learning activities. Theoretically, the plan seems sound and it is consistent with the nature of a human organization. But there are four problems with this solution to the inadequacies of the traditional curriculum:

1. The curriculum of the modern secondary school has become highly specialized. Much of what would appeal to a student would likely fall outside the expertise of his or her set of teacher/advisors.
2. The system would be inefficient. Advocates would argue that efficiency is not a valid objection, that personalizing the instructional setting and teaching students "how to learn" are overriding objectives that more than compensate for any inefficiency. But while we would agree that efficiency should not be the foremost criterion of evaluation, we also would argue that the system requires an inordinate amount of time spent in talking, planning, and implementing. Learning how to learn is certainly a valid objective, particularly in the light of the explosion of knowledge in virtually every discipline today. But too much time would be devoted to organizational and management matters in this kind of instructional setting.
3. The organization and skills necessary for managing such a highly individualized instructional setting do not exist among many faculties—if, indeed, they exist among any at all. It is possible that such a system could be managed by using a computer. But the experience of even master teachers who attempt individualization in one subject indicates that the system could become a nightmare of record keeping and record retrieval. At the least, it would require substantial improvement of teacher/student ratios and the retraining of teachers.
4. Finally, the system places a responsibility upon students for which they may not be ready, requiring them to become self-directed learners. At the high school level, most students do not feel that they can operate independently of teachers. As we have pointed out, students need rules and guidance as well as free-

dom; they need meaningful relationships as well as indepen-
dence. The design we discuss below attempts to fulfill these
diverse needs.

## THE DESIGN OF A RESPONSIVE CURRICULUM

The curriculum design which we shall outline is not offered as an answer to all problems. As we have emphasized before, materials useful
in one school can seldom be adopted whole in other schools. But the design we shall describe can serve as a useful model, for it has a number
of important characteristics:

1.  It uses many traditional elements. It does not "throw the baby
    out with the bath water." Courses are organized into traditional
    time segments—quarter, semester, year. The daily schedule can
    consist of the typical six or seven period day.
2.  It would have a high degree of acceptance from official educa-
    tional authorities at the state and local levels as well as from
    teachers and parents.
3.  It offers a considerable degree of flexibility and individualiza-
    tion. In fact, it is conceivable that a school could have 2000 stu-
    dents without two identical schedules.
4.  It falls well within the management capabilities of most high
    school faculties, given a reasonable opportunity to develop ad-
    visement skills.
5.  It creates a dynamic relationship among students and teachers
    and parents—dynamic because changes in course offerings and
    instructional methods are more feasible and more likely than is
    true in the traditional setting. A "consumer-oriented" accounta-
    bility is built into the design.

As a first element in the design, let us look at the criteria for student selection and placement. In essence, the criteria will be ability and
interest rather than age or grade level. Building on interest is an important element in all human enterprise. The interests of students
should be given much greater priority than has usually been the case.
Student interests should be a basic factor in the design of the curriculum, in the process of matching individual students with curriculum
offerings, and in the teaching methodologies employed in courses. Cap-
italizing on interests does not conflict with the teaching of basic skills.
In fact, a carefully designed curriculum which lets interests become a
significant factor will enhance the changes of students learning basic
skills and attaining academic excellence.

Using both interest and ability means that courses in any particular discipline will, to the extent possible, be set up to reflect both varied interests and differing levels of ability. For example, an ability/interest matrix for art courses might look like that shown in Figure 4.1. The art curriculum is a simple illustration. The student qualifies for admission to any intermediate level course by successfully completing one or both general level courses. Whether a student will opt for one or both of the general interest courses will depend upon his or her interests. The student who is basically interested in sculpture would probably plan to complete the three-dimensional design course.

Students may take as many intermediate level electives as they choose and as seems appropriate within the context of their programs of study. Entry into the advanced level courses depends upon the student's prior achievement and his or her motivation. In some disciplines (as in art), advanced level courses will require approval of the instructor, since there may be special requirements. In art, for instance, students may be expected to produce works for display in school or in specially arranged shows.

The matrices for English, science and other disciplines are, of course, more complex than that for art. The ability level of courses in

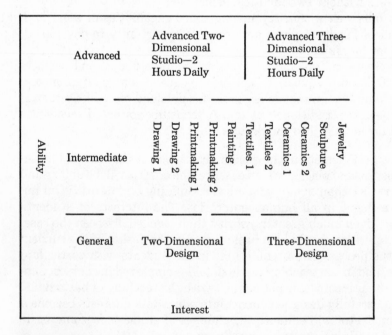

**Figure 4.1**
Illustrative Ability/Interest Matrix for Art Curriculum

English, for example, is much more discretely defined, especially in terms of reading and writing skills. While all course offerings are open to students of all grades, sequences of courses are recommended for students at different levels of ability. Some offerings, however, will draw from a reasonably diverse population.

In order to maximize the effectiveness of a curriculum based on interests and abilities, an appropriate course catalog is necessary. That is, the format of the catalog is important. The catalog should present courses clearly in terms of their position in the ability/interest matrix, their relationship to specific goals (college admissions, careers, honors), and their relationship to other courses. It is essential not only to give adequate information, but also to establish a consistent method of describing courses. A model should be created which can be followed in writing course descriptions, such as that shown in Figure 4.2. A description based upon the model is shown in Figure 4.3.

---

Course Number and Name and Ability Level:

Prerequisites for Course:

Amount of Credit:

When Normally Offered:

Content: A short but helpful statement of what will be covered in the course.

Expectations: A summary of those things a student will be expected to do in the course, so that the student can evaluate the usefulness in terms of his or her interests and abilities. Expectations about reading or other skills, about the kinds of interests addressed, and about relationship with other courses may be included here.

Method of Presentation: A brief statement of some of the teaching methods employed.

Skills Taught: A list of any specific skills that will be taught in the course.

---

**Figure 4.2**
A Model Course Description

---

121 The Isms: Contemporary Ideologies (A)

Prerequisites: None

Amount of Credit: 1/4 in Social Studies

Offered: 3rd Quarter

Content: Capitalism, socialism, communism, and fascism are potent forces in the world. Students will analyze each of them and compare their philosophies and their economic systems.

Expectations: Students will read some difficult materials, deal with abstract ideas and concepts, analyze theories, and take essay tests.

Method of Presentation: There will be some lectures to explain complex ideas. Students will read, discuss, and give individual or group presentations.

Skills Taught: Students will learn to read and listen critically, handle abstract ideas, do research, and write essays.

---

**Figure 4.3**
Course Description Based on the Model

Equally important is the availability of information that helps parents, students and advisors create a *program* of studies rather than a hodgepodge of unrelated choices. Each department, therefore, should include information that will help students plan a goal-oriented sequence. For example, the business department may recommend sequences for various occupations, differentiating between those courses which are highly recommended and those which are useful but not required. These recommendations should be incorporated into the course catalog. Sample sequences are shown in Figure 4.4.

Some programs of study may involve several departments. For instance, students who are planning to enroll in college will need to know the number and kinds of courses they should take in a variety of disciplines. The catalog can include a page that outlines the college preparatory program, indicating which courses should be taken in which disciplines and in what sequence.

RECOMMENDED SEQUENCES OF BUSINESS COURSES
FOR VARIOUS OCCUPATIONS

Computer Operator or Programmer
 Typing 1—one semester minimum
 Introduction to Data Processing
 Beginning Accounting 1
 Beginning Keypunch
 *Beginning Accounting 2
 *APEX Model Office
  (Post high-school training required)

Accounting Clerk
 Beginning Accounting 1
 Beginning Accounting 2
 Advanced Accounting
 *Business Law
 *Data Processing
 *Office Machines
 *Individual Income Taxes

*Useful, but not required.

**Figure 4.4**
Sample Recommended Sequences of Business Department

A second basic element of curriculum design involves the choice between a quarter or semester system. As the materials above suggest, we believe that the quarter system should be used. Much of the flexibility of the design we propose is derived from the use of the quarter system, which offers advantages in the number of courses that can be offered, in scheduling, and in grade reporting. The flexibility may be illustrated by a mathematics curriculum, which includes a combination of quarter, semester, and year-long courses. Basic math would be a quarter course, as would a few other courses such as one in problem solving. Many courses would run for a semester, such as introductory algebra, or analytic geometry. And some courses, such as honors algebra or calculus, would be offered as year-long courses. Information on the offerings of each department, the length of each course, the time normally offered, and the ability level for each should be put into the catalog in summary form as shown in Figure 4.5 for the math curricu-

| MATHEMATICS CURRICULUM | | | | | |
| --- | --- | --- | --- | --- | --- |
| *Course* | *Quarter Offered* | | | | |
| (G) 350 Basic Math (1 or more quarters) | X | X | X | X | |
| (G) 351 Consumer Math (1 or more quarters) | X | X | X | X | |
| (G) 353 Intro to Algebra | | | ───────▶ | | |
| (G) 365 Algebra 1 | ─────────────────▶ | | | | |
| (G) 366 Algebra Review | | | ───────▶ | | |
| (I) 370 Math: Human Endeavor | ───────▶ | | | | |
| (I) 371 Problem Solving (1 quarter only) | X | X | X | X | |
| (I) 372 Computer Application (1 quarter only) | X | X | X | X | |
| (I) 375 Geometry | ─────────────────▶ | | | | |
| (I) 377 Algebra 2 | ─────────────────▶ | | | | |
| (A) 378 Honors Algebra 2 | ─────────────────▶ | | | | |
| (I) 379 Math for Electronics | ─────────────────▶ | | | | |
| (I) 380 Prob. & Statistics | | | ───────▶ | | |
| (A) 385 Analytic Geometry | ───────▶ | | | | |
| (A) 388 Intro to Analysis | | | ───────▶ | | |
| (A) 389 Calculus | ─────────────────▶ | | | | |

**Figure 4.5**
Summary of Math Curriculum for Course Catalog

lum. The letters preceding each course tell the student the ability level—general, intermediate, or advanced. An "X" indicates a quarter course, and tells the student which quarters the course will be available. Arrows show semester and year-long courses and, in the case of the former, whether the course is usually a first- or second-semester offering.

Students who are still functioning at the basic or consumer math level may enter the program in any quarter and may remain for as many quarters as necessary to satisfy the minimum standards required for graduation or the diagnosed needs of the student. It is not uncommon for students in their last year of high school to recognize weaknesses in their math skills and reenter for purposes of relearning and reinforcing their skills. A student may recognize this need through experience with other courses in his or her curriculum (such as business or industrial education), or through the diagnosis of teachers in other courses who are monitoring the development of basic skills, or through the school's formal testing program. Each student, as we have noted previously, will review his or her test results with an advisor, establishing for himself or herself strengths and weaknesses.

Students who attempt the traditional math sequence are encouraged by the offerings to remain in the developmental sequence even when they experience difficulty with aspects of the sequence and fall behind the usual pace of mastering material. Offerings such as Introduction to Algebra and Algebra Review are particular semester offerings designed to give some students more time to establish a strong background at the beginning of the math sequence. Other offerings, such as Math: A Human Endeavor (a math appreciation course), Problem Solving, Computer Application, and Probability and Statistics, give students additional topics in math or encourage students to develop math skills even though they may have dropped out of the traditional sequence leading to calculus.

The quarter system allows such flexibility. In the case of math, such a curriculum is likely to result in higher student enrollments. Rather than a steady loss of math students through the school year, the school may maintain or even increase the number of students in math courses.

Another advantage of the quarter system is the arrangement of double periods for one subject during a given quarter. Double periods can be used to help a student keep up with class progress or review objectives not yet mastered. For example, students will often have difficulty at some stage in the traditional math sequence. Rather than give up or fall farther behind, a student can schedule an additional hour for math for a quarter (and possibly longer). This additional hour each day plus some tutorial assistance may be sufficient in most cases to get the student through the difficulty and renew his or her confidence.

To increase flexibility, credit can be awarded to students on the basis of examinations (objectives mastered) regardless of the time spent in class. A remedial student may be granted 1/8 credit in a given quarter for objectives mastered, which is, in our judgment, a better option than receiving a failing grade for completing only half the quarter's work. An advanced student may agree to work at his or her own pace, and complete by examination a full unit (one year) of math in a semester or three quarters. These curriculum and credit policies allow considerable individualization, but well within the management skills of the math teachers and the advisors. In essence, what we have described is a compromise between a rigidly defined math sequence that all students are expected to cope with (and at the same pace), and the totally individualized program which manages each separate learner by specific objectives.

Yet another important benefit of the quarter system is the opportunities it provides to motivate some students. A student's schedule can change partially or even completely each quarter. The possibility of change gives the student an opportunity to explore course offerings in all areas, perhaps discovering in the process high-interest subjects, activities, and teachers. In a period of two quarters, a student could take such subjects as oceanography, animal behavior, genetics, business law, poetry, speech, creative writing, housewiring, child development, clothing construction, acting, urban problems, and so forth. The only limitations are the amount of time the student has for electives, the student's interests, and the variety of offerings.

When students do explore a variety of subjects and discover a particular interest, they can follow up with additional study in that area and begin to examine, with their advisors, the implications of that interest for their future plans.

We must emphasize that the provision of many different kinds of courses and the exploration of the curriculum in terms of the individual's interests does not mean lower academic standards. We can illustrate this point by the science offerings in one responsive curriculum (Figure 4.6). Note the great variety of courses which can be offered when the quarter system is used. Note also that even a student with little interest in science is likely to find some quarter courses that would be attractive—perhaps consumer chemistry or astronomy or reptiles and fish. A student who is keenly interested in science and who may be planning on a career in science also has an attractive range of courses from which to choose. Students interested in pursuing a career

SCIENCE

Earth Science
  Oceanography
  Nature of Atmosphere
  Astronomy
  Historical Geology
  Physical Geology

Biology
  Plant Kingdom
  Mammals/Birds
  Reptiles/Fish
  Animal Behavior
  Ecology
  Environmental Ecology
  Life in the Ocean
  Genetics
  Anatomy
  Cell Biology
  Physiology
  Field Biology

Physics
  Physics

Chemistry
  Consumer Chemistry
  Chemistry
  Organic Chemistry
  Qualitative Chemistry
  Biochemistry
  Chemistry Calculations

Science
  Research Methods
  Advanced Seminar
  Science Cooperatively
  Planned Unit

**Figure 4.6**
Science Offerings in a Responsive Curriculum

related to health might select genetics, anatomy, chemistry, cell biology, and physiology. Moreover, the student interested in a health-related career will find courses in other departments that supplement those in science—such as the physiology of exercise (physical education department), family nursing and child development (home economics department), and behavioral disorders (psychology department).

Thus, in the quarter system a strong career interest can determine a number of course choices in various departments without sacrificing other goals such as college preparation or a liberal education. The variety of offerings enhances the appeal and usefulness of the curriculum for both students and faculty.

A third element in the curriculum is the Cooperatively Planned Unit (CPU), which creates additional flexibility in all subject areas. The CPU means that a student can, with assistance and approval from his or her advisor, a teacher, and parents, plan a unit of study in any subject around mutually agreed upon objectives and learning activities. In any CPU taken, there should be clear agreement about the evaluation of achievement and the resources needed to conduct learning activities. A CPU usually lasts one quarter and is managed by a teacher who has a scheduled period to supervise learning activity, conduct evaluations, and generally assist students with problems as they progress. The CPU is an alternative that emphasizes learning how to learn—learning to be self-directed.

A student may develop an idea for a CPU as a result of a class. For example, an individual in a quarter course on the Civil War may develop an intense interest in doing further study of some aspect of the war, or the society at the time of the war, or slavery as an institution. A student may also take a CPU because he or she has a particular interest which is not offered within the formal curriculum and which could be realistically pursued in a CPU. It may happen that a subject pursued in a CPU may become very popular and ultimately be incorporated into the curriculum as a regularly offered course. In one school, for instance, weight-lifting was selected as a CPU, became very popular and, eventually, a regular course.

The CPU option is very important for some seniors, who may feel that they have exhausted those aspects of the curriculum which are highly interesting to them and who have completed all their required courses. Some seniors may also need the challenge of engaging in self-directed learning.

A final element in curriculum design is the creation of a number of opportunities which involve the use of off–campus community resources. We will discuss these in some detail in the next chapter. Here we will note that there are basically two kinds of options. One option involves special programs that allow students to spend parts of the school day or school year off campus conducting special research or actually participating in activities as "intern" learners. The other option involves special educational programs offered by other agencies; usually this means the student leaves the high school and transfers to the alternative program on a full-time basis.

These options should be available to students of all interests and abilities. In particular, they are designed for those students who:

(1) can benefit from career exploration opportunities;
(2) are unmotivated by the academic setting and need a new learning environment;
(3) cannot adjust behaviorally to the school's expectations;
(4) need additional academic challenges surpassing those available in the school.

In other words, all students may at some point in their high school programs desire or need to come into contact with educational offerings or settings which can only be found outside the school's walls. In our opinion, these options are of critical importance to adolescent learners who developmentally need contact with people of other age levels and who need to begin assuming greater responsibility for themselves and their growth as learners and persons.

## GENERAL CRITERIA FOR CURRICULUM DESIGN

The above elements are not meant to be rigidly prescriptive. Rather, they reflect the basic notion that the curriculum should be designed in a maner which insures that it will be responsive to the needs and interests of students as well as to the goals of the school and of society. A responsive curriculum must be flexible and must provide optimum choices for students. More particularly, a responsive curriculum will achieve eight things:

1. The curriculum will provide multiple options to individual learners.
2. The options will be communicated in a clear and organized manner to each learner and his or her parents and advisor so that intelligent decisions can be made.
3. The curriculum allows learners to participate in the development of some of their learning objectives, including some which may require the use of resources off campus. This, of course, follows the basic principle of a human organization that each member should participate in the decision-making process.
4. The curriculum should allow continuous evaluation of each student's progress and should provide a means of responding to particular needs as they arise. Some of the particular needs would be partial credit for a course, credit by examination, and credit for experience.
5. Learners are not separated by grade level or by age. Rather, all students should be able to move freely from option to option according to diagnosed needs, ability, and interests.
6. The curriculum should provide opportunities for learners to see the relationships among the various disciplines. That is, there should be provision for multidisciplinary experiences.
7. The curriculum must allow each learner the opportunities to satisfy the formal requirements for graduation. This should include the acquisition of basic skills and of survival skills and the fulfillment of graduation credit requirements.

8.  The curriculum should promote each student's chances of developing those personal traits and understandings which will result in effective, responsible citizenship in the context of one's total environment. The total environment would include, as the RISE Report says, the individual's society and its institutions, the ecological environment, and the global society "in which interdependencies extend beyond national boundaries and languages."[20]

## ONGOING EVALUATION AND CHANGES IN CURRICULUM

In a delightful satire published in 1939, J. A. Peddiwell told of a prehistoric tribe which set up a system of education for children. The curriculum, of course, was designed to meet the needs of the children and, in particular, the survival needs in the local environment. Among the subjects taught was "saber-tooth-tiger-scaring with fire." Over time, various changes occurred in the tribe and in the environment. The saber-tooth tigers all vanished. But people who tried to change the curriculum to make it responsive to the new needs were vehemently opposed. When "radicals" pointed out the need to learn such things as how to make fishnets and antelope snares and how to catch bears, most members of the tribe, and especially the "wise old men who controlled the school," smiled indulgently and told the radicals that such subjects would not be true education. It would only be training, and the curriculum was too full for such fads and frills. One of the most radical members persisted in his efforts to have the curriculum changed. He reminded the wise old men that times had changed and asked them to at least try some of the "more-up-to-date activities," which could have *some* educational value.

> Even the man's fellow radicals felt this was going a little too far. The wise old men were indignant. Their kindly smiles faded. "If you had any education yourself," they said severely, "you would know that the essence of true education is timelessness. It is something that endures through changing conditions like a solid rock standing squarely and firmly in the middle of a raging torrent. You must know that there are some eternal verities, and the saber-tooth curriculum is one of them!"[21]

A responsive curriculum, unlike the saber-tooth curriculum, is—indeed, must be—subject to continuing evaluation and change. Moreover, the evaluation of the curriculum is a participatory process in a human organization, involving members of all groups in the school community.

## PARTICIPANTS IN EVALUATION AND CHANGE

There is widespread responsibility for review and control in a human organization. Members of the organization at all levels share in the tasks of monitoring, evaluating, and changing organizational processes. In the school, this means that students, advisors, and parents all participate in planning, evaluating, and revising the learning programs of students. In that process, a strong sense should develop that the school, its curriculum, and its resources are at the service of the individual. Of course, to the extent that the curriculum is designed to serve the individual, some changes are inevitable over time.

Advisors have an important role in the evaluation and change of the curriculum. They will be sensitive to the needs of individual students as those needs are identified in the advisement process. They can then articulate those needs to the school's administration and to other teachers in advisement team meetings and departmental meetings. In fact, time should be deliberately set aside to solicit this kind of information from advisors.

We want to emphasize that information about *individuals* should be secured. What is happening in the interaction between the individual learner and the school? How are individual learners feeling about and responding to the school's procedures, instruction, and course offerings? The point is that while much of the data we collect formally in schools is important, we may lose much valuable information and significant insights if we only attend to averages and percentages. Furthermore, the formal collection of data may be conducted only on the basis of what administrators perceive the needed data to be. To gather responses of individuals, therefore, is to obtain information that may be the key to important change. If the individual student is to be a true participant in evaluation and change, we must deal with more than averages. A responsive curriculum can only be maintained by taking individuals into account.

This is not to say that the curriculum changes with every expression of individual desire or to accommodate individual idiosyncrasies. We simply want to stress the point that averages can obscure important information and even be misleading. As someone has wryly remarked, an individual with one foot on a hot oven and one foot on a block of ice is, on the average, warm. Similarly, a student questionnaire may show that, on the average, students are satisfied with the curriculum. Information from individuals, however, may reveal that a minority of students, even though generally satisfied, feel the need for more help in basic skills or for a course in some current issue or social activity. Sometimes response from a single individual may ultimately lead to a new course that is useful and of interest to many students.

The varied individual responses do not, of course, always result in changes in the curriculum, but those responses must be secured if the curriculum is to be truly responsive.

## THE PROCESS OF EVALUATION AND CHANGE

Systematic review of curriculum effectiveness can be conducted continually through a formal process for evaluation and change. We will discuss this more thoroughly in Chapter 6. Here, we will note six elements of the decision-making process with respect to curriculum evaluation and change:

1. There should be an annual collection of student and parent responses through questionnaires and follow-up studies of graduates. The evaluation of the curriculum by seniors is particularly important and helpful.
2. Student achievement data should be analyzed, especially the distribution of scores which reflect specific strengths and weaknesses. This analysis should be conducted at the school level for the purpose of setting school-wide instructional objectives and at the individual student level in order to improve the advisement process and the choice of courses or learning objectives.
3. An annual review should be made of enrollment patterns to detect declining or growing interest in various programs and courses. These shifts of interest may be very important. They may reflect weaknesses in advisement, changes in the composition of the student body, changing interests of students, or instructional problems in some areas.
4. Advisement teams and advisement team leaders should meet periodically for the express purpose of discussing informal feedback from parents and students. In addition to gaining and sharing information from individuals, this can be a useful early warning system for emergent problems.
5. There should be an annual review of the course catalog or program planning handbook. Students, parents and teachers can all usefully share in this review.
6. Annual or biannual evaluations should be conducted of community-based learning programs. Community agencies and individuals who participate as sponsors of learners should help with the evaluation.

The above procedures will enable the school's staff to maintain a responsive curriculum by effecting changes as necessary. The procedures will also avoid what Crary calls "strange modes of change."[22] There are three "strange modes" of changing the curriculum, according to Crary. One is the "sugar-coated conspiracy," in which a "well-intended elite group" acts on the basis of its own educational bias to effect change. "Such a group might be convinced of its superior virtue, distrust what they determine are the unprofessional attitudes of *most* of their colleagues, and espouse verbal concessions to democracy but distrust majority rule or open process."[23] The group will work quickly and efficiently, so that the change may be a *fait accompli* before opponents can act.

The "public relations approach" is the second strange mode of change. It is a Madison Avenue or Machiavellian kind of effort:

Like political reform, curriculum change is often the instrument of the big-time operator in office. Such an operator knows the value of associating with present emotions, self-evident propositions, popular current catch phrases, powerful friends with open purses, and newsworthy enterprises.[24]

Finally, there is the mode of "exterior imposition," in which some group external to the school imposes change. The group may be the legislature, colleges and their admission requirements, or various pressure or special interest groups that are able to influence the board or the staff. For example, some schools have been compelled by pressure groups to drop sex education courses, to delete certain books from the required reading list or remove certain books from the library, or to add courses that "get back to the basics." The changes brought about by exterior imposition may be additions, deletions, or modifications.

The three "strange" modes of change identified by Crary all ignore or reject the participation of students and parents and, in some cases, of the school's staff. The processes we have discussed are congruent with our model of a human organization. If the school is to be a human organization, it must have a responsive curriculum. And if the curriculum is to be responsive, there must be participatory evaluation and change.

## SUMMARY

Historically, there has been a struggle between the liberal-oriented and the vocational-oriented curriculum. The contemporary emphasis, as represented by James Bryant Conant, J. Lloyd Trump, and the RISE report, is on the importance of keeping individual differences in mind as the curriculum is developed. The humanistic movement stresses the development of the individual, the relevance of learning, the various dimensions of learning, and interpersonal relationships in the learning situation. There are both formal constraints and personal factors involved in individualizing education. Nevertheless, individualization is attainable. It is possible to develop a responsive curriculum that is orderly and logically organized.

The traditional curriculum offers year-long and semester courses, generally for specific grade levels and ages. Whatever options and flexibility there may be have a group focus. A curriculum that is responsive to individuals will have a number of characteristics. First, the criteria for student selection and placement will be ability and interest rather than age or grade level. Second, a quarter rather than semester system will facilitate individualization. Third, the Cooperatively Planned Unit will be available. Fourth, there will be a number of opportunities that involve the use of off-campus community resources. These characteristics are not meant to be prescriptions, but illustrations of the kinds of things that create flexibility and provide optimum choices for students.

Finally, the responsive curriculum will be subject to continuing evaluation and change. Students, advisors, and parents can all participate in the regular evaluation and revision of learning programs. In order for evaluation and change to be effective, adequate information must be collected. Such procedures avoid the "strange modes of change" and maintain a human organization.

# Endnotes

¹James West, *Plainville, U.S.A.* (New York: Columbia University Press, 1945), p. 80.

²Robert S. Zais, *Curriculum: Principles and Foundations* (New York: Thomas Y. Crowell, 1976), p. 69.

³*Ibid.*, p. 70.

⁴*Ibid.*, p. 71.

⁵A. Harry Passow, *American Secondary Education: The Conant Influence* (Reston, Virginia: National Association of Secondary School Principals, 1977).

⁶James B. Conant, *The Revolutionary Transformation of the American High School* (Cambridge: Harvard University Press, 1959), p. 4.

⁷Quoted in Passow, *op. cit.*, p. 14.

⁸See Passow, *op. cit.*, p. 15.

⁹James B. Conant, *The Comprehensive High School* (New York: McGraw-Hill, 1967), p. 78.

¹⁰Passow, *op. cit.*, p. 48.

¹¹Alfred North Whitehead, *Adventures of Ideas* (New York: Macmillan, 1933), p. 14.

¹²*Ibid.*, p. 26.

¹³J. Lloyd Trump, *A School for Everyone* (Reston, Virginia: National Association of Secondary School Principals, 1977), p. v.

¹⁴*Ibid.*, pp. 16–17.

¹⁵*Ibid.*, p. 18.

¹⁶*Ibid.*, p. 41.

¹⁷*The RISE Report: Report of the California Commission for Reform of Intermediate and Secondary Education* (Sacramento, Cal.: California State Department of Education, 1975), p. 3.

¹⁸*Ibid.*, p. 11.

¹⁹Karl Menninger, *Love Against Hate* (New York: Harcourt, Brace & Co., 1942), p. 186.

²⁰*The RISE Report*, p. 15.

²¹Quoted in Michael Golby, Jane Greenwald, and Ruth West, eds., *Curriculum Design* (New York: John Wiley, 1975), p. 14.

²²Ryland W. Crary, *Humanizing the School: Curriculum Development and Theory* (New York: Alfred A. Knopf, 1969), pp. 147–51.

²³*Ibid.*, p. 147.

²⁴*Ibid.*, p. 149.

# Chapter 5

# Nontraditional Options

In his book on problem solving, Edward Hodnett tells of an innovation at the Chicago stock yards that greatly eased the problem of moving hogs. For decades, literally hundreds of millions of hogs had been unloaded by forcing them down cleated ramps using "blows with poles, prods, electric buzzers, punches, kicks, and curses."[1] A new president of the Stock Yards, a man by the name of Prince, saw the process for the first time and asked the general superintendent why they couldn't make a chute for the hogs in the form of stairs. No one, of course, had ever heard of trying to drive hogs down stairs; but when a stairway was built that accommodated the short legs of hogs, the animals easily and willingly moved down it.

Mr. Prince attributed the success of his innovation to his ignorance of hogs and of the traditional methods of handling them. Had he been more knowledgeable and involved, it might never have occurred to him that hogs, like people, would feel more secure and at ease on a stairway rather than a sloping ramp. The commitment to traditional ways numbs our creative impulses. In addition, there are other factors that weigh against innovative ways. When one is caught up in the immediate and difficult task of moving hundreds of animals, it may be impractical in terms of time and impossible in terms of energy to pause and reflect upon possible alternative methods.

Similarly, in education, the commitment to traditional ways combined with the demands of the task at hand and various other factors can inhibit any consideration of new options for learning. Some nontraditional options, however, can be most effective; they facilitate the educational task. In this chapter, we want to examine a number of options which have proven to be highly effective. First, however, we will briefly discuss the background for these nontraditional options, for in one sense they are very traditional.

## THE ROOTS OF NONTRADITIONAL OPTIONS

What schools now call nontraditional, typically out-of-school learning options, are not novel methods of learning in America. They are nontraditional in the context of the formal school, but they are traditional ways of learning in our society. In other words, the schools have become involved in developing and managing options which historically were handled by other social institutions—business, labor, and the family.

### ACCIDENTAL EDUCATION

Up until about 1840, American young people developed by "accidental education." Their environment was generally "casual and unstructured rather than planned or regulated."[2] James Walker spoke to the American Institute of Instruction in 1831 and warned his hearers against the notion that youth should have a time of protection from the vicissitudes of living, for it is one of nature's wisest arrangements that "every individual is exposed to temptations gradually, and to one temptation after another, and is not thrust on a multitude of new temptations at once."[3] Young people, therefore, should be thrust into the world early in order to learn how to cope with life.

One of the common ways of learning how to cope with life was apprenticeship. For a number of generations, apprenticeship was the primary means of educating the young person. A boy learned a skill or a trade and he also learned how to get along with people. This, according to Shoup, was the first kind of community-based education in America:

In a time when school was not compulsory and families took much of the responsibility for educating their children, most adolescents learned from their parents and other people in the community. Children whose parents owned businesses or farms helped their parents out regularly. Thus, they learned the business or trade thoroughly and, more often than not, eventually took it over. They also learned and practiced enough reading, writing, and ciphering to survive. Those who aspired to a profession arranged to study with a person practicing it. Thus, direct observations, participation, and internships, mainstays of many innovative programs, are hardly novel.[4]

A couple of examples will illustrate the nature of the apprenticeship experience.[5] Baxter Whitney was born in Massachusetts in 1817, the son of an owner of a small woolen mill. Baxter began working at the mill when he was six. He worked full-time at the task of piecing rolls in the mill for the next five years, with the exception of two weeks each summer and winter in school. When he was 11, he learned carding, and when he was 12 he learned how to repair the machines. When he was 13, he was sent by his father to Worcester to help construct looms for the mill. At 17, he entered an Academy for a term, then returned to the mill to work as a repair foreman for the company which had purchased the mill from his father.

John Putnam was born in New Hampshire in 1812. At 14 he became an apprentice to a machinist. According to the terms of the apprenticeship, John was to receive his clothing and board for five years, and he would be able to attend school one month each year. At the end of the five-year period, he became a journeyman with the machinist, and received the pay of one dollar per day. John saved some of his money and eventually hired part of the shop in order to make cotton machinery on contract.

We should note that all young men did not have the orderly experience of the above two. In fact, it was not uncommon for boys to switch from one apprenticeship to another. Education, both formally in the schools and informally in apprenticeships and homes, was a somewhat sporadic affair. The point is, however, that educational opportunities were available and they were primarily community-based educational opportunities.

## LEARNING BY LIVING

Technological advances gradually put an end to apprenticeships. By the 1880s, the predominant mode of education may not have been the schools (only a little over half of the school-aged population was enrolled), but neither was it apprenticeship. The industrialization of the nation meant the inevitable death of apprenticeships as a mode of education. "Whatever its length, the period once devoted to apprenticeship was now taken up with little more than machine tending. Apprentices had become, in effect, child laborers."[6]

In the early industrial era, American youth continued to learn by living—with a vengeance. They were thrust into a world far more vicious than that encountered by the apprentices of an earlier generation. The horrors of early industrial workers generally, and of child labor in particular, are well known. Humans often became objects to be manipulated and used for the sake of the entrepreneur.

There were, of course, a few voices of dissent, a few observers who recognized the inhumane conditions under which children were learning to cope with life. Some agreed with the noted Englishman, John Ruskin, who argued that business and industry leaders have fundamental obligations to treat young workers with the same love and concern as that of the parent for his or her child:

> ... the only means which the master has of doing justice to the men employed by him is to ask himself sternly whether he is dealing with such subordinate as he would with his own son, if compelled by circumstances to take such a position ... supposing the master of a manufactory saw it right, or were by any chance obliged, to place his own son in the position of an ordinary workman; as he would then treat his son, he is bound always to treat every one of his men.[7]

Over the course of time, those who saw the destructive nature of the factory system for the young helped change the situation. Child labor laws were passed. Changing technology itself demanded prolonged schooling, delaying entry into the labor force. Compulsory school attendance laws were passed. The proportion of youth in the schools continued to rise, until nearly all adolescents in the present are in school or in some other alternative program. Thus, as the relationship of youth to the economy changed, their relationship to education also changed. By the time compulsory school attendance laws were passed, schools gained a kind of parental authority over youth—they were to perform custodial as well as educational functions.

As a result of increasing numbers of youth spending an increasingly long time in formal schooling, living and learning separated for the young. American youth remained in an artificial school environment for a longer and longer amount of time. We say "artificial" to point out that the schools traditionally have not exercised much creativity in establishing alternatives for young learners, particularly alternatives which have viable connections with work and people in the larger society.

Youth subcultures developed along with the prolonged containment in schools. The subcultures tend to reinforce and perpetuate the separation between the generations. But many adolescents view their separation as undesirable. In some respects, in fact, the search—even demand—for alternatives in the 1960s and early 1970s can be interpreted as a search for some way of reestablishing continuity between young and old and between school and society. Many young people reject the validity of a social system that relegates them to the periphery of social, political, and economic matters. Unfortunately, many adults interpreted the efforts simply as rebellion and not as attempts to become more meaningfully involved in the society.

The separation of learning and living (or, to be more accurate, of learning by experiences outside the classroom) may be coming to an end. There is now wide acceptance of the idea that schools should provide optional programs and that they can do so without sacrificing standards or crucial competencies. There has been a legitimization of the idea that young people can learn from experiences outside the classroom. School-directed education does not mean school-encased education. National organizations such as the National Association of Secondary School Principals and various state departments of education have endorsed the value of experience-based programs. This endorsement means the acceptance of at least three basic ideas:

1. Adolescents need contact with people of other age groups.
2. Adolescents need to experience firsthand the responsibilities that go with maturity and adulthood.
3. Adolescents need to learn how to learn, to learn "on the job," to see learning as a lifelong process.

The various commissions and panels of the early 1970s to which we referred in the last chapter also recognized the importance of experience-based programs. The United States Office of Education National Panel on High School and Adolescent Education suggested that young people be provided with actual jobs that would involve real work. This would be achieved by a program that stressed "job-knowledge, on-the-job training, occupational citizenship, and job placement."[8] Similarly, the RISE Report recommended:

> Learners should have the opportunity, upon request, to be assigned to an actual work situation related to that learner's interests, career objectives, and maturity. For example, a learner interested in veterinary medicine or in caring for confined animals might gain experience at a municipal animal shelter, learning while performing a public service and possibly earning a salary.[9]

There are certain obvious parallels between such recommendations and the old apprenticeship system. It is for this reason that we speak about the traditional aspect of these nontraditional options. Community-based or out-of-school learning programs are not novelties. The basic idea is rooted in our history, and it is an idea whose time has come once again.

## CURRENT OPTIONS

The options we shall discuss in this section are currently available. Some are widely available, and some are atypical (available primarily in alternative schools). We should note that, in spite of the legitimization of nontraditional options, and in spite of the current options, many schools have not developed viable community-based programs or other kinds of nontraditional options. That is, in many schools there are no programs available that allow students to establish significant relationships as learners and workers with people and places outside the school.

## SOME TYPICAL OPTIONS

The typical exceptions to the lack of nontraditional options include work/study programs, field trips, and guest speakers. Most schools today have established the first of these, the work/study program. Typically, students are placed in courses of study such as vocational education, business/office occupations, or distributive education, and are helped to find part-time employment by their teacher/coordinator. Credit is given for class work and for time spent successfully on the job (using employer evaluation of the student's performance). Extracurricular clubs, such as DECA (Distributive Education Clubs of America), may be used with the work-study program. Frequently, the program may be coordinated by state-level officials and may receive special funding. The work/study programs are extremely effective in most schools, providing an important option for many students. Unfortunately, this option is viewed as a kind of second-class program in some schools, as a step below the normal academic program for those students who cannot or will not function effectively in regular courses.

Field trips, the second typical nontraditional option, have been a way of using community resources to bring students into contact with various kinds of extraschool activities. One of the major problems with field trips is their inconvenience. Arrangements must be made for a substitute teacher, for transportation, and for supervision of students on the trip. One teacher may not be able to supervise 30 to 45 students. Field trips are also expensive and school budgets generally provide little money for transportation or for substitutes. These difficulties are often sufficient to discourage the development of field trip programs. Another drawback of the field trip is the duration. As a rule, a few hours on a site for interviews, tours, or observations can only give a superficial understanding of the activity or the people who are visited.

In spite of the limitations, field trips can be valuable educational experiences if carefully planned. Schools need to explore the idea of letting students assume more responsibility for planning and conducting their own trips. Not only would this eliminate some of the problems, but it would also increase the effectiveness of the experience. One or a small number of students can visit many more places, often without prior arrangements. The students would be much more personally involved, which means they would probably pay closer attention to details at the site of the visit. At any rate, greater student participation enlarges the possibilities for learning from field trips, and should be utilized.

Finally, the use of guest speakers is a nontraditional option often used by schools. In this case, of course, the learning usually takes place within the school rather than in the community. But it is not the traditional teacher–student relationship. In fact, one could think of it as bringing the community into the school.

Many schools and instructors have probably not tapped fully this readily available resource. There are thousands of experts in the community who would be pleased by occasional invitations to talk about themselves and their expertise or experience. Many businessmen and professionals would like to have contact with schools and with young people.

As examples of how guest speakers can be utilized for particular classes, consider the following (each of which has been done in a particular school). A class on writing essays can interview a panel of successful business women as they develop papers on new roles for women in our society. Government classes can invite political candidates from both parties, creating opportunities for students to participate in the campaign of their own candidates. Foreign language classes can hold a career day that features guests who use a second language in their jobs. If the staff knows the community and its resources, there will be manifold opportunities to bring those resources into the classroom. And as the examples above show, guest speakers can be used in a way that does not merely consume time but that is directly pertinent to the purposes of the class.

The use of both field trips and guest speakers can be valuable, but the value is limited because the experience is too brief to allow any significant relationship or personal growth to develop. They also limit the responsibility which the learner can assume; the learner cannot fully participate. Within such limitations, however, field trips and guest speakers are useful educational tools.

## SOME ATYPICAL OPTIONS

Programs which give young learners the opportunity to develop a sustained relationship with community resources are the exception rather than the rule in most American high schools. Shoup, however, has described a number of successful programs which have been implemented primarily by alternative schools. She discusses in some detail such things as community classes (an arrangement in which an expert teaches a class at a community site), internships, group service projects, community action projects, student publication projects, student exchange programs, and the "Walkabout model."[10] In some cases, comprehensive high schools have used one or more of these options, but, as pointed out above, they are more likely to be found in alternative schools. Let us briefly look at what they involve.

First, the community class can be taught weekly or biweekly for several hours at a time. Parents or people in various positions and jobs in the community may be called on to teach the class. Since the teacher's time is given on a volunteer basis, the quarter system may facilitate the task of finding people willing to teach. What can be taught in such classes?

> As with so many community-based learning activities, there are infinite subject areas for classes. Examples run the gamut from glass blowing, auto mechanics, and karate, to law, writing for publication, and banking. Students may learn practical skills like how to do their own income tax returns, explore special interest areas like needlework or Renaissance art, or gain some insight into a possible career.[11]

Internships are similar to the old practice of apprenticeships. They give the student the opportunity to get involved in a responsible way in some kind of work. Again, the kind of work can vary widely, from the professions to the trades. Students themselves participate in the process of selecting and implementing an internship, thus gaining skills other than those of the work of the intern. Internships work best when they are long-term experiences. A weekly visit for two quarters, with each visit lasting about half a day, will allow the student to have a valuable learning experience.

Group service projects are essentially volunteer activities for some agency or organization. They are, however, more personal than some efforts such as collecting recyclable materials or walking or biking for charity. In a group service project, students engage in such activities as being volunteer guides for a museum, manning a booth during a fund-raising drive for a charity or hospital, serving as an aide at a nursing home or hospital, or helping with the mechanics of production and performance for a local theater group. All such activities, of course, must be evaluated for their educational contribution. Nontraditional options are not to be used as an easy way to consume students' time (thereby facilitating the custodial task of the school) nor as a way of providing a pool of cheap labor for community organizations. Planning, analysis, and evaluation are necessary so that students who engage in the options have a valuable educational experience.

Community action projects differ from service projects in that the former imply a commitment to changing things whereas the latter imply a commitment to meeting needs within the existing social system. As Shoup suggests, many people who would happily view service projects become rather nervous in the face of action projects. Students engaged in an action project are likely to challenge the power structure or to insist on changes in business practices or to identify an unethical policy of a corporation and so forth. In one class on consumer rights, the students and teacher began a consumer advocate program. They dealt with 54 problems which were reported to them, and resolved 80% of them. (They also found that in some cases the consumer is wrong.) Needless to say, action projects are fraught with hazards for both students and the school. They must be approached with special caution.

Student publication projects were stimulated by the work of Eliot Wigginton, the teacher in rural Georgia who motivated his students by having them write about the people in their own community. The students became involved in and excited about the project, soon began to publish a magazine—*Foxfire*—and eventually saw the magazine become a book. Students in other communities have begun since then to interview, photograph, and publish information about their own local people and places. As Shoup points out, the information which is gathered can be used in various ways other than publishing a magazine. Some students have begun collections of oral histories. Some have made contributions to state historical societies. And one group made a slide/tape show for their city's information center. As with all options, there are numerous variations; the only limits are the limits of the imagination.

Student exchange programs are well known. The exchange allows each student to become fully involved in a different culture. Exchanges are often made with a foreign country, but, as Shoup notes, they can also be set up within the nation. In one case, for example, an urban teenager from Indianapolis exchanged places with a student from a small town in Indiana, and found the experience most enlightening and rewarding.

Finally, the "Walkabout model" forces students out of the school and into the larger society to confront a number of challenges. "Walkabout" is a survival ritual employed by Australian aborigines. Youth are left alone in the wilderness for six months. When they return to the tribe, they are received as adults. Applying the idea to an American high school (James Walker, whom we quoted early in this chapter, would strongly advocate it), one Midwestern school offers a Walkabout course for seniors. The students must create experiences in five areas—adventure, creativity, logical inquiry, service, and practical skills. Each student creates his or her own set of experiences, based on interests, goals, and ability. In some cases, a student may create experience by venturing far from home, as the young man who traveled alone for three weeks in the Southwest and California in order to experience the "wild west." As this suggests, the Walkabout model may involve the creation of risky experiences; considerable care and planning are required in order to minimize the possibility of disastrous consequences.

In her discussion of the above options, Shoup frequently extols the flexibility and creativity of the alternative school as a vehicle for offering nontraditional programs. At one point she discusses the division and conflict which developed between a successful alternative school and the regular school from which it sprang. We believe, however, that the options not only have a place in the educational setting but that many of them can be successfully implemented in the comprehensive public high school.

In addition to the above suggestions, we shall now describe in detail two options which have been successfully implemented in a comprehensive public high school—Deliberate Psychological Education and the Community Learning Program. Both options have been supported strongly by parents, by the community, and by the Board of Education. The two programs are simple in design, allow students to participate in varying degrees depending on individual needs or interests, and effectively combine certain academic objectives with a significant experience in community placement.

## DELIBERATE PSYCHOLOGICAL EDUCATION

As noted in Chapter 3, Deliberate Psychological Education combines a practicum experience and a seminar. We shall look a little more at the background of the program, and then show how it can be an effective part of the school's curriculum.

### BACKGROUND AND NATURE OF THE PROGRAM

Bronfenbrenner echoed the concerns of a number of observers when he argued, in 1970, that

> if the institutions of our society continue to remove parents, other adults and older youth from active participation in the lives of children, and if

the resulting vacuum is filled by the age-segregated peer groups, we can anticipate increased alienation, indifference, antagonism and violence on the part of the younger generation in all segments of our society.[12]

Deliberate Psychological Education is an answer to the concern for age segregation, for it deliberately involves the student with people at various stages of life. Fundamentally, the program aims at positive psychological growth for all students:

> Our objective is to make personal development a central focus of education, rather than pious rhetoric at commencement. . . . Our long-term objective is to create from a development framework of growth stages, educational programs which address the major aspects of personal, moral and ethical domains.[13]

There are a number of assumptions in a program of Deliberate Psychological Education. First, we assume that students will continually improve themselves by examining and reflecting on what matters in life. Second, we assume that there are developmental stages in personal growth (such as those identified by Piaget, Erikson, and Kohlberg), and that students will benefit by examining their own growth in the light of such stages. Third, we assume that human relations skills can be taught. Finally, we assume that the personal growth of students can be facilitated through experiences with people at various stages of life.

In Deliberate Psychological Education, then, each student has a practicum experience. The practicum has three objectives:

(1) to teach material from psychology and other subjects that enhances an understanding of individual development;
(2) to provide the student with systematic personal experience and responsibility;
(3) to help students make conscious what they learn about themselves from their formal study and their experiences.

The weekly seminar that is part of the practicum may include a variety of activities. The leader (teacher or counselor) may give information and assign readings on developmental stages, or may use a session as a time for training in empathy, or may generate a discussion aimed at clarifying values.

An important aspect of the practicum is that students are encouraged and expected to develop responsibility. Each student who desires to participate in the program may be interviewed prior to enrollment in order to identify expectations. For instance, students should be expected to attend each day, to call in when sick, to practice talking with people in order to maintain effective communication, and to write a journal and behavioral contract. In addition, specific expectations will be made for specific kinds of experiences. For example, a student who will be working in peer counseling or a geriatric center must recognize the importance of confidentiality.

Students who become involved in such a program often show rapid behavioral change, closer relationships with the school's staff, more initiative and a greater sense of responsibility in their work, and a tendency to use the experience as a way of testing potential careers. Part of the success of the program is that the students have a chance to become intensely involved with staff members and to combine traditional, classroom methods of learning with experiential learning.

Thus, a student can emerge from this program a more moral and sensitive individual than he or she was before—a statement that cannot be made of many programs in our schools. As the student becomes personally involved with people of other ages, he or she also becomes involved with issues and problems of other ages, such as how children develop morally and physically, how people learn, how to listen, and how to help someone in need.

## AN EXAMPLE: COMMUNITY OUTREACH

In this section, we will look at a particular example in a specific school. A decision was made in the school to offer some kind of program in Deliberate Psychological Education. The result was a course called "Community Outreach." The catalog description of the course is shown in Figure 5.1. Students may petition to take a community outreach program for more than one semester. If permission is granted, the student is normally expected to move to a different agency which serves a different age group or different special needs.

There is a seminar leader, usually a counselor and sometimes a trained teacher. The leader has the following responsibilities:

1. Coordinate with the agency supervisor a written contract outlining the objectives of the program and the responsibilities of students while working and learning at the agency.
2. Visit the agency periodically to observe firsthand the students' work—both the nature of the work and the way in which the student is performing it.
3. Read and respond to students' daily journal entries.
4. Assist students in their study of readings which are assigned to help them understand and function more effectively with respect to their placement or agency's clientele.

## 971-976 COMMUNITY OUTREACH

1 credit in Social Studies or elective credit; semester course, 2 hours per day.

Prerequisites: Permission of counselor in charge of the program.

Content: See "content" for each of placements below.

Students can expect to (these apply to all placements):
spend four days per week working at their placements;
spend one day per week in a seminar at school;
set behavioral goals;
keep a daily journal;
plan weekly activities;
do book reports.

1. Child Development
   Content: In this practicum, students will be assigned to work with very young children in a local nursery school, preschool or day care center.
   Students will learn to:

   a. recognize physical and emotional development of children through age 5;
   b. plan and teach a full day of activities;
   c. increase their awareness and personal growth;
   d. function with a team of peers;
   e. relate with children and adults in assigned agency.

2. Elementary Aide
   Content: This practicum will provide students with an opportunity to work with children in an elementary school. Tasks may include helping children with reading, math, art, or working with them in sports or playground activities.
   Students will learn to:

   a. work with children ages 6 through 12;
   b. function as an assistant to a teacher;
   c. help children work in art, reading, math, sports or playground activities;
   d. explore career goals;
   e. recognize different styles of teaching.

(cont.)

3. Child Development in Special Education
   Content: This practicum provides the student with the opportunity to work with children who have physical, mental
   or emotional handicaps. Placements will be in Special
   School District's schools and in private schools for the handicapped. The age range of the children is 3 to 17.
   Students will learn to:

   a. read about topics of special interest and concern to
      those in special education;
   b. study the psychology of exceptional children;
   c. recognize and accept physical handicaps;
   d. explore special education as a career;
   e. use referral sources and schools relating to similar prob-
      lems.

4. Mental Retardation
   Content: This practicum is a volunteer service with the
   mentally retarded, including intensive training in special
   teaching techniques and a general exposure to the entire
   field of mental retardation.
   Students will learn to:

   a. write intelligibly about special needs;
   b. use special techniques in working with the retarded;
   c. develop concern for the handicapped;
   d. explore career goals.

5. Adolescence
   Content: In this practicum, students can be placed at a cor-
   rectional institution for boys as a teacher's aide. In addition, there will be a focus on the process of listening to
   another individual, listening for feelings and ideas, and
   learning to respond to others' feelings and ideas.
   Students will learn to:

   a. tutor juveniles in math, reading, science and writing;
   b. listen to feelings of others;
   c. be aware of their own personal growth;
   d. deal with adolescents;
   e. be familiar with adolescent psychology;
   f. be familiar with the juvenile court.

*(cont.)*

6.    The Study of the Aged
      Content: This practicum provides an opportunity to work with, and get involved in, the lives of the aged who are living in geriatric centers. Activities range from giving physical assistance to providing company and friendship.
      Students will learn to:

      a.    help an elderly person write letters, communicate with others, etc.;
      b.    transport patients to planned activities;
      c.    function as friends and companions of the aged;
      d.    assist staff in necessary chores;
      e.    plan group activities;
      f.    understand life in a nursing home.

7.    Health Services
      Content: This practicum provides practical experience in a health service facility, where students will become familiar with rules and regulations and work under the direct supervision of staff members, learning how to meet the needs of people.
      Students will learn to:

      a.    care for the sick;
      b.    use medical terminology;
      c.    know about medical careers;
      d.    know how a hospital is run;
      e.    serve meals, read to patients, and help transport patients.

**Figure 5.1**
Catalog Description of a Program Based on Deliberate Psychological Education

5.    Help students share their experiences and connect theory and practice.
6.    Help students understand their own developmental needs and issues as they emerge from their experiences and relationships with others.
7.    Encourage students to gather information on careers in human services.
8.    Train students in the practice of setting goals and solving problems.

One person, probably a counselor, should be assigned to the role of program coordinator. The coordinator should be a persuasive, energetic leader with a deep commitment to the program goals and the patience to deal with problems as they (inevitably) occur. Among the responsibilities of the program coordinator are the following:

1.  Set up field placements by contacting various organizations in the community that need volunteers, explaining the program objectives to key personnel in those organizations, and arranging visits for students.
2.  Schedule and assign students. This includes the initial screening interview, conferences with students who express interest in the program, and the assignment of students to an appropriate field placement.
3.  Coordinate seminar groups and practicum leaders. For this task, the coordinator needs to know about the strengths and special interests of individual counselors. The coordinator will assign groups of students to practicum leaders.
4.  Provide in-service training for practicum leaders. Practicum leaders need to be familiarized with the rationale and goals of the program and oriented toward goal-setting procedures and behavioral evaluations.
5.  Coordinate practicum leaders in terms of observing seminar meetings, scheduling group meetings for practicum leaders, and scheduling individual conferences to review the progress of each leader's group.
6.  Consult with field site supervisors. Meetings need to be set up to evaluate the program and to maintain communication with site supervisors.
7.  Implement follow-up procedures. The coordinator needs to get feedback from program participants, consider various changes, communicate any program changes, and reinforce positive experiences.
8.  Develop positive community relations. There are various ways to achieve this goal, including a presentation of the program at a PTA meeting, publicity in the media, workshops at guidance association meetings, and a plan whereby participating students share their experiences with parents, staff, and other students each semester.
9.  Consult with administrators for budget appropriations. Funds will be needed for transportation, inservice training, curriculum development, field trips, and the purchase of books and supplies.
10. Integrate the program into the Guidance and Counseling services of the school. The program provides opportunities for ca-

reer exploration and is a type of preventive counseling for students; as such, it naturally fits into the work of the counselors.

Obviously, there is a considerable amount of work to be done in running this program. The implementation and management of the program can be facilitated by developing a number of important forms. As indicated above, students who are interested in the program are given a screening interview. Prior to the interview, they fill out a form like that shown in Figure 5.2. Note that the form helps identify

---

## APPLICATION

Please read the information on the Out-Reach Program before completing this application.

Name:_____(Circle one: Soph. Jr. Sr.)

Address:_____Telephone:_____

Advisor's Name:_____

Please write your area of interest (for example, nursing, teaching, social work, geriatrics, delinquency, child care, retardation):_____

What specific things would you like to do or learn during your two hours away from school?_____
_____
_____

List your strengths and/or special talents:_____
_____

Briefly state why you want to work with the community outreach program:_____
_____
_____

To Parents: By signing this form you give permission for your child to become involved in a supervised learning activity which takes place out-of-school.

Parent's Signature:_____Date:_____

---

**Figure 5.2**
Application for Community Out-Reach Program

student interests and also insures parental knowledge and approval of the program.

Once in the program, students are given a number of forms to facilitate a valuable educational experience. For example, students should have a written statement of how to prepare their journals (Figure 5.3). A weekly activity planning form (Figure 5.4) will help them make effective use of their time. A contract for personal growth and learning, on which students state what they hope to learn, how they hope to grow personally, what they will do to accomplish their goals, and what kind of help they will need, will be of value to both the students and the seminar leaders.

Another helpful form is one upon which students state a behavioral objective for each week. Whether or not a standard form is used, students in this kind of program need to write out their objectives for each week and evaluate their success in achieving those stated objectives.

---

## PREPARING YOUR JOURNAL

The journal is a crucial part of the course work. It is important that you understand the purpose of keeping a *daily* journal. The journal will:

(1) serve as a record of events which occur at the field site.
(2) include a description of how you *feel* about your work at the field site.
(3) give you the opportunity to reflect on your behavior and how your behavior affects others at the field site.
(4) serve as a record of events and changes that occur in the practicum group.

You will refer to your journal when you write your nine-week behavioral evaluation. You will have a record of specific incidents that show you have mastered a skill or developed an insight. Journal entries should also help you understand the development of those with whom you are working and help you gain a greater understanding of yourself.

---

**Figure 5.3**
Student Instructions for their Journals

---

### COMMUNITY OUTREACH
### WEEKLY ACTIVITY PLANNING FORM

Name_____Date of Activity_____

(Be sure to tell a Center teacher to watch your activity before presenting it.)

Description:

  Type of Activity:

  Describe the Activity:

  Age and name of children:

  Number of children:

  What area of classroom is to be used:

  Amount of time needed (do not exceed 15 minutes):

  Materials (kind and amount needed):

Plans:

  What the children will do for themselves:

  What I will have to help the children do:

  How will I get the children's attention?

  How will I introduce the activity?

---

**Figure 5.4**
Weekly Activity Planning Form for Elementary Aide Practicum

Some kind of standardized forms, such as those shown in figures 5.5 and 5.6, are needed so that site supervisors can evaluate students and programs. As the various items on the forms suggest, feedback from site supervisors can also pinpoint problem areas, providing infor-

---

COMMUNITY OUTREACH STUDENT EVALUATION


Student's Name:_____

1. Attendance                                    A   B   C   D   F
2. Arrival on time                               A   B   C   D   F
3. Cooperative with teachers                     A   B   C   D   F
4. Cooperative with other aides                  A   B   C   D   F
5. Copes with problem situations                 A   B   C   D   F
6. Willing to try new things, activities         A   B   C   D   F
7. Plans and carries out activities and
   new experiences for the children              A   B   C   D   F
8. Willing to help with daily routines           A   B   C   D   F
9. Adheres to rules and policies                 A   B   C   D   F
10. Accepts responsibility for actions
    and behavior                                 A   B   C   D   F
11. Understands needs and behavior
    of the children                              A   B   C   D   F

12. What changes in behavior have you noticed in the student
    since the beginning of the quarter?


13. In what areas has the student increased knowledge?


14. Additional Comments

---

**Figure 5.5**
Student Evaluation Form for Elementary Aide

mation that can be used to strengthen the program and help subsequent students be more effective in their work. The forms may vary depending upon the particular program (geriatrics, child care, teaching, etc.). Those who prepare the forms need to think carefully about what kind of information is needed for proper evaluation of the work of the students and the effectiveness of the programs.

## COMMUNITY OUTREACH PROGRAM EVALUATION

1. How helpful was your aide?

| Very | | Somewhat | | Not at All |
|------|---|----------|---|------------|
| 1 | 2 | 3 | 4 | 5 |

2. How do you view the residents' response to the aide?

| Positive | | Neutral | | Negative |
|----------|---|---------|---|----------|
| 1 | 2 | 3 | 4 | 5 |

3. How well prepared was your aide?

| Very | | Adequately | | Not at All |
|------|---|------------|---|------------|
| 1 | 2 | 3 | 4 | 5 |

4. How would you describe your aide's attitude?

| Positive | | Neutral | | Negative |
|----------|---|---------|---|----------|
| 1 | 2 | 3 | 4 | 5 |

5. Would you request another aide next year?

| Yes | | Unsure | | No |
|-----|---|--------|---|----|
| 1 | 2 | 3 | 4 | 5 |

6. Which activities are most helpful with aides?

    a. establishing a good rapport with residents
    b. leading discussion groups
    c. visiting with residents on an individual basis
    d. developing a relationship with new residents
    e. showing respect for the resident
    f. other

7. Which three traits do you consider most important in order for an aide to be effective?

| enthusiasm | sensitivity | patience |
|------------|-------------|----------|
| creativity | intelligence | responsibility |
| warmth | cooperation | willingness to |
| promptness | | work |

*(cont.)*

8. How many times were you contacted by the student's practicum supervisor or program coordinator?

9. Do you feel contacts with the student's supervisor were

| too frequent | | frequent enough | | not frequent enough |
|---|---|---|---|---|
| 1 | 2 | 3 | 4 | 5 |

10. Do you find the over-all aide program to be

| very effective | | somewhat effective | | not effective |
|---|---|---|---|---|
| 1 | 2 | 3 | 4 | 5 |

11. Do you have suggestions for increasing the program's effectiveness?

**Figure 5.6**
Program Evaluation Form for Geriatrics Program

## COMMUNITY LEARNING PROGRAM

The Community Learning Program is similar in design to Community Outreach. Students work at a field site with a community sponsor three hours daily for four days each week. In addition, the students spend one day each week in a seminar or in an individual research activity. The program lasts one quarter and can be extended to one semester with the approval of the community sponsor, the program supervisor, parents, and the advisor. Students also keep daily journals and research information regarding careers related to placement. In the seminar the students share their observations and experiences, helping each other solve problems and set goals. The catalog description for the program is shown in Figure 5.7. In the following sections, we will look at some of the practicalities involved in setting up and managing the program.

---

### 011-029 COMMUNITY LEARNING PROGRAM

1/4 credit per hour: 3 hours daily for one quarter

Prerequisites: Permission of CLP instructors, appropriate background skills, and transportation.

Content: This program emphasizes the use of community resources. Under the guidance of school and community sponsors, students plan learning opportunities that are not possible in the regular school program, such as self-directed programs related to vocational interests. The program also helps students discover new interests.

Students can expect to:
write and meet learning goals
be assigned to a community sponsor
participate in weekly seminars
keep a daily journal
demonstrate responsible behavior

Students will learn to:
do independent learning under self-direction
improve written and oral communication skills
develop specific skills related to one's own program and goals

---

**Figure 5.7**
Catalog Description for Community Learning Program

## FUNCTIONS OF THE CLP SUPERVISORS

The supervisors for the program can be any staff members who have a strong commitment to the program and who have the skill and enthusiasm to manage CLP learning. The supervisors have a number of important functions:

1. Develop community placements for students. In order to insure an adequate number and variety of opportunities for students,

the supervisors will have to use diverse methods for securing placements. Some helpful methods are:

(a) call on various businesses and other agencies to explain the program and ask for participation;

(b) speak before community groups such as Rotary, Kiwanis, and the Chamber of Commerce (a method which is particularly important in the early stages of implementation);

(c) develop a brochure and business card;

(d) gain the cooperation of students and parents in finding additional sponsors;

(e) maintain contact with sponsors and potential sponsors by means of an annual update report;

(f) develop a recognition program for active sponsors.

2. Publicize the program and its benefits. Again, a variety of means can be employed to achieve this goal:

(a) arrange meetings with advisement teams;

(b) allow participating students to make presentations to the faculty and other students;

(c) develop news releases in cooperation with the school community relations staff;

(d) develop listings of available sponsors;

(e) invite community sponsors to speak to school groups.

3. Visit community sponsors before and during each placement. Such visits should be used to clarify expectations for all concerned parties—the student, the sponsor, and the school supervisor.

4. Organize a student evaluation process. The program is not meant to be inferior in an academic sense. The process of evaluation can include the following:

(a) establish clear guidelines for daily journal entries (which should be read weekly);

(b) establish objectives for seminar participation and career research;

(c) develop means for community sponsors to submit evaluations of students' performance, progress, and attendance;

(d) develop means for conducting an end-of-the-experience assessment, such as an oral examination by other seminar members, other faculty members, and the supervisor.

5. Establish the nature of the weekly seminars, including expectations and goals. For instance, students can be trained in problem analysis and goal setting during the seminars. And each seminar group can develop its own project (a display or slide show or presentation of some kind).

## IMPLEMENTING A COMMUNITY LEARNING PROGRAM

If a school has decided to set up a CLP, the following points will prove valuable:

1. The CLP should have its own location—a special room with a telephone, files, message boards, and appropriate furniture for group discussions.
2. Program supervisors need to be carefully selected. The skills needed to manage and develop community learning are quite different from skills employed in classroom instruction. Some enthusiasm and salesmanship are essential in addition to good communication and organizational skills. Moreover, the program should not be built too heavily around one person. The quarter system will allow the use of several teachers over a period of a year or two. If a number of teachers are jointly supervising the program, one needs to be assigned as coordinator.
3. Student registration procedures should be developed in a way that insures adequate communication of the program's expectations to students, parents, and advisors. Special attention should be paid to the transportation arrangements agreed upon by parents and students.
4. A CLP does not require additional expense, a point which may be important in gaining approval of the board of education for the program. The ratio of students to supervisor is about equal to a typical class. (It would be best to keep the ratio a little smaller at first. As the program develops and more sponsors are secured, the ratio can be equal to that of a normal class.) An effective supervisor can manage 25 students and parent volunteers can also be solicited to assist.
5. Develop an out-of-school learning program coordinating council. Representatives from all programs that use community sponsors can meet twice annually (or more often if necessary) in order to:
   (a) avoid any unnecessary overlapping of programs;
   (b) act as a sounding board for proposed changes in the programs;
   (c) determine relationships of programs to each other and to other programs in the curriculum;
   (d) set up criteria for student participation;
   (e) coordinate community contacts; and
   (f) consider evaluative methods.

## USEFUL FORMS AND MATERIALS

As with all programs, community learning can be managed more effectively if a number of prepared materials are available. For one thing, an outline of the students' responsibilities, the sponsors' role, and the staff's role should be prepared and made available to all interested parties. One school uses the material shown in Figure 5.8.

Students will find it helpful to have a suggestion sheet that lists some activities for the time they spend at school on their "day-in." Typically, part of their grade will be based on what they do on the day in. Among other things, they might read and review a book, review an article on CLP, work on a scrapbook of articles related to their CLP, interview and write an account of someone with expertise in the sub-

---

### COMMUNITY LEARNING PROGRAM

*Student Responsibilities.* The student is expected to:

(1) attend the learning site four days per week, as reliably as if he or she were an employee.

(2) call the sponsor on those rare occasions when he or she cannot attend.

(3) complete any reading, research, or work assignments given by the sponsor.

(4) dress appropriately for the kind of learning site he or she attends.

(5) accept any responsibilities for which his or her sponsor feels he or she is ready.

(6) maintain a high level of interest in learning.

(7) develop a realistic set of learning objectives.

(8) be in attendance at the CLP office one day each week for his or her day-in seminar or day-in activity.

(9) write a daily journal and turn it in for grading each week on his or her day-in.

(10) call the CLP office on those rare occasions when he or she cannot come to school on the day-in.

(11) come to the CLP office for the assigned time on days when he or she cannot go to the learning site because of transportation problems or because the sponsor requested that he or she not attend on a particular day.

(12) prepare one or more day-in projects.

---

*(cont.)*

*Sponsor's Role.* The sponsor is encouraged to:

(1) provide the student with a learning opportunity through appropriate means (observation, participation, student-directed activities, etc.).

(2) expect the student to do any activity of a regular employee as long as the student is capable and can learn from the activity.

(3) expose the student to as much of the business or activity as possible without detracting from the regular operation of the business or activity.

(4) assign reading or tasks to be mastered that would benefit the student whenever possible.

(5) evaluate the student at the end of the program on qualities such as performance, attendance, punctuality, willingness to work, and courtesy.

(6) call the CLP office for questions or problems.

*The CLP Staff's Role.* CLP instructors will:

(1) lead day-in seminars with students.

(2) counsel with students to expand on-site learning.

(3) make efforts to visit each learning site.

(4) assist sponsors whenever requested.

(5) evaluate student's journals.

(6) evaluate day-in activities and projects.

**Figure 5.8**
Outline of Responsibilities of CLP Participants

ject of the CLP, arrange to spend one day-in at a different location "shadowing" an expert in the area of the CLP, or work on a formal research paper.

Other useful forms would include a progress report (to be filled in periodically by the instructor), an extension request form (for students who wish to continue a particular CLP for a second quarter), and an agreement form to be signed by the sponsor (Figure 5.9). The discussion of various prepared materials and forms may not be particularly exciting, but such materials are an essential component of an effective program.

COMMUNITY LEARNING PROGRAM
AGREEMENT WITH COMMUNITY SPONSOR

1. Name of student:_____Phone:_____

2. Name of business or organization:_____
   Address:_____Phone:_____

3. Student's Learning Program:_____

4. General objectives of student:_____
   _____

5. Scheduled time for student's program:
   Dates:_____to_____
   Days and hours:_____
   (Note: the student will be with you four days each week and
   will attend a seminar at school the other day. Please arrange
   the schedule to fit your own convenience.)

6. Type of activities student may be involved in under your
   supervision:_____
   _____

7. Signature:_____

Thank you for your willingness to work with this young person
and help him or her discover the potentials of your profession.
Please contact us at any time you have questions about the program or the student.

Figure 5.9
Form for Agreement with CLP Sponsor

## MERITS OF OUT-OF-SCHOOL LEARNING

Both programs, Community Outreach and Community Learning, have
similar designs. They are easily scheduled into the school program, do
not require excessive funds, and place realistic responsibilities upon
school supervisors, students, parents, and community sponsors. The
programs satisfy criteria for community-based learning programs established by some state departments of education. Moreover, the programs have many positive consequences for sponsors, parents, and

students. We shall discuss some of these consequences below. Some of them are the kind that would have been expected; others may be a pleasant surprise to the school's staff.

## EFFECTS ON COMMUNITY SPONSORS

The director of a large medical clinic reported that shortly after students began reporting as intern/learners the efficiency and quality of work improved noticeably among regular staff members. Presumably, he thought, the workers were modeling for the young learners. The students were observing, asking questions, and eagerly waiting to participate. The interest of the students testified to the significance of the work. The regular workers responded by attending more carefully to their tasks.

A number of community sponsors have ultimately hired some of the students who were placed with them as interns. The sponsors indicate that they get better employees as a result. The internship period initiated a relationship that led to a mutually satisfying result for both the employers and the students.

Community learning has also been an important public relations tool. In one case, an influential businessman was an outspoken critic of public education. The man had unique skills in his field (design), however, so the program coordinator and principal called on him. After considerable effort, the man was persuaded to allow a student to work with him. The experience was so rewarding that he hired the student for part-time work and asked to become a permanent sponsor. He subsequently became a strong advocate of the CLP and developed a positive attitude toward the school's programs.

A considerable variety of sponsors can be secured by a hardworking staff. At one school, the CLP has over 300 community sponsors (not all of whom are utilized in any one quarter, of course), ranging from auto body repairmen to architects, surgeons, and policemen. The program is a network of community contacts built around a strong common interest—the young people of the community. The result has been a great number of educational opportunities for students and a more positive attitude toward both the school and the students by numerous sponsors.

## EFFECTS ON THE PARENTS

One random survey of parents whose children participated in a CLP failed to elicit a single negative response. All of the parents reported an increase in communication with their children about school and about the child's future. All of the parents reported that the experience was significant in helping their children develop career plans and self-confidence. Apparently, many students will talk with their parents about CLP experiences where they would be more reticent about traditional school activities.

We are suggesting, then, that one of the outcomes of a CLP is a number of cases of improved family relationships. We can illustrate this by two actual cases. In one, a mother who was a single parent brought her son to the principal's office one day and asked for help. There was a sense of desperation in her request. The boy, who was just 16 years old, was being dropped for non-attendance. He had no desire to remain in school. The principal suggested the CLP as a possible way to stimulate some interest in the boy. The boy expressed an interest in police work, but all the placements were taken at the time. Furthermore, his age and school record did not satisfy the police department's criteria for interns. The CLP coordinator looked for some other opportunity, and found a police dog training firm that was willing to accept the boy.

After several weeks, the mother returned to the principal and reported that her son was not only responding to the placement with great enthusiasm but also was changing in a number of other ways. He appeared to want to spend more time with his mother at home, assume more responsibility, and talk about his future. One of the things the community sponsor had done which seemed to make a critical difference was to give the boy a set of keys and make him a responsible member of the team.

The second case involved a girl. During her first two years of high school she spent an increasingly large amount of time with a group of friends who were experimenting with drugs. She also grew increasingly alienated from her family, and increasingly bored with school. Partly because school was "such a drag," she arranged for a CLP to study horse training and stable management. Though initially skeptical, the parents supported her plans, and they quickly saw their daughter's enthusiasm for the work, which they began to share. Eventually, they purchased a horse for themselves. They began to study horses, developing an interest that was more than a response to the girl's need. Most important, the mother later reported, the CLP had become a catalyst for positive change in their daughter and ultimately in the family relationships. In a real sense, the CLP had rescued the girl from total alienation from her family.

We do not intend to be overly sanguine about the program. It is not, and is not meant to be, a tonic for the intra- and interpersonal ills of students. Nevertheless, one of the extra benefits of the program is the positive psychological or interpersonal outcome it has for at least some students and their families. More than one distraught parent will find the program to be an answer to a perplexing problem with a child, whether the problem is career uncertainty or alienation.

## EFFECTS ON STUDENTS

As the above cases illustrate, the effects on students can be dramatic. At the least, students will experience a number of positive consequences through their participation in CLP (even if nothing more than recognition that they do not like a particular career option after all). One of the best ways to see the effects on students is to look at their daily journal entries. We shall look at two examples, and then at some more extended excerpts.

A senior girl had long hoped to become a nurse. But after a CLP in a pediatrics ward she realized that she really didn't like the work: "I know I could be a nurse if I really wanted to be, but I'm sure glad I found out that I don't want to be one." She went on to college to study French and English and become a teacher.

A senior boy who had been disinterested in school and who had a very poor academic record found his occupation in a CLP for auto body repair. He was hired by his sponsor after graduation to be an apprentice. Within two years, he had a journeyman's license. He declared that the program "saved my life. I don't know what I would have done if I had not joined it."

A senior boy who participated in a Community Outreach program tells of how he and a three-and-a-half-year-old boy influenced each other. As a result of the senior's attention and concern, the young boy received the extra help he needed. The journal entries of particular interest begin on December 18.

*December 18.* This time even Ben joined in. Ben is a funny kid. I can't figure him out at all. I've tried being nice to him, but it doesn't seem to be sinking in. Until today he wouldn't join in anything. If I talked to him, he just sticks up his nose and grunts. He's a loner.

*January 14.* Today was fantastic. I've finally gotten through to Ben. He's very independent. I bet he never got much attention from his parents. He gives the impression of "nobody can hurt me, I don't need anybody." Some one said the other day, "It's the people who need love the most, who are the hardest to love." Most people would see Ben as a spoiled brat. I see him differently. I have been sure to include him in my activities. Today we went to the Zoo. Ben crawled out of his shell for awhile. As I was about to leave today, Ben asked if we could go for an airplane ride. I was shocked. He'd actually come to me to play with him. It was a Happy Day.

*January 16.* Ben is becoming increasingly friendlier as the days go by.

*January 31.* Today my thoughts about Ben's relationships with his parents were verified somewhat. Ben cried a lot today, more than usual. The last week or so, whenever he cried, he'd tell me he wanted to go on an airplane. He said that he wanted to sleep on a plane with Dad. Ben yearns for his parent's love, I just know it. I think this bit with the airplane was an isolated case when his father really paid attention to him. He needs it so bad, it just kills me to know he doesn't get it.

*February 5.* Today I brought my camera. As far as Ben goes it was a big mistake. Ben wanted to "play" with the camera. I tried to explain to him that it was not a toy. He cried and kept saying "I want to play with it." I tried everything. He wouldn't listen. He got a distant look in his eyes and wouldn't look at me. I was so frustrated, I could have burst.

*February 6.* Ben was great. He didn't hit anybody. He behaved really good all day. Today when things didn't go his way, instead of throwing things and hitting people, he came to me and told me about it. I think he's gonna make it.

*February 20.* Today was really a bad day. Ben slipped away from me, because he was home too much. I've spent weeks and weeks trying to help this kid and it all goes down the drain in a few days. I give him all the love I can, but it just isn't enough. He seems to get better and better and then it's ruined by missing a day. I thought he was just about getting to the point where he wouldn't need so much special attention. I was wrong. He was totally unpredictable all day. Why does all this have to happen now? Well, tomorrow I start over.

*February 21.* Today I spent the entire day alone with Ben. He went in a room and played with a bat and ball, and talked all day. I taught him how to throw the ball up himself and hit it, so he could play after I left. I think it helped him let out a few frustrations. I also taught him my name which he didn't know until today and will probably have forgotten by tomorrow. As the end of the day was near Angelique stepped in. He was so proud of how good he could hit the ball he wanted to show her. Angelique loved it and laughed with Ben and me. The first step in getting along with others. It's too bad he hasn't got a father to teach him how to bat.

*February 27.* Ben was pretty good today. I actually got him to do something he didn't want to do. I think I've been a little easy on him.

*February 28.* I hate having to leave in the middle of my work with Ben. I guess it doesn't matter anyway. Ray said I couldn't do anything else for him. He's going to have to leave the day care center. Ray is going to try to get him into a special school, because Ben can't be helped until the situation at home is changed.

*March 12.* This will probably be my last entry. Yesterday and today I had to really control myself from crying. I'll never see my kids again. I really love them. They've really become a part of me. I'm going through a big change in my life and unfortunately it means losing them, but I know deep down they have given me something special I can keep forever. I've finished my work with Ben. I've done all I can with him, now it's out of my hands. I've left my mark though. I gave Ben all the love I could, and it's paid off. Ray said Ben is going to spend part of the day at the center and half at a special school. I'd really like to find out what becomes of him. I knew he wasn't just a little brat.

Obviously, the above journal records the unusual experiences of a particularly sensitive young man. But the journal shows the kind of meaningful experiences possible in out-of-school learning. The following are excerpts of entries made by a boy who participated in a CLP in a medical research lab. The young man has subsequently gone into pre-medical studies at a university.

*March 28.* Today was the first day we went to the hospital. It was a very interesting experiment that was being done when we arrived at the lab. At least it looked interesting. We hadn't the faintest idea of what was going on. The doctor gave us a brief explanation of the experiment. We spent the rest of the time with two of his assistants. While the two women messed with the experiment, we proceeded to dissect a rat completely. It was a big mess. The heart was still beating after we had taken it out and the muscles were still contracting. The rat was anesthesized by phenol-barbitol.

*March 30.* Today was fun and very tiring at the same time. As soon as we got to the lab, we were given some calculations to punch into the computer. At about 1:00 ten fish (live rainbow trout) were delivered to the lab. I had to net a fish and put it on a wooden platter, holding it down tight with a dry towel in the left hand and by the gills with the right hand. Miss Lee then took a needle and syringe and inserted the needle into the center of the heart. As much blood as could be drawn was taken and put into a small test tube. Meanwhile I was practically wrestling with the fish who was internally hemorrhaging from the heart. Miss Lee then cut the belly of the fish open with a scalpal and pulled all the guts out of the fish. Keep in mind that the brain and spinal cord are still intact and the fish is twitching horrendously. The guts, especially the reproductive cells, were carried to another lab for further experiments along with the blood. After she had taken the kidneys out of the fish and placed them in a special solution, I was told to take the fish (still squirming) and put it in a tub of ice to keep it fresh for good eating. This was repeated nine more times. My hands felt like meat hooks; they were so tired.

*April 4.* Today was very boring and blah. All we did was calculations on the computer.

*April 5.* Today was less boring than yesterday. There were calculations to do on the computer. That's routine. But Miss Lee decided to teach us how to operate the PH meter after we finished the daily computer work. It was a lot of fun because it really is a remarkable machine. It costs about $900. The machine needs to be adjusted every time it is used.

*April 18.* Today was absolutely the most boring day so far. We had missed a week from spring break and a lot of calculations had built up. There were six or seven big sheets of numbers to punch into the computer. I can hardly wait until Thursday when the fish are delivered. It is an assured fun day.

*April 20.* Today was finally fish day. While waiting for the fish we were introduced to a machine called an ionization calcium counter which, when injected with blood samples from the fish, analyzes the blood and detects the calcium ion concentration due to varying diets.

*April 24.* Today was a bomb. I'm sorry that things aren't jumping like frogs every day. We must all learn to accept bad days however. It's the bad days that make the good days so fantastic.

*April 25.* Today we did some dreadful calculations on the computer then dragged ourselves across the lab where one of Miss Lee's assistants was working with an interesting, box-shaped green machine sitting on the counter. It was a "Fluorometer." The girl working this gadget would take a test tube with the ionized calcium solution in it and put it in a slot inside the door, close the door, and record a reading from a dial on top of the box. This is called measuring the fluorescence of a substance. I decided to see how much some of the lab equipment cost. I was astounded. The flurometer, which is no more than a foot high, long, or wide, cost $1200!

*May 16.* There were attempts to add variety to the routine work with the computers. We were given new kinds of computations to do. They involved a linear regression program. What happens is there are certain quantitative characteristics in blood serum and intestines etc. which are recorded in large amounts of examples from rats and fish. The numbers that we are concerned with measure the general calcium content of the organism. Then, these calcium characteristics are compared with many other characteristics of the organism. The computer puts out the information needed to form a graph. The slope is read. If a pattern forms on the graph, then the relationship between the calcium content and, let's say, the age of the organism is a significant one and there is possibly a lead to discoveries of the nature of calcium, which is what we are attempting to find.

As the above entries show, different students have diverse kinds of experiences in out-of-school learning. But in all cases we have used, there was an important educational experience. Furthermore, the students we have used for illustrations ranged from those doing very poorly to those who were honor students. Out-of-school learning programs can be stimulating and helpful to all kinds of students. The programs are not merely for those who cannot cope well with the normal curriculum.

## SOME ADDITIONAL OPTIONS

In this last section, we will briefly look at a few additional options for the nontraditional part of the curriculum. Some additional options include:

(1) adult night school-community school, with high-school credit by arrangement with the principal;

(2) correspondence courses for high-school credit;

(3)   credit for travel/experience by prior arrangement;
(4)   dual enrollment with local colleges;
(5)   college courses for credit offered at the high school.

There are also some options which can be offered off campus on a full-time basis for those of high-school age. One is the alternative school which is managed by school personnel. Basically, this involves tutorials and small groups. It can be used for fifth-year seniors who are finishing their credits for graduation, for young women with infants who cannot attend the school full time, and for students who are disruptive or who refuse to follow reasonable guidelines. In some cases, the latter group will include students who are able to develop more positive relationships through the alternative program and who later request readmission to regular school programs. Even if the students do not return to the regular program, the alternative school can reduce problems of violence and vandalism, as a Congressional report noted, by "offering a more suitable educational model for students who find the traditional approach to learning unrewarding and frustrating."[14]

The last option we shall note is the Job Training Program which was funded by the Comprehensive Educational and Training Act. Initially, training was done by Chrysler Corporation on a subcontract basis. Currently, the training is handled by school district personnel. A six-week training program is offered to habitual truants or to dropouts with assistance in job placement after the training. Some of these young people may also join Adult Basic Education programs for completion of high school equivalency.

In sum, the curriculum of the high school can offer something for every kind of student. The various options we have discussed are all practical. At the same time, they allow for the great range of interests and abilities that will be found in any high-school student body. A diverse, stimulating, beneficial set of options can be offered without the least sacrifice of academic standards. And for at least some students, the options may mean a door of opportunity in an otherwise (for them) meaningless situation.

## SUMMARY

Out-of-school learning is a traditional American method, going back to the apprenticeships of Colonial America. Technological change ended the apprenticeship system, but young people continued to learn by living—with a vengeance in the early industrial era. After compulsory school laws were passed and the schools assumed custodial as well as educational functions, living and learning became separated. The separation may be coming to an end as increasing numbers of people recognize the legitimacy of learning from experiences outside the classroom.

There are a number of options currently available for learning experiences outside the classroom. These include work/study programs, field trips, and guest speakers, all of which are used rather widely. There are also a number of successful programs which have been implemented primarily by alternative schools: community classes, internships, group publication projects, student exchange programs, and the "Walkabout model."

Two options which have been successfully implemented but not widely used are Deliberate Psychological Education and the Community Learning Program. Both programs are simple in design, allow student participation in accord with individual needs or interests, and effectively combine certain academic objectives with a significant experience in community placement. Furthermore, both programs have been shown to have positive consequences for community sponsors and parents as well as for students.

Finally, there are additional options for the nontraditional part of the curriculum, some of which can be offered on a full-time basis for those of high-school age. The variety of options which are practical is sufficiently large that the high school's curriculum can offer something for every kind of student.

# Endnotes

[1]Edward Hodnett, *The Art of Problem Solving* (New York: Harper & Row, 1955), p. 97.

[2]Joseph F. Kett, *Rites of Passage: Adolescence in America, 1790 to the Present* (New York: Basic Books, 1977), p. 111.

[3]*Ibid.*, p. 112.

[4]Barbara J. Shoup, *Living and Learning for Credit* (Bloomington, Indiana: Phi Delta Kappa, 1978), p. 4.

[5]These two examples are from Kett, *op. cit.*, pp. 25, 27–28.

[6]Kett, *op. cit.*, p. 145.

[7]Peter Quennell, ed., *Selected Writings of John Ruskin* (London: The Falcon Press, 1952), p. 81.

[8]A. Harry Passow, *American Secondary Education: The Conant Influence* (Reston, Virginia: National Association of Secondary School Principals, 1977), p. 49.

[9]*The RISE Report: Report of the California Commission for Reform of Intermediate and Secondary Education* (Sacramento, Cal.: California State Department of Education, 1975), p. 11.

[10]Shoup, *op. cit.*, pp. 26–42. As with any program, there are many problems and pitfalls associated with these options. Those considering implementing the options as well as those interested in the problems should consult Shoup, for she discusses briefly some of the advantages and some of the hazards of each option.

[11]Shoup, *op. cit.*, p. 26.

[12]Urie Bronfenbrenner, *Two Worlds of Childhood: U.S. and U.S.S.R.* (New York: Russell Sage Foundation, 1970), pp. 116–17.

[13]Ralph L. Mosher and Norman A. Sprinthall, "Psychological Education: A Means to Promote Personal Development during Adolescence," *The Counseling Psychologist* 2 (no. 4, 1971): 3, 9–10.

[14]Quoted in the *NAASP Curriculum Report* 8 (October, 1978): 6.

# Part

## 3

# ADMINISTRATION:
# MANAGING A HUMAN ORGANIZATION

# Chapter 6

# Decision Making: Freedom and Responsibility

In 1961, a contingent of Cuban exiles who had been trained and equipped in the United States invaded their former homeland in an attempt to overthrow the Communist government of Fidel Castro. The attempt not only failed but also raised embarrassing questions about U.S. involvement in such ventures, for the abortive invasion, known thereafter as the Bay of Pigs incident (after the place at which the invasion took place), was discussed and approved by the President and other high-level officials. How could this elite group, given the intelligence base from which it was operating, have made a decision to proceed with an operation that was virtually certain to fail and to embarrass the nation?

In his discussion of the Bay of Pigs case, Whyte points out that President Kennedy asked himself a question that is not very fruitful: "How could I have been so stupid?"[1] The question is not fruitful, argues Whyte, because it focuses our attention on thinking ability, and we are likely to conclude nothing more than that we make better decisions if we are smart rather than stupid. A useful approach is to look at the process of decision making rather than at the thinking ability of individual decision makers. In the Bay of Pigs case the decision was made as a result of the advice of men who held key positions in large bureaucracies:

> No one of these men was free to give his full attention to an uncommitted analysis of the proposal. Like any good organization man, each of these executives had to be concerned also with his relations with members of his own bureaucracy and with interagency relations . . . there was no one called upon to speak whose only loyalty was to the President himself.[2]

In other words, the participants were caught up in a decision-making structure that precluded an objective analysis. The plan was developed in the CIA. The men who evaluated it had to consider the relationships between their own organizations and the CIA. If, for example, a representative from the Defense Department had rejected the proposal, the rejection could have been interpreted as interagency rivalry and could have affected subsequent relationships between the two organizations in a negative manner.

The Bay of Pigs decision was not a unique set of circumstances, however. The point is that decision making is a social process. In every organization, there is a structure of decision making that is of critical importance independent of the perceptiveness or bumbling of individual decision makers. Furthermore, the decision-making structure affects not only the nature of the decisions that are made but also the quality of member participation in the organization. In essence, the decision-making structure may be primarily either authoritarian or democratic (participatory). Those in a democratic structure are likely to find their membership more rewarding than those in an authoritarian structure, a point we will discuss in more detail below.

A democratic decision-making structure is an integral part of a human organization. It assumes that people, including adolescents, operate most effectively in a context that maximizes their freedom and responsibility. Such a maximization requires that a balance be maintained among the needs of the individual, the abilities of the individual (including stage of individual development), and the functioning of the organization. Unfortunately, some school administrators believe that the only way to maintain a proper balance is for them to make the necessary decisions in an authoritarian manner. We would argue, on the contrary, that while democratic decision making has its risks, a comprehensive high school can function effectively—in fact, most effectively—by a system of decision making in which staff, students, and parents all enter into the process. We have already noted one way in which students and parents share in important decisions, for participatory advisement is a decision-making system. In addition, the school can allow broad participation in decisions about curriculum, administrative procedures, rules and regulations, student activities, and faculty inservice.

We shall begin our discussion of decision making in this chapter by first looking at the way in which typical educational organizations in this country have mirrored typical industrial organizations—both have been hierarchically organized for authoritarian decision making and both have suffered the consequence of alienated members. This typical structure and its attendant problem of alienation is the basis for our argument that schools should adopt participatory decision making. We shall then discuss the elements of participatory decision making and illustrate the significance of those elements by detailing their role in participatory advisement. Finally, we will show the kind of organizational structure that allows democratic decision making.

## AUTHORITARIAN ORGANIZATIONS AND ALIENATION

An organization needs positions of authority, but those in such positions need not be authoritarian. Someone must have the authority to make and to implement decisions, but that does not mean that decisions must be made arbitrarily or unilaterally. Many people believe that an authoritarian structure is necessary if the organization is to be viable. As an engineer said to one of the authors at a discussion on democracy in organizations, "If our corporation tried to be democratic we would be broke in two months." The engineer's attitude is shared by many principals, who say, in effect, "If our school tried to be democratic we would have chaos in two hours." Because of such attitudes, organizations—both industries and schools—have been more authoritarian than democratic.

## AUTHORITARIAN ORGANIZATIONS

Large comprehensive high schools, developed over the last century, have been patterned architecturally and organizationally after the industrial model. The organization has been structured in an authoritarian way in order to create an efficient assembly line that will maximize output. In the schools, this means that each teacher is a specialist in charge of dispensing a prescribed portion of the curriculum. The teacher, like an assembly line worker, waits in a 25' × 30' cubicle called a classroom for sets of students to arrive on an hourly schedule via a conveyor system called a single or double-loaded corridor.

There has been, of course, a good deal of rhetoric about democratizing classrooms. But democracy and shared decision-making exists, if at all, in extra-curricular activities and in clubs. Even there, activity can be organized *a priori* in order to achieve efficiency and limit the number of decisions that are necessary.

Schools, like most factories, leave little time or opportunity for shared, participatory decision making. Students and teachers are encouraged to practice democracy in the classroom and in after school activities. Democracy is heralded in the classroom as a superior mode of social interaction. But few teachers and administrators are convinced that students are capable of participating in responsible decision making. Principals make decisions arbitrarily or unilaterally because "you *have* to if you want to keep control over things." Teachers and advisors tell students what to do rather than discuss what can be done because adolescents "don't have the experience necessary for making the right decisions." After all, the worker does not consult with the product. The worker does what is necessary so that the product will turn out as it ought. In a factory system, the worker obeys the orders of the superiors, functioning according to directions in order to manipulate materials properly and produce the desired product —whether the product is a machine, a gadget, a package, or a student. And what is the result of the authoritarian factory system?

## AUTHORITARIANISM AND ALIENATION

In an authoritarian industrial organization, the worker may produce a good product but he or she often has problems of satisfaction and morale. In the authoritarian school, both the worker (teacher) and the product (student) may have such problems. At best, an authoritarian organization may be tolerated by the members (at least, by those members not in the elite positions). At worst, an authoritarian mode of organization can be inhuman, involving what Robert Presthus called "organized irresponsibility:"

> Decision making in the big organization becomes abstract and impersonal, the instrument of an anonymous, fragmented intelligence. . . . In extreme cases the condition may lead to arbitrary and immoral behavior, particularly when compounded by intense personal identification with some polit-

ical ideology, the state, the party, the church, or the "organization." In every case, the probabilities that the organization may act unjustly are increased by the weakening of individual responsibility. Only "the system" is responsible.[3]

As an example, Presthus refers to the authoritarian Nazi chain of command that led to numerous atrocities. More recently, the well-known experiments of Milgram have shown that a considerable number of Americans can perform cruel acts when directed to do so by a legitimate authority.[4]

More commonly, however, members of authoritarian organizations are likely to experience negative emotions and attitudes, ranging from job dissatisfaction to a sense of alienation. For example, in his effort to systematize social scientific research findings pertinent to social action, Rothman set forth the following as one of his generalizations: "Increased hierarchy of authority (centralization and lower degree of worker participation in decision making) is correlated with greater job dissatisfaction and work alienation. Hierarchy of authority is also correlated with expressive alienation."[5] Alienation from work is a sense of powerlessness and isolation from decision making, while expressive alienation was defined as dissatisfaction with relationships at work. People prefer to have some involvement in decisions that affect them and their work. When they do not have the opportunity to participate in decisions, they are likely to have lower levels of satisfaction with their work, lower team spirit, lower morale, and less motivation to be productive.[6]

There is also some evidence that people perform less effectively in authoritarian structures. An experiment with teams of airmen showed that problems were more quickly solved when responsibility for the task was shared equally by all team members than when the responsibility was centered in one member of the team.[7] A study of salesmen in three different organizations showed that the more centralized the authority the less likely the salesmen were to experience self-actualization, the more likely they were to perceive higher amounts of anxiety and stress, and the less efficiently they worked.[8] Such studies support Likert's claim about productivity in a human organization, namely, that workers will exhibit more loyalty and higher motivation, have higher performance goals, and achieve higher levels of productivity.[9]

There is also evidence of negative consequences of authoritarianism in schools. Students may find their educational experiences oppressive and meaningless. They may become apathetic about academic achievement. They may even become chronic rebels. We are not suggesting that all such problems are merely due to an authoritarian administration. But if authoritarianism has negative consequences for people generally, it would be surprising if we did not find such consequences in schools. What is the meaning of a student council, which contains some of the most involved students in the school, developing an adversary role? Why does a student council try to find ways of wresting from administrators some "rights?" When even those who serve on the student council do not perceive themselves as genuine participants in determining the nature of their educational experiences, it is likely that the administration is an authoritarian one.

## TREATING THE SYMPTOMS

Recognizing the negative factors in their organizations, some managers and school administrators have attempted to resolve the problem of alienation. Unfortunately, they have tended to treat the symptoms rather than to attack the problem, for they have applied various social analgesics while retaining the authoritarian structure. Riesman noted this tendency in his analysis of leisure and work in a postindustrial society:

> In the high-wage industries given over to "conspicuous production," management has the resources to be concerned with the amenities of work—the group harmony, the decor, the cafeteria and other ancillary services—and to make provision for the worker's leisure, such as bowling teams, golf courses, and adult education courses too; in fact, a whole range of extracurricular pleasures and benefits. Sometimes these benefits include profit-sharing, but they are much less likely to include decision-sharing.[10]

Since Riesman wrote his analysis, the notion of participatory management (that is, management in which workers share in the decision-making process) has become more popular in theory but not widespread in practice. Riesman's plea is still relevant: "What I am asking for now are explorations in reorganizing work itself so that man can live humanely on as well as off the job."[11]

Similar points could be made about schools. Authoritarian administrations have attempted to make education more meaningful for a larger number of students by providing such things as extracurricular activities. We are not saying that extracurricular activities and other kinds of programs are unimportant. But they will not resolve the alienation experienced by many students. Schools, like industries, need reorganizing if the participants are to live humanely within them.

Specifically, there is a need for participation in the decision-making process, so that all members of the school can have a sense of belonging to and having an impact on the organization.

## THE ELEMENTS OF DEMOCRATIC DECISION MAKING

As pointed out in the Introduction, in a human organization individuals and groups who will be most affected by decisions have a part in making those decisions. Such participation is based on the principle that people should have a voice in any decision that affects their well-being. In addition, decision makers in a human organization are generally aware of problems at lower levels in the organization. There are organizational processes and structures that insure the flow of adequate information—information that flows up as well as down.

Participation in the decision-making process is a motivating force of considerable importance, because it is an acknowledgement that the individual is capable, has some control of a given situation, and is entrusted with responsibility. In a school environment, there is no better means of learning about the relationship between freedom and responsibility than by sharing in the process of making decisions and living with the consequences of those decisions. Participation in decision making by students is not only an antidote to alienation but also an invaluable experience for personal growth.

## A CAVEAT

Before discussing the important elements in a system of shared decision making in a school, we need to pause for a caveat: beware of the revolving door syndrome. The syndrome was expressed poetically by Omar Khayyam in the Rubaiyat:

> Myself when young did eagerly frequent
> Doctor and Saint, and heard great argument
>   About it and about: but evermore
> Came out by the same door where in I went.[12]

In other words, in spite of his activity and in spite of all the rhetoric he heard, he learned nothing and nothing changed. Thus, we define the revolving door syndrome as a set of activities and rhetoric that mask the fact that nothing has really changed.

In terms of shared decision making in a school, the revolving door syndrome means that democracy is espoused and organizing or reorganizing occurs, but the school remains authoritarian. "There is a difference between theoretical democracy in patterns of organization and democracy in action, and a democratic administrator will help plan an organization in which democratic principles can be applied in daily practice."[13] We agree, and will show below how democratic decision making can be implemented in a high school. But we need to be aware of the possibility of providing the appearance of democracy without the reality.

One way to give the appearance without the reality of shared decision making is to give students opportunities to provide input without the responsibility of voting or of actually making a decision. For example, students may be brought into a policy making committee in order to share their thinking but may be given no vote on the committee. Or an advisor might insist on making the final decision about the student's program, giving the student opportunity to express an opinion but not the power to make the final decision (and learn from the consequences). A facade of democracy over an authoritarian structure may be worse than unvarnished authoritarianism. The student who comes in with the eager expectation of responsible sharing and discovers that he or she "came out by the same door where in I went" may be more alienated than the one who knows that he or she must learn to cope with authoritarianism.

## ORGANIZING FOR SHARED DECISION MAKING

Given the desire for implementing a democratic decision making system, what are the necessary elements? How does one go about organizing for such a system? We believe that there are three crucial elements necessary—time and opportunity, information, and training.

First, organizational change must take place that gives individuals and groups both the time and the opportunity to make appropriate decisions. While this may seem to be an obvious statement, there are cases, as we shall note below, where schools have tried to implement some kinds of shared decision making without providing the necessary time and opportunities.

Second, information must be freely available in the necessary form at all levels of decision making. We pointed out that information must flow both up and down in a human organization. In most cases, there is no problem with the downward flow of information. Upward flow may prove problematic, however. Whyte notes that large organizations typically have "filtering effects" with respect to the upward flow of information.[14] Middle-level managers with aspirations to be upwardly mobile tend to restrict information that suggests problems or troubles in their areas of responsibility. Rather, the managers try to emphasize the desirable and positive aspects so that they will appear to be doing excellent work.

All of us want to "look good." Schools are as likely as other large organizations to experience some problem with the upward flow of accurate information. Of course, inaccurate and inadequate information inhibits or even precludes optimal decision making. Expecting people to make decisions without appropriate information is like expecting them to engage in target shooting in the dark.

Third, even when appropriate information is available, decision making requires training. Training is necessary for both individual and group decisions. People need to learn how to make rational decisions as individuals, and they must learn about the complexities of group decision making (including the way in which the decisions of one group are likely to intersect with those of other groups).

The significance of the three elements necessary for organizing a democratic decision-making system can be illustrated by their role in participatory advisement. We will look at each in turn.


## TIME AND OPPORTUNITY

Building in the time and opportunity to make decisions is crucial to the success of participatory advisement. Some schools have adopted the goals of participatory advisement but do not provide adequate time or settings for participants to make the decisions which are expected of them. In some cases, for instance, schools have set up home-room type structures (15 minutes daily). Such a structure is simply not adequate in amount of time, in the way the time is allocated (small daily amounts) or in the setting provided (groups of students, who may be isolated from adequate resources). The time must be adequate to the task, and the setting must be conducive to individual decision making. Even in schools that adopt the weekly two-hour individual conference periods that we described in Chapter 3, occasional adjustments in scheduled conference time may be necessary in order to insure that advisors and students have adequate time to make good decisions.

Periodic assessments are necessary in order to ascertain whether parents, advisors, and students are satisfied with their decisions and feel that the system is providing appropriate time and opportunity for them. Parents in particular must be fully aware of their role in the advisement process and know how to participate. Not all parents will take the opportunities provided, but they should be aware of each one and have the chance to evaluate their role and potential participation.

In our society, the amount of time allocated to anything is a measure of the importance attached to it.[15] Time is said to be a scarce resource that is carefully distributed according to what we value. The school that refuses to allocate sufficient time for shared decision making in participatory advisement, then, is clearly saying that it does not consider such an activity to be of prime importance.

## INFORMATION

Even if we allow sufficient time and opportunity for shared decision making, the activity will be of little value unless adequate and accurate information is provided to all the participants. An effective participatory advisement system requires:

(1)   a carefully designed catalog of school offerings, including information on graduation requirements, special honors, and general college/career entry requirements;

(2)   access to more detailed information regarding college/career entry;

(3)   knowledge of student records and registration procedures; and

(4)   knowledge of all school policies and procedures.

A school with a participatory advisement system will probably find over time that the greatest demand for change is for better and more information. In one school, evaluations repeatedly uncovered weaknesses in the format of information and in the quantity of information available. Among the criticisms were the following:

1.   The first course catalog did not have a standard format for course descriptions. Various complaints and evaluations revealed a need to simplify the descriptions and to clearly identify the level of difficulty (particularly with reference to reading and writing levels which would be expected of students).

2.   Evaluations revealed that incentives to take the most challenging courses in each subject were weak; an honors program was therefore developed. Students and faculty worked together to develop the program.

3. Some parents and advisors indicated that setting up three-year plans was difficult and required an inordinate amount of time. Subsequent catalogs, therefore, included sample three-year plans for various career or college options. The sample plans were to be used as models or guides, of course, and not as a limited set of fixed options.

As the above suggests, problems are certain to occur in democratic decision-making systems (just as they are certain to occur in authoritarian systems). In some cases, the problem may be rooted in the participants, who are not accustomed to functioning in a democratic decision-making system or who may even oppose such a system. Like the engineer mentioned earlier, some people believe that shared decision making is inappropriate or even deadly to an adequately functioning organization. But frequently the problem will arise because of inadequacies in the area of information. Conflict may arise when people are asked to make decisions without having adequate information. Breakdowns in functioning may occur when people make decisions on the basis of inaccurate or inadequate information.

The significance of information in an organization has been detailed by Harold Wilensky, among others. Wilensky said that one of the fundamental problems for an administrative leader is that "of gathering, processing, interpreting, and communicating the technical and political information needed in the decision-making process."[16] He details various kinds of "intelligence failures" in organizations, that is, the failure to gather the information necessary to successful achievement of organizational goals. Interestingly, he shows how a highly centralized, hierarchical organizational structure can be one of the causes of intelligence failure. In such an organization, there is a tendency for upward communication to be inhibited and for a good deal of irrelevant or even misleading information to circulate. The administrator who actually makes the decisions may therefore be overloaded (though not necessarily with appropriate information) and out of touch with the real problems. Those who have expertise or appropriate knowledge may be isolated from the decision makers, so that even though the necessary information is theoretically available it is in practice unlikely to reach the decision maker. The outcome may range from inconsequential to disastrous in terms of achieving organizational goals.

Of course, an authoritarian administrator may be willing to run the risk of having inadequate information in order to maximize his or her own power. And such an administrator may maintain maximum power by convincing others that he or she not only has adequate information but more information than anyone else in the organization. Government leaders do this when they act on the basis of "top-secret" information. They say to us, in effect, "If you knew what I know, you would make the same decision that I have made." How can we disagree as long as we acknowledge the validity of keeping certain information secret? The same kind of process can occur in a school. A principal may say to a teacher, "On the basis of enrollments, I am going to have to switch you to different courses next year." The decision may or may not be a good one in terms of the education of students. And it may or may not be a necessary decision, but what recourse does the teacher have if information on enrollment is not generally available except to the principal? Or an advisor may tell a student that some activity in which the student is interested cannot be pursued because it will violate school policy. The decision may or may not be a valid one, but how can the student respond if information on policies is not generally available?

If the goal is to maintain and exercise power, information must be guarded. If the goal is to provide opportunities to participate in decisions that affect the individual, information must be generally available. We would argue that a democratic decision-making system will facilitate the personal growth of the participants and enhance the solidarity and sense of community of the school. But if adequate information is not available, the experience will be attended by aggravations, frustrations, and conflict.

In some cases, administrators learn by trial and error the kind of information needed. Procedures are established, problems arise, and the administrator investigates to see if there is a problem of information. Sometimes the problem may be minimal and easily resolved. For example, administrators in one school with participatory advisement initially sent out registration information each semester reminding all participants of deadlines for program planning decisions. Advisors frequently expressed surprise at the nearness of deadlines and began asking for earlier warnings. In other words, they had an information problem; it was the timing rather than the amount of information that generated anxiety and frustration. The problem was easily resolved by developing a calendar for registration and program planning. The calendar was posted throughout the school. It gave the dates for the entire year for such things as student registration, parent conferences, deadlines for setting up the master schedule, and deadlines for resolving schedule conflicts.

Not all problems of information are as easily resolved, of course. In fact, not all problems are rooted in information. But the flow of information is an integral part of any shared decision-making system, and the sensitive administrator will always be alert for information problems.

## TRAINING

The third crucial element of a shared decision-making system is training. In the participatory advisement process itself there are several decision-making models that parents, advisors, and students are encouraged to review or consider periodically. The models help all participants to become more aware of themselves as decision makers, which means awareness of oneself as a responsible individual. The models also help participants to evaluate their decision-making style.

The models may need to be the focus of several inservice training sessions for advisors if their full potential is to be realized. Counselors may offer seminars on parent-child communication and use the decision-making models as a partial basis for helping parents relate more effectively to their sons and daughters. And advisors should schedule at least one session with advisees in which the decision-making process is discussed.

Students have been known to decide the answers on a true–false quiz by flipping a coin. People have been known to decide how to vote on the basis of the appearance of two opposing candidates. Individuals sometimes decide between alternative courses of action on the basis of their current emotional state. A student may decide to abandon previous interest in a career because of a poor teacher of a course related to that career. We make decisions on any number of bases, ranging from the inappropriate to the bizarre. Decision making that is conducive to our own well-being and to the effective functioning of our schools must be learned. It is unlikely that many people already possess the requisite skills. The democratic administrator, therefore, will plan for adequate training of all the participants—staff, students, and parents.

## BUILDING A STRUCTURE FOR SHARED DECISION MAKING

The participatory advisement system, by making all participants thoroughly knowledgeable of the school's total program, prepares many participants to play a greater role in the decision-making process. In fact, principals in schools with effective participatory advisement sys-

tems will find many people expressing personal involvement and a
sense of responsibility for the quality of the school. Often, such people
will also display an eagerness to play a greater role in those larger decisions that affect the goals and operations of the school.

The following structure for shared decision making in a comprehensive high school has proved to be workable and effective. The structure pulls in participants from all aspects of the school, including the
participatory advisement system, the student activities programs,
student government, departments, administration, counseling, and
parents. The various groups that make up the school's decision-making structure must be examined in terms of the three crucial elements
discussed above—time and opportunity, information, and training. In
addition, the structure must be examined in terms of the functions for
each group, particularly in terms of any overlapping which may occur
between groups. Figure 6.1 shows the structure in chart form. We will
look at certain groups in some detail.

## THE INSTRUCTIONAL IMPROVEMENT
## COMMITTEE

As the chart shows, the Instructional Improvement Committee is a
key group. Its members—six faculty members, six students, and one
parent—are chosen at large from the school community. This committee has overall responsibility for sharing in those decisions which
transcend all special interests and set policy or direction for the entire
school. An IIC manual sets forth the committee's rationale and purpose:

> One of the major problems in education today is that of making decision-
> making structures responsive to the people whom they serve. More than
> ever before individuals recognize and insist that they have a right to par-
> ticipate in decisions that will profoundly affect them. In the past decisions
> have been made by the principals, who have attempted to establish re-
> lationships and to maintain contact with many people so that their deci-
> sions would be as sound and just as humanly possible. But in the end, these
> decisions were necessarily dependent upon the perceptions, the knowledge,
> and the good judgment of one humanly fallible individual.
>
> In our school the principal is still the pivot, still the spark, but he ad-
> ministers through leadership rather than through supreme authority. The
> decision-making process becomes just that—a process, a process which at
> one time or another will involve the entire school (students and teachers)
> and the community.
>
> To achieve this end, we have formed a representative body known as the
> Instructional Improvement Committee. It meets regularly to discuss

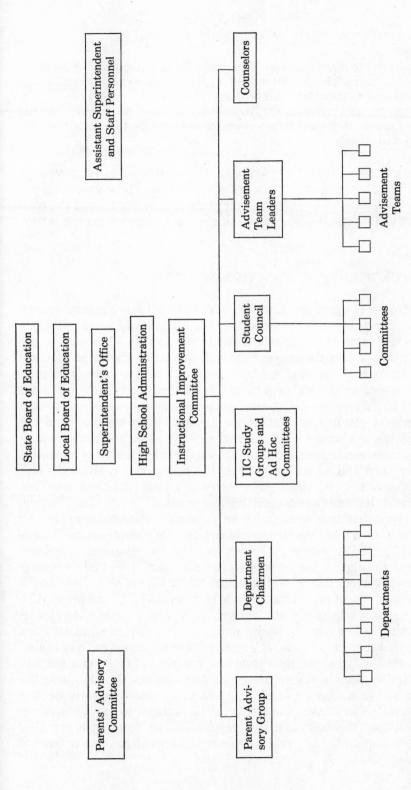

**Figure 6.1**
Structure for Shared Decision Making in a Comprehensive High School

issues and to make decisions. This group assumes responsibility for creating and maintaining liaison with all people, groups, and organizations with an interest in the educational process of the school. Through a carefully designed "modus operendi" the IIC insures that school decisions are fair and practical solutions based on fact and consistent with the school's philosophy and goals.

In order to function effectively, the Instructional Improvement Committee must operate by a set of guidelines. These guidelines are shared with the entire school. Their purpose is to insure that the committee will be responsive to individuals and groups within the school.


## FUNCTIONS AND FUNCTIONING OF THE IIC

One of the primary functions of the IIC is to be a central agency which is responsive to all elements in the school. Any person with any legitimate interest in the school and its operations has access to the committee. When the student council decides to challenge a school rule, when an individual student seeks redress for some grievance, when a teacher questions a current educational practice, when the school board requires assistance in making a policy statement, when a community group has suggestions for improving something in the school, when a school employee can no longer tolerate certain activities—whenever, in sum, anyone wants and needs a review of any situation in which the school is involved, that person may petition the IIC.

One of the IIC members is chosen to be the agenda leader. That member is responsible for receiving any petitions. Many times individuals experience frustration with an existing system because they do not know where to take their problems, and they may become the victims of an endless round of referrals. The IIC meets this problem through the agenda leader, who acts as a listening post and a clearinghouse for various issues. Not all issues can or should be brought to the IIC as a whole. Many matters can be best dealt with by the principal, a department chairman, a student group, or various other individuals and groups. The agenda leader may consult with an administrator, with other members of the IIC, or with other personnel as he or she solicits, consolidates, and refers matters brought to his or her attention.

If the agenda leader brings an issue before the IIC, it is the leader's responsibility to make sure that the issue is clearly defined and stated. The leader then forwards the problem to the study group coordinator. The coordinator is responsible for forming a group of capable, impartial individuals to research the problem. A basic tenet of the group is that anyone in the school is capable of studying issues. Teachers, students, and administrators may all serve on a group and each is an equal member of the group (*not* a representative of a vested interest). The coordinator has the authority to assist the research process in any way that he or she deems necessary. In very serious issues, the coordinator might even request substitute teachers so that study group members may be free for one or two entire days. But the coordinator's primary responsibility is to insure that the appointed group will work to produce the information that will enable the IIC to make an intelligent decision.

Each study group (there may be several functioning simultaneously) approaches an assignment with the knowledge that they must issue a written report within a specified length of time. The written report has six elements:

1. a clear statement of the problem. This statement may be worded exactly as it is received. If new information provides new insights, however, the problem may be reworded to reflect a more accurate description of the situation.
2. a statement proving that the problem exists, including how it was identified and how it has manifested itself in the school.
3. a reference to the specific "We Agree" statement or to elements of school goals that are relevant to the problem.
4. a list of people contacted and references used in securing information about the problem.
5. a list of alternative solutions or courses of action developed by the group.
6. a majority opinion and, if appropriate, a minority opinion of the group.

The above six elements are vital to problem solving. The problem cannot be solved if people do not understand clearly what the problem is. The IIC would not be interested in the problem unless there is clear evidence that such a problem does exist and clear indications of the extent to which it influences the school. A noting of appropriate "We Agree" statements permits the IIC to consider actions in keeping with pre-determined overall goals and objectives. A list of references enables pertinent data to be reconfirmed should there ever be any doubt about the validity of the information reported. A list of alternatives reveals the depth to which the study group has researched the problem and speeds the final decision-making process. A majority opinion becomes the recommended course of action; a minority opinion records opposition and opposing rationales.

Copies of the study group report are sent to all members of the IIC, to all teachers in the school, and to the student council. Thus, when the report and its recommended action are placed on the IIC agenda, all IIC members will have been able to consider it prior to a formal meeting and all teachers will be able to make their thoughts known to their IIC representative prior to formal consideration. At the formal (usually weekly) IIC meeting, the chairperson directs the discussion, attempting to elicit all viewpoints and discuss each thoroughly until a decision is made by consensus. In most situations, of course, people are not totally for or against a proposal. The aim is for the group to arrive at a decision that is appropriate, acceptable, and in keeping with the spirit of the "We Agree" concepts.

To insure that the IIC discusses matters fully and that it does function in an open democratic manner, one of its members is designated as "process observer." The process observer withdraws from active participation to monitor the decision-making process. At the conclusion of the meeting, the process observer reports his or her observations, commenting on such matters as participation, maintaining attention, ability to listen, and so on. For example, the process observer might say that during a particular meeting

(1)   three members left to answer the phone;
(2)   one member left for a few minutes to meet with a student;
(3)   one person took detailed notes that seemed to distract and inhibit others in the group;
(4)   two members seemed very fidgety and unable to concentrate on the discussion;
(5)   three times the chairperson asked for comments and no one responded;
(6)   one point on the minority report seemed to be largely ignored;
(7)   there did seem to be genuine consensus at the end.

Such statements enable the IIC to see itself and recognize the circumstances that undermine group cohesiveness and make decision by consensus more difficult. It is a self-improvement technique for a democratic decision-making group.

In addition to study groups for specific problem areas, the IIC usually sponsors a number of ad hoc groups focusing on specific areas of concern. Many such groups might be formed regarding curriculum development. One group might be responsible for making recommendations concerning short course topics and/or structures. Another group might be assigned the task of determining what specific study skills are being taught and whether the school environment encourages the learning of study skills. Still another group might theorize on new kinds of structures that might be of value to the school. A school's catalog of objectives usually needs updating and a group might be formed for this purpose. Curriculum development can never be left to chance, and it is very difficult for all staff members to become adequately knowledgeable about all aspects of curriculum, particularly new materials. Ongoing study groups in such matters are invaluable aids to IIC decision-making in the area of curriculum.

An ad hoc group could also be formed in the area of school-community relations and communications. In addition to researching the area, such a study group might also coordinate the program. Student activities include everything from the athletic program to the drama club, from the Honor Society to the Candy-Stripers program in the local hospital. Here too study groups can research new areas for student involvement, coordinate the use of school facilities, work with and for a student government, and undertake various assignments in behalf of the IIC for the enrichment of student opportunities.

Other areas of concern in which study groups might get involved include reporting to parents, scheduling facilities, budgeting, and in-service. The IIC is responsible for so many areas of school life that only through the study group system can all areas be adequately considered. And through the study group system all staff members and many students and community members become actively involved in the decision-making process.

In sum, the IIC functions as a democratic decision-making group that is accessible to the total constituency of the school. Anyone, including members of the IIC, may bring a problem or issue or proposal to the agenda leader. All matters brought to the agenda leader are handled in accord with the process outlined above, a process summarized in graphic form in the flow chart (Figure 6.2). As the chart shows, there are a number of points at which matters may be terminated and a number of different avenues by which they may be resolved.


## AN EXAMPLE: REPORTS OF IIC STUDY GROUPS

Two actual study groups and their outcome will illustrate the way matters are handled through the IIC. The first case involved study halls. The agenda leader was given a proposal to provide alternatives other than arbitrary assignment to study hall for students who drop a class after the quarter begins. The matter was referred to the

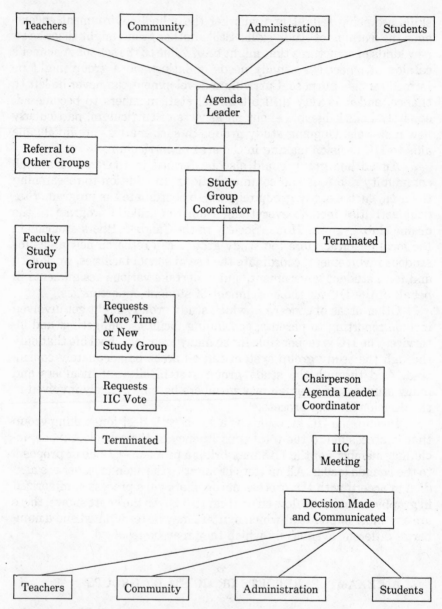

**Figure 6.2**
Flow Chart for Matters Handled by Instructional Improvement Committee

study group coordinator who established a group to study the problem. The group met twice for a total of six hours and agreed that a problem existed. Evidence that arbitrary assignment was problematic included the following:

(1)   ineffective in preventing students from dropping classes;
(2)   some students have two study halls;
(3)   study hall is viewed as punishment;
(4)   students fail to find something to do;
(5)   attendance is poor;
(6)   lack of uniformity in how study halls are conducted.

The study group forwarded the following recommendations to the IIC. First, students should not be placed automatically in a study hall. Second, when dropped from a class for reasons other than discipline, a student should be asked to choose, with his or her advisor, to do one of the following:

(1)   enroll in another course with teachers' permission and amount of credit to be determined by time remaining in the quarter;
(2)   audit a course;
(3)   participate in a service program run by the student council;
(4)   take a course of study overseen by the study hall teacher;
(5)   tutor or be tutored;
(6)   do additional work in a class already being taken;
(7)   investigate career or college information under assignment to a guidance counselor;
(8)   take a study hall.

The recommendations were discussed by the IIC at length. Ultimately it was decided that one of the assistant principals would handle all students who drop a class. He might assign a student to a study hall, but he would present the student with the above list of options before a final decision was made about the student.

A completely different kind of problem was handled by another study group—drug abuse. The group met five times, agreed that drug abuse was a problem at the school, and presented four recommendations to the IIC:

1.   Give a student drug attitude and usage inventory to a random sample of the student body, with date dependent upon IIC approval.

2. Contact the school district's attorney to determine legal responsibility for all personnel in the district in dealing with such situations as confiscation of drugs, witnessing the taking of drugs, or having knowledge of someone taking drugs on campus.
3. Designate a half day workshop during orientation week for the faculty, using community personnel who are familiar with the local drug problem.
4. Prepare a drug packet for each teacher which would include such information as the guidelines to be followed in dealing with a drug problem.

During the IIC meeting a fifth recommendation was suggested: select a committe to study approaches to educating students. Students on the IIC said that marijuana was the main drug used at school, that hard drugs were used off campus, that students with emotional problems take drugs, and that students who confide in a teacher about a drug problem expect that information to be confidential. Eventually, the committee decided to table the report and assign a number of tasks to various individuals. The principal was asked to obtain legal information, prepare a drug packet for each teacher, and publicize and encourage participation in on-going drug abuse programs. A teacher was asked to implement the drug usage survey and prepare a workshop.

These two examples show the range of matters that can be considered by the IIC and the variations in outcome that are possible. The committee may or may not fully accept the recommendations of the faculty study groups. This can cause some frustration in faculty members who have worked hard to produce a report, but they must be reminded that such experiences are inevitable in any democratic process and that the value of shared decision making far outweighs the occasional frustration of seeing one's work rejected.

THE IIC AND MAJOR ISSUES

As we have indicated, the range of matters handled by the IIC is considerable. One of the best features, in fact, is the ability of the system to respond to major issues which may be imposed on the school from outside. Here we will give an example from a court-ordered desegregation case. The court ordered an all-black high school closed and annexed to a neighboring school which had been primarily white. The school receiving the black students had an IIC. Consequently, through the IIC and a series of study groups there was close communication and a sharing of key decisions even before the actual desegregation occurred. Students and faculty from both schools formed a series of study groups which were assigned the tasks of making recommendations on school rules and regulations, curriculum, extra-curricular activities, school traditions, inservice training for faculty, and reciprocal visitation of students prior to desegregation. The new IIC and its study groups, formed by personnel from both schools, did more than make the recommendations for implementing desegregation. The participants developed friendships and mutual trust which greatly helped to overcome later problems.

One of the important actions of the new IIC was the establishment of an ad hoc committee on student relations. The committee was composed of equal numbers of black and white students. Over a period of four years, the committee initiated a number of programs and activities that encouraged the development of racial understanding, friendships, and full participation by both races in school events. Thus, a shared decision-making apparatus such as the IIC can cope with major as well as less significant matters. But as with any other group, the IIC can only function effectively if the three elements of time and opportunity, information, and training are attended to.

## TIME AND OPPORTUNITY

The IIC meets one hour weekly. It may call special meetings as necessary. The committee meets during the school day, with schedules of student and faculty members being adjusted to make participation possible.

Study groups generally conduct meetings after the last class of the day. Occasionally the membership of a study group may be such that the meetings can be held during school hours. One of the school secretaries is assigned the job of typing and distributing IIC minutes and study group reports.

## INFORMATION

The IIC has access to all information available to the administration. In addition, the committee may (and on many occasions will need to) collect or generate information for itself through such things as questionnaires and interviews. Depending on the agenda item, the administration may need to provide special information on school law, school finance, board policies, and other matters.

The principal should make a concerted effort to keep the IIC informed of the activity of other decision-making groups, particularly if a group is considering an idea that is contrary to current school goals or practices or that overlaps the work of other groups. For example, it is possible that a student council committee, a department, the parent advisory group, or the advisement team leaders would want to initiate a curriculum evaluation for the same or for different reasons. Periodically, representatives of other groups may be asked to report on their projects or activity directly to the IIC to prevent overlapping or conflicting activities.

## TRAINING

The membership of the IIC will change regularly. With each change the principal should, with the help of past members, conduct several sessions on IIC operations. The sessions would clearly identify the school's decision-making structure, the role of the IIC in that structure, and the appropriate procedures for democratic decision-making groups.

## OTHER DECISION-MAKING GROUPS

The structure for decision making as outlined above (Fig. 6.1) achieves several important goals. It respects the traditional roles of teachers as subject matter specialists (departments) and of students (student councils). But it gives an equal opportunity to students and teachers to participate in other roles—as advisors (advisement teams) and members of study groups or ad hoc committees. This should decrease the chances that any particular group's vested interests or power will have undue influence on the school's program.

The administrators each share in the process of keeping in touch with the various groups. Generally, an administrator should attend a group's regular meetings for liaison and coordinating purposes. For example, at an English department meeting where teachers were discussing the development of objectives in basic English skills that could be taught in all subjects, the administrator facilitated the goal by placing the idea on the agenda for departmental chairpeople and advisement team leaders. This shared thinking led to broader support and ultimately the IIC requested that the English faculty develop objectives and conduct inservice training for all departments. In this case, it also helped that an IIC study group on basic skills instruction had already recommended similar goals for school-wide adoption.

Each group in the school should have a statement of purpose and a procedure for conducting meetings. The chairperson for each group is responsible for maintaining contact with the administration and the IIC. A ground rule for all IIC study groups is that the group consults with administrators before making a final list of recommendations. Such a procedure has proven useful in revealing problematic alternatives before people developed a commitment to an impractical plan.

The above procedures will not prevent disagreement and debate over alternatives. In fact, the school would suffer under any arrangement that stifled vigorous debate. There is a good deal of evidence that opposing viewpoints make a group more creative than it would be otherwise. For example, two researchers discovered that the most effective producer (in terms of sales, profits, and new products) among six organizations in a plastics industry had the most serious problem of integration and highest degree of conflict.[17] Two others identified conflict as a mechanism of beneficial change in the welfare agencies they studied.[18] There is evidence that scientists in organizations are more effective under conditions of competition and intellectual rivalry.[19] And Boulding reported an experiment in which groups were created to test problem-solving ability. Some of the groups contained a "deviant," an individual who forced the group to consider conflicting views and integrate them. The other groups lacked a deviant member. In all cases, groups with deviants devised "a richer analysis of the problem and a more elegant solution."[20] We should also note that when groups were given the option to cut out one of their members, they invariably chose the deviant. Unfortunately, we tend to feel uncomfortable with someone in the group who persists in bringing up contrary ideas, but the presence of such an individual is likely to make the group's work much more creative.

If anything, therefore, we want to be wary of too little disagreement and debate. As long as alternatives are being defended and debated, the school is likely to have richer solutions to problems and more creative proposals for change. Thus, consultation of study groups with administrators does not, and is not meant to, minimize debate. Rather, the consultation insures that all ideas will undergo the test of manageability and receive some degree of cost-benefit analysis. In addition, the administrator will examine proposals for political, legal, financial, and social effects. Involvement of administrators, then, does not mitigate the democratic thrust of decision making, but insures that important, larger considerations will not be neglected in the decision-making process.

## ADVISEMENT TEAM LEADERS

The advisement teams are crucial groups in the school's decision-making structure. Within the weekly two-hour conference period provided (see Chapter 2), advisement team leaders conduct regular meetings once or more each quarter. The team leader has four basic responsibilities. First, the leader conducts regular meetings. This responsibility includes setting an agenda, delegating special duties to other team members, and making various announcements at the meeting. Second, the leader maintains positive team attitudes and activities. This responsibility includes assessing group needs, setting team goals, taking an inventory of team members' skills, and setting up inservice activity. Inservice activities appropriate to the advisement team would include such things as visiting a local technical school and having a counselor review college/career files.

Third, the team leader facilitates the exchange of ideas, information, and concerns. To fulfill this responsibility, the leader must see that concerns are channeled to appropriate groups for action or response. The leader also communicates information from the administration or other groups to the team. And the leader should collect various ideas for discussion—ideas surrounding such questions as: what are students complaining about most often? what are the most common parent concerns or comments?

Fourth, the team leader is responsible for developing leadership skills. To do this, the leader will probably have to attend some training sessions and encourage team members to attend team leader training groups.

The principal should meet regularly with advisement team leaders about once a month. Prior to each meeting a brief note can be circulated to solicit agenda items. If no items are suggested, and administrators have no concerns or information to communicate, the meeting can be cancelled. While cancelled meetings can be a subtle way of subverting the democratic process, we do not believe that meetings should be held mechanically when they have no purpose.

At some meetings of advisement team leaders the style of leadership itself can be the agenda, with team leaders sharing among themselves techniques for running meetings, for setting goals, for evaluating advisement, for conducting parent conferences, and so forth. While the advisement team leaders are usually concerned about the advisement process itself, they are free to consider any aspect of the school or community and make recommendations. Advisors are interested in and should find out about the students' total interaction with the school—curriculum, activities, grading, discipline, and other facets of school life.

Advisement teams and their leaders have both the time and the opportunity to meet and participate in decision making. They have access to all school information plus the unique and valuable information generated through their own activity as advisors. They should have sufficient training opportunities so that they feel comfortable and adequate in their role.

## DEPARTMENT CHAIRPEOPLE

Department chairpeople meet more infrequently as a group (perhaps once a quarter, or as necessary), but they wield considerable influence as individuals in their own subject areas. Each department is heavily involved with a number of daily and annual issues and tasks that demand decisions. The following are typical:

(1)  development of curriculum materials;
(2)  selection and purchase of supplies and equipment;
(3)  designing new instructional methods;
(4)  evaluating effectiveness of instruction;
(5)  responding to changing needs of students, parents, and others with new curricula and methods;
(6)  selection and assignment of personnel (helping to establish master schedules); and
(7)  allocation of space and equipment.

The concerns tend to focus on instruction and instructional logistics, although chairpeople as a group will also participate in other issues such as discipline and attendance policies; setting priorities for building or program improvement; and teacher inservice programs on new ideas and methods. Many decisions regarding instructional materials, instruction, and teacher assignments are made by chairpeople and teachers in the department (all, of course, within the parameters of decisions which have been already established regarding course objectives and course offerings).

Department chairpeople are typically experienced teachers with considerable knowledge of their subjects and of instructional methodology. Their expertise is crucial to a large comprehensive high school with a considerable number of separate subject specialists, each special area with its own peculiar problems and needs. In the decision-making structure we have outlined, however, the various departments, each with its own vested interests, do not compete for influence or power. They have complementary relationships with other groups, such as advisement team leaders, IIC ad hoc groups, and parents. All the various groups have cross-departmental membership and concerns that transcend the special concerns of one department.

Departments and department chairpeople meet regularly throughout the school year. Usually an administrator will attend to assist in providing information and liaison with other groups. Typical meetings of department chairpeople would have the following:

(1) a review of the results of student achievement tests, identifying strengths and weaknesses in the total curriculum;

(2) responses to proposals such as that of teaching basic English skills in all subjects; and

(3) a review of past enrollment in all courses in order to detect any trends (wanted or unwanted) and to adjust the schedule to achieve more balanced enrollments and more effective use of space, materials, and teachers.

## STUDENTS

In addition to the decisions they make with parents and advisors, students have two primary means of participating in the decision-making process. One is the student council and its various committees and the other is the IIC and its study groups or ad hoc committees. The student council has the basic task of coordinating and developing student activities. Periodically, the student council may form special committees of its own to evaluate curriculum, advisement, or some other aspect of the school. In such cases, their efforts may be coordinated with department chairpeople or advisement team leaders to insure cooperation for evaluation and effective use of results. Student council committees might also be of help in the ongoing evaluation of the school's discipline policy and social climate. In any case, it is important that the student committee be treated with the same seriousness and respect as a faculty committee. As we noted above, student participation in the decision-making process should be real, not a facade of democracy in an authoritarian school. It should also not be a facade of democracy in what we would call a split-level school, i.e., a school where democracy prevails among the staff but the students remain powerless because of a patronizing or disparaging attitude toward their participation. Ancient Athens showed us the possibility of combining democracy for the few in the midst of slavery for the majority. A human organization must be democratic for all of its participants, not just some of them.

## SPECIAL AD HOC COMMITTEES

We have already mentioned one special ad hoc committee—the student relations committee. Another effective ad hoc committee is the school focus committee, which is a group of selected teachers charged with the following tasks:

(1)  collecting and organizing all evaluative data available on student achievement, attitudes (of parents, students, teachers, and community), career interests, graduate followup information, etc.;

(2)  analyzing the data in a systematic manner to determine strengths and weaknesses;

(3)  converting needs uncovered by the data analysis into a set of proposed goals;

(4)  presenting the data and proposed goals to the faculty at large and to various groups (such as the parents' advisory groups, department chairpeople, advisement team leaders, student council, the IIC) for their response; and

(5)  assisting the principal in developing an action plan for implementing agreed-upon goals.

The school focus committee helps provide some focus for overall improvement efforts based upon careful consideration of various data. The data come from various sources:

(1)  standard achievement tests given to students (it is important to look at distributions and not merely at group means when interpreting scores);

(2)  evaluations of advisement, including student and parent responses;

(3)  annual evaluations of the school completed by sophomores and seniors;

(4)  community polls or questionnaires conducted by the Board of Education, Superintendent, or other groups;

(5)  followup studies of graduates;

(6)  informal feedback collected by advisement teams; and

(7)  special evaluations conducted by any group.

As our examples of the student relations and school focus committees show, ad hoc groups can be invaluable in making decisions that enhance the effectiveness of the school. The kind and number of ad hoc groups in any school must be determined by the particular circumstances of that school and is limited only by the imagination and concern of those in the school.

## PARENTS

Parents participate most significantly in the advisement process, helping to make those decisions which most affect their children. Parents may also play an important role as members of the IIC, IIC study groups, and the parent advisory council. The parent advisory council can be a most vital part of the decision-making and communication processes. Among other things, the parent advisory council can:

(1) review and respond to evaluative data collected by other groups;
(2) give feedback and recommendations on improvement goals;
(3) determine ways of reporting the school's progress and programs to parents and to the community; and
(4) help communicate the concerns of parents and the community to the school.

As in the case of students, parent participation must not be viewed patronizingly, as a symbolic gesture to those who really know little about what is necessary for good education. Some of the more vocal parents may indeed be advocates of the "saber tooth tiger" curriculum. But many parents, by their intimate knowledge of their children and the social world in which their children are developing, have important contributions to make to good education.

## A CONCLUDING COMMENT

The shared decision-making structure described above does not negate the principal's authority or power to act decisively when necessary. At the same time, it provides a means for making and evaluating decisions in the light of the school's stated goals and philosophy. It provides a means for administrators to exercise leadership in managing the school while simultaneously providing administrators with help, understanding, and support as they attempt to improve the school. Finally, the structure makes the school truly a school for all participants—it is the school of all those parents, students, and staff who care enough to participate in the decision-making process.

# SUMMARY

A democratic decision-making structure is an integral part of a human organization. Typically, however, American schools have mirrored American business and industrial organizations, for both have been hierarchically organized for authoritarian decision making. Consequently, those in the schools—both staff and students—are likely to experience some negative emotions and attitudes, ranging from dissatisfaction to alienation.

In a human organization, alienation is resolved through participation in the decision-making process. If there is to be real participation, however, the school must be organized to insure that participation. Individuals and groups must have the time and opportunity to make appropriate decisions. Information must be available at all levels of decision making. And people must be trained to make rational decisions.

Various kinds of structures might facilitate a democratic decision-making process. One structure that has been proved effective utilizes the Instructional Improvement Committee as a key group. The IIC is a central agency that is responsive to all elements in the school. All those connected with the school have access to the committee, including individuals, the Parent Advisory Group, department chairpeople, various study groups and ad hoc committees, the student council, advisement team leaders, and counselors. Advisement teams are particularly important in the decision-making structure.

The structure outlined does not negate the principal's power to act decisively when necessary. At the same time, it makes the school a school of all those who care enough to participate in the decision-making process.

# Endnotes

[1]William Foote Whyte, *Organizational Behavior* (Homewood, Ill.: The Dorsey Press, 1969), p. 688.

[2]*Ibid.,* p. 689.

[3]Robert Presthus, *The Organizational Society,* revised edition (New York: St. Martin's Press, 1978), pp. 39–40.

[4]Stanley Milgram, *Obedience to Authority* (New York: Harper & Row, 1973).

[5]Jack Rothman, *Planning & Organizing for Social Change* (New York: Columbia University Press, 1974), p. 173.

[6]Paul E. Mott, *The Characteristics of Effective Organizations* (New York: Harper & Row, 1972), pp. 85–97.

[7]Thornton B. Roby, Elizabeth H. Nicol, and Francis M. Farrell, "Group Problem Solving Under Two Types of Executive Structure," in Henry Clay Lindgren, ed., *Contemporary Research in Social Psychology* (New York: John Wiley & Sons, 1969), pp. 489–500.

[8]John M. Ivancevich and James H. Donnelly, Jr., "Relation of Organizational Structure to Job Satisfaction, Anxiety-Stress, and Performance," *Administrative Science Quarterly* 20 (June, 1975):272–80.

[9]Rensis Likert, *The Human Organization* (New York: McGraw-Hill, 1967), chapter 4.

[10]David Riesman, *Abundance for What? And Other Essays* (Garden City, New York: Doubleday & Company, 1964), p. 173.

[11]*Ibid.,* p. 171.

[12]In *Immortal Poems of the English Language* (New York: Pocket Books, 1952), p. 354.

[13]Harl R. Douglass, Rudyard K. Bent and Charles W. Boardman, *Democratic Supervision in Secondary Schools,* 2nd edition (Boston: Houghton Mifflin, 1961), p. 33.

[14]Whyte, *op. cit.,* p. 692.

[15]Leonard W. Doob, *Patterning of Time* (New Haven: Yale University Press, 1971), p. 64.

[16]Harold L. Wilensky, *Organizational Intelligence* (New York: Basic Books, 1967), p. 3.

[17]Paul R. Lawrence and Jay W. Lorsch, *Organization and Environment* (Boston: Harvard University Press, 1967).

[18]Jerald Hage and Michael Aiken, *Social Change in Complex Organizations* (New York: Random House, 1970), pp. 37 and 39.

[19]Donald C. Pelz and Frank M. Andrews, *Scientists in Organizations* (New York: John Wiley & Sons, 1966), pp. 7, 151, 259ff.

[20]Elise Boulding, "Further Reflections on Conflict Management," in Robert L. Kahn and Elise Boulding, eds., *Power and Conflict Organizations* (Ann Arbor: Foundation for Research on Human Behavior, 1964), pp. 147–48.

# Chapter 7

# Discipline in
# a Human
# Organization

According to one secondary principal, discipline continues to be a major concern in public schools and "teachers complain that discipline and discipline referrals consume a major portion of their instructional time."[1] In their efforts to deal with this vexing problem of discipline, teachers and administrators have tended to employ one of two opposed models. One model is the authoritarian. In this model, there are detailed rules which are strictly enforced by school authorities. There is an effort to monitor and control all student behavior. Suspension is a basic form of punishment. The other model is the democratic. There is an emphasis on trust, freedom, and participation. There is an effort to develop the kind of school climate where problems will be unlikely to emerge.

Either model can be carried to an extreme. It is said of one school-master that during the fifty-one years he served as superintendent of a large school he administered 911,500 canings, 121,000 floggings, 136,000 tips with a ruler, 10,200 boxes on the ear, and made 700 boys stand on peas, 6,000 kneel on a sharp piece of wood, and 5,000 wear a fool's cap.[2] To him, and to those generally who hold to the authoritarian model, discipline is punishment for infractions of the rules. An extreme example of the democratic model is the contemporary "free school." Those who run the free schools assume that behavior is largely a function of school climate and that discipline problems will not occur when an atmosphere of freedom and trust has been established. There are no sanctions for breaking the rules in such schools, because there are no rules to break.

Both models contain valid points. And both contain invalid notions. In our view, a human school must have sanctions. As Table 1 in the Introduction shows, control is a part of a human organization. But we reject a number of aspects of the authoritarian model. We do not, for instance, believe that physical punishment is appropriate at the secondary level. Many educators apparently feel differently. In 1976-76, the first national survey to gather data on the use of corporal punishment in schools was conducted. In a preliminary analysis of 116 schools, there were 4335 reported formal incidents of corporal punishment, a figure that can "be taken to mean that 5.9% of the students, or 1 in every 17, received corporal punishment."[3] There were also 5737 suspensions in the schools, with about 12 percent of the secondary students being suspended during the year.

We do not agree that control demands corporal punishment. In a human organization, the emphasis is on shared responsibility for control and on the development of self-control rather than on punishment. On the other hand, to say that authoritarianism should be rejected because it is not conducive to maximizing the well-being of students or staff does not mean that the school lacks authority, including the authority to enforce rules and punish rule-breaking. Adolescents, like the rest of us, do not function well or develop optimally in either a rigid, authoritarian context or a context of anomie.

In a human organization, then, discipline involves what one person has called "authority without authoritarianism."[4] As another observer has put it:

> Successful organizations, from Macy's and Gimbels' to the United States Marine Corps, are built on a healthy respect for authority. Without it little progress and much confusion would exist. If respect for those in positions of authority is not maintained, then those in authoritative positions have a *responsibility* to take measures which dictate desired responses. In concise terms, such authoritarians command respect by their behavior and their exercise of discipline. The more the teacher has of the former the less he will need of the latter. Without the respect-discipline combination teaching can become a veritable hell on earth.[5]

We do not agree with all of the above quote, but the author has made some valid points: authority is necessary for a viable organization; an atmosphere can be developed in which the need for punitive kinds of discipline is minimized; and discipline problems have indeed made teaching a "veritable hell on earth" for many teachers.

Given the need for maintaining control, how is authority exercised in a school that is a human organization? We will answer the question in this chapter by first looking at the meaning of the term "discipline." We will then discuss in some detail the process of enforcing rules. Finally, we will look at preventive discipline, that is, at those measures which can be taken to minimize the need for punitive action by those in authority.

## WHAT IS DISCIPLINE?

As we noted in the Introduction, Gallup polls have shown that the public's major concern in recent years with respect to education has been discipline. Generally, this seems to mean the exercise of control. But behavior can be controlled in various ways. When we inquire more specifically into the meaning of discipline, therefore, we find that the meaning varies considerably.

### DISCIPLINE AS CONFORMITY TO RULES

For some people, discipline simply means those measures which are necessary to insure conformity to the rules. Most often, such discipline will be punitive in nature. The rules are not to be questioned but obeyed. Those who do not obey must suffer the consequences. Presumably, the punitive consequences or the threat of such consequences, are sufficient to gain conformity.

Often, those who view discipline in this way also believe that there is a rather narrow range of behavior among students that is acceptable. They believe that control is being properly exercised only when students sit quietly and obediently in fixed rows with a stern teacher hovering over them and drilling them in what they need to know. For example, an older woman came to a humane school as a substitute one day. She had taught school at one time. At the end of the day she came by the principal's office, visibly upset. With a mixture of indignation and distress she reported that she had had a terribly upsetting experience that day. She said that she had never seen behavior so bad. The principal had heard no reports of problems that day and was accustomed to very positive comments from both visitors and substitute teachers. Complaints about student behavior had been rare. When he asked her to tell him specifically what had happened, she said: "In every one of my classes there were some students who chewed gum."

The woman's view of discipline evokes memories of another era, an era of rigidity, of paddles, of strict enforcement of rules regardless of whether those rules could be rationally defended. But unfortunately such things are not merely relics of another era. Attitudes and practices that reflect this view of discipline are still found in the nation's high schools (including corporal punishment of high school students). There are high schools today which remain like the one described by Friedenberg:

> It is a big, expensive building, on spacious but barren grounds. Every door is at the end of a corridor; there is no reception area, no public space in which one can adjust to the transition from the outside world. Between class periods the corridors are tumultously crowded; during them they are empty; but they are always guarded with teachers and students on patrol duty. . . . Between classes, no student may walk down the corridor without a form, signed by a teacher, telling where he is coming from, where he is going, and the time, to the minute, at which the pass is valid. A student caught in the corridor without such a pass is taken to the office where a detention slip is made out against him, and he is required to remain at school for two or three hours after the close of the school day. He may do his homework during this time, but he may not leave his seat or talk.[6]

The school, Friedenberg continues, offers students no physical freedom at all. The students have no privacy, no time or place where they may merely go about their own business.

In such a school, the staff learns to specialize in the "control of large groups of students even at catastrophic expense to their opportunity to learn."[7] The students obviously have no opportunity to learn and practice self-discipline. And many of the controls do not, directly or indirectly, facilitate instruction or learning. What, then, do students gain by such rigid controls? Control-oriented schools tend to teach conformity. Students learn to obey, or at least to act as if they are conforming to the rules. But there is little room for students to exercise their judgment enough to experience growth. The use of punishment and fear may keep the adolescent in a childlike state. Ironically, such schools may praise self-directed, self-regulated behavior even while they maintain a system that precludes the development of such behavior. The school rhetoric will unfailingly include the objectives of preparing students for mature adulthood and citizenship, but the school policies and practices will enforce childlike obedience and dependency.

## DISCIPLINE, SELF-DISCIPLINE, AND ORDER

A different view of discipline is that it is not simply conformity to rules or enforcement of rules, but a process in which the school helps students internalize those values and norms that facilitate a free and orderly society. In this view, discipline is not simply punishment. We discipline, as the Madsens put it, "to provide for social order and individual productivity."[8]

A good set of principles of secondary school discipline has been offered by Knute Larson, who points out that he first articulated them in a 1963 book. By 1972, he says, much of the material in the 1963 work was outdated by subsequent events, but the principles remained valid. We believe that they are still valid. He offers six:[9]

1. Disciplinary policies should reflect the educational goals of the school. That is, discipline should not become an end in itself, but should contribute to educational goals and be consistent with good educational practice.
2. Disciplinary policies should reflect sound social scientific knowledge.
3. Disciplinary policies should reflect democratic principles such as "equal justice for all, respect for the rights and dignity of the individual, humanitarian treatment for all."
4. Disciplinary policies should reflect the fact that individuals are expected to assume responsibilities as well as enjoy rights.
5. Disciplinary policies should aim at the development of self-discipline.
6. "Disciplinary policies should be primarily preventive, secondarily corrective, and never retributive."

Thus, disciplining is educational in the broadest sense—including all practices and environmental factors that contribute to the development of self-disciplined, purposeful behavior and to cooperation between students and staff. It must include what Larson called "corrective" measures, but it is primarily preventive.

In the remainder of this chapter, we will show specifically what such a view of discipline entails in terms of policies and practices. We want to first stress the point, however, that the kind of discipline being discussed here is consistent with the goals of a human organization. There are rules, and they are maintained, but the discipline is not a unilateral process. For example, students should be able to appeal the decision of a teacher or administrator and know that other staff members in the school would not automatically side with their colleague.

Students should know that they may challenge regulations or policies without fear of embarrassment or retaliation. The school's regulations should be open and available to all, and those regulations should be constructed rationally in accord with the goals of promoting instruction and learning and of protecting students and teachers from disruption or threats to persons or property. There should be an emphasis on obtaining agreement with the regulations so that control is primarily a matter of self-discipline rather than externally imposed discipline. Most educators would agree with these points. The question is, how are the above principles translated into concrete policies and practices?

## THE PROCESS OF DISCIPLINING

In a school that promotes the idea that students can share in the responsibility for maintaining a secure, safe, and orderly environment that is conducive to learning, the firm but judicious enforcement of rules is very important. Student satisfaction with school rules and with their enforcement is an important indicator by which the staff can measure the climate of the school. Table 2 in the Introduction showed that satisfaction with rules in a humane high school was markedly higher than in schools generally throughout the state. This greater satisfaction is not the result of nonenforcement of rules, or the lack of rules, or laxity, or permissiveness. The school has rules and they are enforced. But the enforcement occurs in a context that includes:

(1) careful communication of all rules and regulations to the school community;
(2) student and faculty involvement in reviewing and evaluating rules and in enforcing rules;
(3) knowledge that the appeal process works, that individuals are not subjected to the arbitrary judgment or biases of one person, even if that person occupies a powerful role.

Interestingly, one of the more frequent concerns about rules expressed by students in a school familiar to the authors was a number of instances in which they believed that the rules had not been enforced. Students as well as staff recognize the importance of enforcement. If enforcement is to be effective, that is, if a situation is to be created in which the rules are generally kept because they are enforced legitimately and equitably, there must be clear guidelines for enforcing the rules.

## GUIDELINES FOR RULE ENFORCEMENT

In Oceania, George Orwell's fictional society, language was manipulated in order to control people's thinking. One of the practices involved the linking together of opposites: "Even the names of the four Ministries by which we are governed exhibit a sort of impudence in their deliberate reversal of the facts. The Ministry of Peace concerns itself with war, the Ministry of Truth with lies, the Ministry of Love with torture, and the Ministry of Plenty with starvation."[10]

A typical reaction to Orwell's description is that words should reflect and not mask reality. The torture chamber should not be called the Ministry of Love, nor should the love bed be called a pallet of hate. And rule enforcement should not be masked by giving it some more acceptable label such as "corrective guidance." Some people object to the coercive and authoritarian connotations in the term "enforcement." Obviously, we too reject those connotations. But we retain the term because it suggests the reality of discipline in a secondary school. That is, the rules are not to be taken lightly. Everyone is expected to comply with them, and compliance is maintained with equity but also with certainty and firmness. In other words, we do not view rule enforcement as deviation from the model of a human organization. On the contrary, a human organization cannot be maintained without the formulation and enforcement of rules.

### FORMULATING RULES

The principal and faculty should develop a written set of policies and procedures. This must be done, of course, within the framework of school board policies and school law. Using a decision-making process like that described in the last chapter, the principal should see that broad participation (students, parents, faculty and other staff members) occurs in the formulation and evaluation of the written statement. Furthermore, it will be necessary to evaluate the statement with some regularity. Otherwise, students will be subjected to rules which were formulated by other students who are no longer in the school and perhaps by some faculty members no longer in the school. Every few years, the rules will need to be restudied, readopted, and perhaps rewritten to some extent.

In deciding what regulations are necessary for the conduct of a safe, orderly school and what basic rights students have as individuals in and out of school, the following California court decision (Myers v. Arcata Union High School District, 1966) well expresses the basic attitude of the courts:

The limits within which regulations can be made by the school are that there must be some reasonable connection to school matters, deportment, discipline, etc. or to the health and safety of the students. . . . They must reasonably pertain to the health and safety of the students or to the orderly conduct of school business. In this regard, consideration should be given to what is really health and safety . . . and what is merely personal preference.[11]

It is not our purpose here to examine the legalities of various kinds of regulations. But the principal should be sensitive to the basic legal issues. Pertinent resources should be available to the principal and to the committees that are deliberating such matters. Legal questions regarding school regulations and their enforcement may involve such matters as dress, school publications, corporal punishment, locker or personal searches, due process in suspension or expulsion cases, and sexual or racial discrimination.

The fact that such matters are now legal questions demonstrates the radical changes that have occurred in the area of students' rights. Historically, the doctrines of *parens patriae* and *in loco parentis* legitimated the state's right to provide for children's welfare and the school's right to employ whatever disciplinary action deemed necessary. But in the 1960s and 1970s a series of court decisions established new principles in the matter of discipline. The decisions generally make the point that students have constitutional and human rights that must be respected. In a human organization, of course, respecting a student's rights is fundamental. But such respect does not mean a loss of control in the school, nor does it justify an undisciplined school. The thrust of the court decisions is to protect students from the arbitrary exercise of power. Some educators believed that the courts were depriving them of the authority they needed to maintain order, but the essence of the new legal situation is well captured by Mahon:

The student rights decisions have affirmed the constitutional rights of students, provided that the exercise of such rights is not disruptive of an atmosphere conducive to learning. These decisions also support the duty of educators to make and enforce rules which provide such an atmosphere.[12]

## APPEAL AND TYPES OF INFRACTIONS

Proper guidelines must also include specific provisions for students to appeal and to receive an adequate hearing prior to being disciplined. The primary objective is to assure, even in the case of minor punishments for infractions of rules, that procedures protect against errors in judgment. In one court case, the decision said that a student who is given a short-term suspension has the right to "(a) effective notice of the charges (which may be either written or oral); (b) an explanation of the evidence in support of the charges; (c) an opportunity to present his/her side of the story."[13] Moreover, these rights apply prior to the suspension unless the student's continued presence poses some kind of danger or threat.

There are three kinds of offenses or situations, each of which requires a different degree or level of attention to due process rights:

(1)   simple infractions of rules, which might result in a short-term suspension;
(2)   serious infractions which could result in long-term suspension or expulsion;
(3)   serious infractions that involve a violation of the criminal law. These infractions could also result in long-term suspension or expulsion but, in addition, they require the use of law enforcement agents.

Briefly, we will look at how each of these kinds of offenses may be handled.


SIMPLE INFRACTIONS

These infractions include such things as truancy from classes, smoking in unauthorized places, and disruption of a class. Any behavior defined by the school as resulting at most in a short-term suspension is a simple infraction. When such infractions occur, teachers and principals should always explain to a student what regulation appears to have been violated and give the student an opportunity to present his or her side of the issue. If discussion with the student creates doubt about the facts involved, a decision should be delayed until a more thorough hearing can be conducted. Certainly, in such cases more than rudimentary procedures will be required.

In the court case noted above, an "unusual situation" as well as a factual dispute demands more than rudimentary procedures. An "unusual situation" is probably one in which the suspension would result in unusual harm, although the court did not specify the meaning of "unusual situation." Unusual harm could include such things as a damaged reputation or being excluded from important school events.[14]

In any case, simple infractions are not to be handled summarily. At a minimum, students have the right to know the specific charges, the evidence of their infraction, and the opportunity to defend themselves or rebut the charge. In some cases, the protection of student rights will demand an additional hearing or hearings. The manner in which these hearings are conducted is significant in terms of their long-range effects on the student, his or her view of the school, and the school's climate.

In the case of any kind of infraction, simple or serious, it is important that the staff member listen carefully and openly to the student's point of view and explanation of behavior before reaching a decision. It is to be hoped that the staff member involved will weigh the facts of the matter as well as the effects of various kinds of punishment on the student. Like a citizen caught speeding, a student who is caught in a violation of the rules will expect punishment of some kind. But the manner in which the charges are made and the disciplinary action is taken can vary widely. In a human organization, both the well-being of students and an orderly, productive school climate must be maintained. Neither can be sacrificed to the other.

For example, student well-being is maximized if a student suspected of rule infraction is approached in a questioning rather than accusatory manner. Let us suppose that a student's name appears on the absence report for one period of the day. The student can be approached with the question, "John, why did you skip the fifth period yesterday?" which is an accusation. Or the student might be approached with the statement, which is also an implicit question, "John, your fifth period teacher marked you absent yesterday." Statements of fact rather than accusatory questions give students an opportunity to explain. Implicitly, they request an explanation, but they do not presume the student's guilt. Frequently, the student may provide information which completely explains or changes the situation. The student has given an appropriate account of the situation, has not felt accused, and knows that regulations are being enforced fairly. This kind of "hearing" not only protects the student's rights to due process but also maintains good human relations, thereby supporting the goals of the school to provide a learning environment that is humane as well as academically sound.

## SERIOUS INFRACTIONS

These infractions include such things as persistent truancy or disruption of classes, violent behavior or the threat of such behavior, vandalism, and drug possession or sales. Whatever behavior is defined by the school as requiring long-term suspension or expulsion is a serious infraction. When such infractions occur, more care should be taken to ascertain facts and to give the student a full opportunity to present his or her side of the case. In these matters, students should also be fully informed about their right to appeal. Roos has suggested that, based on various court decisions, students who are faced with the possibility of long-term suspension or expulsion have at least seven rights:

(1) written notice that details the evidence against the student;
(2) sufficient time to prepare for the hearing;
(3) witnesses who can testify in the student's behalf;
(4) opportunity for cross-examination;
(5) the right to be represented by counsel;
(6) a disinterested arbiter who can decide what the facts of the case are; and
(7) the right "to specific findings of fact."[15]

The legal status of each of the above rights is not yet clear. But it is clear that serious infractions involving more severe disciplinary action require more formal procedures than those which are appropriate for simple infractions.

### CRIMINAL OFFENSES

If a student's action is clearly a serious criminal offense (drug sales, assault, extortion, robbery, and so forth) the school authorities should request assistance from the police or other authorities to insure that the offense is properly prosecuted. Certainly, there should be no feeling that a school can be a kind of haven for the person who has committed a criminal act. School officials who ignore criminal offenses are not helping the offenders. At the same time, they are allowing the school to develop an atmosphere in which the rest of the students will be subject to fear, harrassment, or pressure to engage in criminal behavior.

To avoid conflict over how a situation of criminal offense should be handled, the school should have a prior understanding (a written understanding, if possible) with law enforcement agencies. The understanding should include a clear statement of the student's and parents' rights that need to be protected, particularly with respect to self-incrimination and interrogation. For instance, an opinion of the Michigan attorney general stated that school officials cannot permit a student to be questioned without the consent of the student's parents or guardian. "Only the parent or guardian can waive the privilege against self-incrimination of the child."[16] On the other hand, in the same opinion the attorney general said that law officers do not need a warrant to remove a student from the school if there is reasonable cause to believe that the student has committed a felony, or if the student has committed a misdemeanor in a law officer's presence.

## THE ROLE OF PARENTS AND ADVISORS

The principal has the responsibility in disciplinary action to be sensitive to the legal and human rights of all parties involved. The principal works to maximize the well-being of the offender, the offender's parents, and the rest of the school. In all cases, therefore, parents should be notified quickly of disciplinary action and should have the opportunity to be present during any discussion. In some cases, parents may even participate in the determination of the disciplinary action that is to be taken. Indeed, if discipline is to fulfill its purpose of maintaining order and enhancing individual productivity and well-being, the involvement of parents is mandatory.

Advisors should also be a part of the disciplinary process. At a minimum, advisors should be:

(1)  informed of the disciplinary action;
(2)  encouraged to talk with students about the situation and their feelings about the situation; and
(3)  encouraged to assist the offender in an appeal if appropriate or needed.

In some instances, advisors will assume an advocacy role on behalf of the student. As an advocate, the advisor helps the student articulate his or her position (rather than attempting to excuse the student's behavior or the infraction of the rules). An advisor's support of the student can create or strengthen an effective relationship, which may lead to insight into the cause or causes of the problem. The advisor's work with the student can also involve a search for alternatives which are motivating to the student and which lead to successful learning rather than to continuing disciplinary problems.

## THE QUESTION OF SUSPENSION

It is generally agreed that suspension is necessary in certain cases. As Larson put it: "The common practice of suspending students for a short period of time in order to force a parent conference needs no defense, educationally or legally, unless it is overused or utilized in trivial cases."[17] However, much has been written about alternatives to suspension, and those alternatives should be given serious consideration.[18] The National Education Association has recommended a considerable number, categorizing them under the following headings: short-range, intermediate-range, long-range, and long-range solutions with other agencies.[19] We will look at a few examples out of the list of 41 alternatives to show the possibilities.

The short-range solutions suggested by the NEA are temporary measures used to maintain order while waiting for the implementation of longer-term solutions. For example, the school might provide a quiet place such as a small room or retreat. Or there might be an agreement on alternatives for the immediate future worked out by the student and a teacher. Or a team of adults (which can include parents and staff members) might counsel with a disruptive student until the student is prepared to function properly again. Or the school might provide various kind of alternative programs, such as those we described in Chapter 5, for students who are turned off to typical programs.

Intermediate-range solutions suggested by the NEA attempt to go beyond the immediate amelioration of problem behavior and get at some of the deeper causes of the behavior. The association suggests, for example, that staff and students share in the development of disciplinary policies and procedures, a point which we have already made. They also recommend that staff, students, and parents should all be involved in developing good interpersonal relationships and implementing the disciplinary policies. Finally, training programs of various kinds should be available for the various members of the school community (e.g., crisis intervention training or training for teachers in coping with the threat of physical violence).

As we move to long-range solutions, the purpose is to strike more deeply at the root causes of problem behavior. The first suggestion is one that we have already recommended—"full involvement of students in the decision-making process" of the school. The association also recommends student and staff involvement in the changing curriculum, the development of various nontraditional options for learning, and more meaningful, personal relationships between staff and students. In other words, in order to minimize the use of suspension as a disciplinary practice, the NEA recommends that a school develop the kinds of programs, policies, and climate that are markedly similar to those we have been describing in previous chapters. The implication of the various alternatives is that the school environment can be a cause of the problem and that it should be the focus of concern as much as the student who is engaged in problem behavior. In support of this line of reasoning, we might note that teachers who supervise work–study students have often observed that some of the most unruly and unsuccessful students in the classroom receive outstanding evaluations from their job supervisors in the community. Students who were uncooperative, disruptive, and inadequate in their performance in the classroom have often been commended by supervisors for their hard work, cooperation, and loyalty.

If a school employs one or more alternatives to suspension, some attempts should be made to evaluate their effectiveness.[20] Some of the questions that should be asked in evaluation are the following:

1. Do the alternatives develop a greater amount of self-discipline?
2. Do the alternatives actually reduce the number of suspensions given or perceived to be needed?
3. Does the alternative seem to solve the problem that created the need for disciplinary action?
4. Does the alternative seem to meet the needs of the student who would have been suspended?
5. Does the alternative have educational value for the student?
6. Do the alternatives facilitate the general goals of the school, including the maintenance of a humane atmosphere?

As noted before, we agree that every effort should be made to find alternatives to suspension. Certainly, a human organization is designed to help students have a meaningful, productive educational experience, and that is not possible with those who are suspended or who have been expelled. Nevertheless, suspension remains an effective disciplinary measure, particularly when efforts have been made with other alternatives. The school cannot be expected to succeed with every student. There are simply too many variables that are outside the control of school personnel. And principals must also be concerned with the rights and the well-being of those teachers and students who will be adversely affected by the problem behavior. There will be cases where suspension is the only option left if the total school community is to be protected.

We should note that keeping suspension as an option has value even if it is not frequently used. The *threat* of suspension has disciplinary value. For there are some students who, in spite of any other alternatives available, behave reasonably only when they know that their choice is either to respect the rights of others or to be removed from the school. Particularly at the high school level, chronic offenders may need to make a decision either to abide by reasonable guidelines or to seek alternatives which are completely outside the school setting. In the latter case, it is helpful when alternatives such as high school equivalency programs, alternative schools, and job training programs are available.

When, then, must suspension or expulsion be used? Those students who fail to respond to alternatives and who represent a constant threat to other students and teachers or who continuously cause disruption may have to be suspended or expelled. In some cases, suspension is necessary for another reason. As Larson says, suspension can force a parent conference. Unfortunately, many parents will not assume much responsibility or share in the problems occurring at school until suspension occurs. Thus, suspension may be an effective way of getting parents or others who are significant in the life of the student to become involved in dealing with the problem, including the exploration of alternatives to suspension or expulsion. Parents are not necessarily indifferent. They may simply be unaware of the severity of the problem or of the importance of home/school cooperation. They may have unreasonable expectations of the school—more than one principal has frequently heard a parent say such things as "Why don't you *make* my son go to class?" or "You can't suspend her; that's what she wants you to do." Suspension may be the only way to convince some parents that their help is required in dealing with the problem.

## EVALUATING THE DISCIPLINE PROCESS

We have already indicated that alternatives to suspension need to be evaluated. In this section we will look at the evaluation of the total process. The entire rule enforcement system, like every other aspect of a humane high school, needs periodic evaluation.

First, instruments which measure school climate may include specific items regarding various aspects of rules and the procedures for enforcing the rules. At times a sizeable percentage of students may perceive that rules are unevenly enforced. Clearly, whether students perceive it or not, differential enforcement has occurred on numerous occasions. For example, in his classic study of adolescents in an Illinois town, Hollingshead noted that discipline could vary considerably, depending upon students' social class background.[21] The daughter of a prominent family did not show up at detention hall one day. When the principal asked her if she had forgotten, she said no but that she had had an appointment to have her hair set and could not change it. "All right," said the principal, "but don't let this happen again." Similarly, the principal decided not to put the son of a wealthy resident in the detention room, but kept the boy in his outer office and then apologetically sent him home. In contrast to such deferential treatment of the children of the well-to-do and prominent people in the town, the children of the poor residents were treated strictly in accord with the rules and might even be physically abused.

Students will generally, as they did in the school studied by Hollingshead, recognize any differential enforcement of the rules and will resent it. Sometimes, on the other hand, the students may believe that there is unequal enforcement when in fact there is not. It is important, therefore, for the administration to tap student attitudes on the matter at some point. When students indicate that they see differential enforcement occurring, some kind of administrative action is needed. A principal may set up a seminar with the teaching staff and with students and review with them a number of typical disciplinary cases. The principal may have to provide evidence to the contrary in a case of misperceptions of the treatment of different students.

Student and staff understandings of rule enforcement can also be enhanced by simulating the process of reaching decisions in disciplinary situations. When people are given an opportunity to take the administrative role and reach a decision they may gain a more realistic view of the administrative task of maintaining a just system of discipline. They will probably develop a greater empathy for the administrators who have to make the decisions. And, finally, they may be able to make some creative suggestions for improving the disciplinary process. Thus, a first step in evaluation is to secure student attitudes about the enforcement of rules, to respond as needed to their attitudes, and to involve staff and students in activities that will enhance their understanding of the administrative task of enforcing rules.

Second, at the end of each year administrators and teachers should analyze a summary of discipline cases which have arisen during the year. A careful review of the process of disciplining and of the incidence of various kinds of discipline cases will assist school personnel in setting goals and changing procedures. The aim, of course, is to improve the disciplinary process and to reduce the number of discipline problems. For example, in one school that conducted a year-end review of disciplinary actions, the staff noted that many of the problems and the suspensions were occurring with greatest frequency in the early part of the school year. A number of students, in spite of the fact that written guidelines had been distributed, claimed ignorance of certain rules. The following year, therefore, the administrators of the school visited classes during the first week and conducted brief discussions of those regulations that had been troublesome. This simple approach greatly reduced the number of problems experienced with those regulations. At the same time, the administrators were able to let students know that they were accessible and willing to talk openly about school procedures.

Third, administrators should meet periodically with advisement teams and counselors to discuss discipline. These meetings need not have a predetermined line of inquiry, but can simply be open-ended discussions that provide the administrators with continual monitoring of the disciplinary process. The administrator may simply ask the group a series of probe questions: how are we doing in the area of discipline? what are the students' major concerns about discipline or school regulations and practices? are there some rules which may need to be reviewed?

## PREVENTING DISCIPLINE PROBLEMS

As the old adage says, an ounce of prevention is worth a pound of cure. Preventive programs of various kinds testify to our belief in the adage. Well-developed safety programs in industry aim at prevention of accidents. Community health centers attempt to prevent physical illness. Preventive psychiatry has emerged in recent times as an effort at early detection of mental disorders and the prevention of serious emotional illness. And school administrators are advised by numerous experts to implement a program of preventive discipline.

In general, preventive discipline is the active promotion of a positive school climate. Of course, we cannot be certain exactly what it is that such a climate has prevented. But we can say that discipline problems will occur less frequently in such a school, and we can identify the nature of such a school climate. In a 1965 report, Vredevoe identified a number of common practices among those schools—whatever their size, their location, or the composition of their student body—that were chosen for best citizenship and teacher-student relationships. The schools tended to share nine characteristics:

1. Those in the school knew the rules and understood the purpose and the value of those rules.
2. Self-discipline rather than externally imposed discipline was stressed.
3. Appropriate behavior, including such things as courtesy, respect, and neatness of appearance, characterized the faculty as well as the students.
4. Rules could be changed by due process, but until changed they were enforced.

5. When discipline problems arose, the focus was on the individual (this person needs help) and not on condemning the behavior (wasn't this a terrible thing to do?).
6. Disciplinary action was certain but fair when rules were broken.
7. Disciplinary action took account of the individual involved and not simply the nature of the infraction.
8. Faculty and students shared in the responsibility for generating, maintaining, and changing rules.
9. The school's program presented a challenge to all groups within the school.[22]

At one point or another we have argued for all of the above. In the following sections we shall give five general principles that form the basis for preventive discipline. These general principles legitimate not only the above nine practices, but some other practices that we shall discuss.

## MAINTAIN OPEN COMMUNICATION

We have repeatedly emphasized the importance of open communication in a human organization. We do not view communication as a kind of magic potion that will cure all problems but as an indispensable element in developing understanding and effective relationships. A positive school climate, which is synonomous with preventive discipline, demands good relationships between staff and students.

### ADVISEMENT AND STAFF-STUDENT RELATIONSHIPS

Many discipline problems grow out of and are exacerbated by a general alienation of students from the school's staff. Creating a school where each student is treated as a person with unique needs and an important point of view is a way of attacking the problem of alienation. Such a positive attitude towards students is conveyed powerfully by the advisement system we have discussed. The system allows:

(1) close personal relationships between each student and his or her advisor;
(2) a means of identifying the particular needs of the individual and responding to them as such, rather than treating the student as, say, just another sophomore; and
(3) a means of keeping abreast of each student's progress, particularly his or her feelings about things as they happen.

Because of the close relationship an advisor develops with each advisee, the system can provide an early warning of problems before they become serious (a goal of many preventive programs). Furthermore, the advisement system sets the tone for all relationships in the school, emphasizing the fact that individuals are important, that people are expected to express their ideas and feelings, and that staff and students are expected to solve problems and be responsive to each other.

## ACCESSIBILITY

Open communication depends largely on creating accessibility. We have emphasized a number of times the significance of the advisor's accessibility, including times outside of scheduled conferences. Advisors should always be sure to inform each student of his or her usual location in school each day and encourage each student to seek him or her out if a problem arises.

Other personnel should also communicate their accessibility. An open communication system that is effective will require all staff members to be accessible to students and to convey that fact to the students. Administrators and counselors can accomplish this in a number of ways. First, they can spend time in visiting various areas of the school regularly and talking informally with students and other staff members. One practice that seems particularly effective is to be visible and accessible as students arrive and leave the campus each day and during the lunch periods. These are peak times for making contact with a variety of students. At a school where an area was established outside the building for students to smoke, administrators daily spend time in or near the area, even in bad weather, in order to keep in touch with those students.

Second, administrators and counselors can visit classrooms, particularly early in the school year, to introduce themselves and to indicate the kind of services they render. Third, they can periodically call together small, randomly selected groups of students for brief discussions. The use of a process observer may be helpful in assessing the effectiveness of such sessions. Students may also be asked to evaluate the session and to indicate whether they would attend again if invited.

As we noted earlier, open communication means free flow in all directions. Everyone has access to everyone else. In fact, it is a good practice for administrators to share some concerns or problems with students and staff. In this way, administrators are saying to others:

"Just as you have access to me to discuss your concerns and problems, I have access to you. The responsibility for successful school operations falls on all of us."

## INSERVICE TRAINING AND COMMUNICATION

It would be a mistake to assume that open communication can be achieved simply because everyone agrees that it is desirable. Communication skills and the nature and functioning of an open communication system must be taught. A good deal of important teaching occurs outside formal instruction. Administrators and staff members who are skilled in communication teach others by their own practice. For instance, an administrator who listens to a teacher with obvious concern, as evidenced by demeanor and by such questions and statements as "I'm not sure I understand your position on that point; explain it to me again," exemplifies good communication habits. The sensitive teacher will pick up those habits and use them in his or her relationships with students and other staff members.

The practice of open communication must be supplemented with inservice training for those who need to improve their skills. Some training sessions can focus directly on communication skills. Other training sessions may contribute indirectly to effective communication. For example, a school that set up inservice training one year on developing diagnostic procedures for classroom use was contributing to effective communication. The inservice training focused on careful diagnosis of where the students are in relationship to course objectives early in a course. One of the requisites of good communication is awareness of individual differences. The diagnosis enables a teacher to treat students differently in terms of the expectations communicated to each student. The teacher can identify particular needs that could become serious roadblocks to successful completion of assignments. In some instances, the teacher might even conclude that the student was misplaced. Many conflicts and problems originate in classrooms where no diagnosis or assessment is conducted and where a single, rigid set of expectations is conveyed to all students. The teacher cannot communicate effectively because individual differences are ignored. Thus, training that is basically designed to achieve some other purpose may also contribute to more effective communication. Wherever this is true, those conducting the training should point out the value of the sessions in improving communication.

RESOLVING CONFLICTS

Maintaining a system of open communication does not eliminate conflict, but it does provide a means for resolving conflict. At the same time, because there is a means of dealing with conflict, the possibility of alienation is further reduced.

A case study will illustrate the way in which open communication in a high school can resolve conflict. A young man in a typing class complained to his advisor that typing teachers were unfair in one of their grading policies. He said that he refused to follow the policy even if it meant a lower grade for him. The policy was that each class would begin with a five-minute, timed exercise which would be counted toward the student's grade. That aspect of the policy was acceptable, but some of the teachers were encouraging students to arrive in class before the exact starting time (in other words, during the time allowed for passing from one class to another). Students who arrived early were allowed to begin the timed exercises early.

The student presented two arguments against the practice. First, some students were more likely to arrive earlier than others because of the proximity of a preceding class. Second, even if all of the students could arrive at the same time, the passing time was for students to use for a variety of legitimate purposes. It was unfair, therefore, to expect students to begin before the official starting time.

The advisor listened to the complaint and suggested that the student first talk with the teachers and the department chairperson. The teachers and chairperson listened to the student's argument, but decided to retain the practice. They gave three reasons:

(1)  really motivated students were being rewarded by the practice;
(2)  students who needed additional time to make a passing grade were able to get it; and
(3)  a reasonable number of students could complete the timed exercises with excellence within the five minutes after the official starting time.

The student was not convinced by these arguments. In fact, he felt that the teachers' response was irrelevant to the substance of his complaint. He returned to the advisor, who told him that he could carry his appeal to the principal. After hearing the student's case, the principal informed the chairperson of the business department that the student's appeal would be considered by the administrative team and put on the agenda of the IIC for consideration. Shortly thereafter, the business department met and reconsidered the practice. They decided to abandon it, allowing students in the future to arrive early but only to warm up.

This case exemplifies a number of important points. First, the student had access to staff members in the school who would listen to him and help him receive a fair hearing of his point of view. Second, a process existed in the school's decision-making structure for handling grievances and appeals. Third, policies and practices could not be imposed arbitrarily by an individual or small group with impunity. Finally, a potentially alienating situation was rectified. We cannot say, of course, that the student would have become a discipline problem if he had not had recourse for his grievance. But we do know that systems that lack mechanisms for resolving conflicts in an acceptable way are fertile ground for the growth of increasingly serious problems.

RESOLVING PROBLEMS

Not only conflict, but a wide range of problems are more likely to be resolved when open communication is maintained. As mentioned above, administrators can often facilitate the resolution of particular problems by their accessibility to and communication with staff and students. Two cases will illustrate this point.

In one case, a principal was getting increasing reports of vandalism throughout the school during the fall quarter. He called in the maintenance supervisor and asked for a complete report of all vandalism, including an itemized list of instances and costs. He then translated these costs into other terms such as science equipment, books, student council expenses, and the students' annual fund raising for autistic children. The principal then called a special advisory (each advisor meeting with all advisees as a group) throughout the school, gave everyone a copy of his report, and asked each advisory to help him identify causes and possible solutions to the problem.

Before any of the proposed solutions could be explored, the problem was largely resolved. For a number of weeks there was no case of vandalism and only occasional instances thereafter for the remainder of the school year. The problem was resolved because the total school community assumed responsibility for it after the principal shared the problem with the rest of the school and showed them the costs in concrete, meaningful terms. Peer pressure developed among students to maintain an attractive school and to eliminate the costs (and loss of funds for other purposes) of some students' destructive impulses.

In the second case, the administration was faced with a growing number of rumors about grievances developing among the students.

The grievances, it was said, reflected differential treatment of white and black students. According to some of the rumors, there was a threat of disruption of the school and the possibility of intervention by outsiders. The school's administrators tried to work through normal channels and through discussions with various student leaders, but were unable to identify the source of the grievances or the threats.

The situation began to look potentially explosive. The principal decided to open up all possible lines of communication in the school. He held "open assemblies" for up to one hundred students at a time during the school day until all students who wished to participate did so. In the assemblies, the principal shared his concerns and set forth the ground rules for the assembly. The assembly was to be an open forum in which every student would have the opportunity to express himself or herself freely about the school. Notes were taken and the principal pledged to the students that every grievance would be thoroughly considered by an appropriate group or groups in the school. Reports of the results of the open assemblies were made to the faculty. Later, reports were made to the student body regarding what, if any, action had been taken with respect to each grievance.

The process helped sharpen some issues that needed particular attention. More importantly, it utilized a process of open communication to bring a good deal of covert complaining and threatening by a few small groups into the school's formal decision-making process. Again, we cannot be certain what kinds of problems, if any, were prevented by the action, but those who participated felt that anything from serious conflict at a minimum to disaster at worst had been averted.

## KEEP DISCIPLINE PRIVATE

The public correction of student behavior should be minimized. Public reprimands often create more problems and contribute more to a negative school climate than does the behavior which is being corrected. No one, teenagers or adults, likes to be corrected in front of others. The humiliation of public discipline does not belong in a human organization.

Obviously, there are many instances where private discipline is not possible. Rule infractions in the classroom may demand quick, public disciplinary action. On the other hand, there are many situations, including some in the classroom, that allow for private action. Our tendency to respond immediately to misbehavior may lead us to overlook the possibility of avoiding a public confrontation by quietly talking with the student aside or by waiting to confer with the student in a private setting. This issue is so important that the staff should consider its significance deliberately. Techniques and strategies for handling a variety of situations should be developed. The key is to handle the problems in a manner that will not intensify disjunctive emotions or make the problem more difficult by creating issues in addition to the original behavior. Severe disciplinary cases sometimes develop from simple situations such as requesting a student to pick up a piece of paper. There have been instances where a staff member winds up confronting not only one student but a number of others, who become hostile and threatening. This is not to suggest that one should tolerate an infraction of the rules or ignore some infraction out of expediency or fear of a student's reaction. Rather, we are suggesting that the manner in which discipline is handled can prevent a student's behavior from becoming a bigger issue that involves others. Discipline should be a private affair. Each student will then recognize that the staff is concerned about his or her feelings and respects his or her right to be free of the threat of public embarrassment. This approach contributes to a positive school climate.

## GIVE STUDENTS RESPONSIBILITY

Giving students responsibility is a crucial part of the development of self-discipline. In fact, responsibility is a crucial part of becoming a mature person generally. All of us, if we are emotionally healthy, resist having things done for us that we can do for ourselves. At any age, the assumption of responsibility is an integral part of healthy development. One psychiatrist has commented that mothers err if they assume too much responsibility for a child rather than allowing the child to grow through increasing amounts of responsibility. The result may be an individual who does not dare to "make the responsible choice which . . . is one of the characteristics of personal life. So the flow of life is arrested."[23]

We have already referred to a number of ways in which students can be given responsibility:

(1) sharing in the decisions made in advisement;
(2) participating in the decision-making process of the school;
(3) making appropriate use of commons time; and
(4) participating in classes set up to promote self-directed learning, especially out-of-school learning.

A faculty should examine areas where students can effectively be given more responsibility and develop means of assessing their effectiveness and of helping students learn from their experiences.

The commons, in particular, is a powerful device for helping students learn the relationship between freedom and responsibility. The degree of freedom that students may exercise in a commons program can be in direct proportion to their willingness to assume responsibility for it. A well organized commons program sets high expectations for student behavior, letting the students know that the staff believes in their ability to make good decisions and in their trustworthiness. At the high school level, a commons program can be viewed as providing a transition between the world of the child and adulthood. Students at the age of sixteen are learning to drive and at eighteen they are learning to vote. It seems to make sense that those students can also learn to manage some free time in a responsible manner. And as they do, they are developing increasing amounts of self-discipline, which is one of the essential components of preventive discipline.

## PRAISE GOOD BEHAVIOR

There is an abundance of evidence that praise is extremely important in preventive discipline. Whether one calls it positive reinforcement, positive feedback, motivation for growth, or anything else, praise is an essential ingredient in developing a healthy, creative, self-disciplined individual. Unfortunately, there is a tendency for us to remind others of their undesirable but not of their good behavior. In a laboratory experiment of maternal attitudes and behavior, 80 mothers were observed in interaction with their children during a time of play. The mothers and children were observed through a one-way mirror and various kinds of maternal behavior were recorded. Out of nearly 9,000 recorded contacts between the mothers and the children, only 42 involved the category of "giving praise or affection."[24]

Teachers may be less likely even than mothers to give praise. One of the authors had a drawing teacher who boasted of his ability, which had come from years of experience, to quickly spot errors in the work of students. He handed back all student work with errors noted in bright red ink. There were no words of praise.

Constant attention on mistakes can inhibit learning. Consequently, one of the rules of the classroom should be, as LaGrand says, "praise before criticism."[25] The teacher does not ignore the mistakes, but neither does he or she ignore the praiseworthy efforts. LaGrand gives the example of a math problem. Rather than saying or implying that all of the student's work is wrong, the teacher can show the student those parts of the work that are correct or at least point out that the student has made an error only at a particular point. "Praise before criticism opens the path to further learning. Pick out the good points first, then give meaningful suggestions for improvement."[26]

We should note that, as the Madsens point out, many teachers probably are not aware of how little they praise students:

> Many teachers who believe they use more approval than disapproval do not (monitored by trained observers in classroom). It is necessary to practice delivering responses and to give yourself time cues or cues written on material you are teaching. A mark on every page can remind you to "catch someone being good."[27]

Praise can be a significant part of the development of self-esteem of adolescents. To praise a student is to express interest in that student and, ideally, some warmth towards the student. Studies of the parental role in the self-esteem of children show that such interest and warmth are crucial: "parental warmth, respectful treatment of children, and other expressions of concern for the child's well-being [are] all associated with the development of self-esteem."[28] Self-esteem, in turn, has been found to be associated with such things as academic achievement, aspiration level, good interpersonal relationships, emotional health, and acceptable rather than deviant behavior.[29] We recognize that a teacher's praise may not overcome the effects of a debilitating home environment. Nevertheless, praise from a teacher may be the one spark of hope some students have and it may contribute to the developing self-esteem of many others. As such, it will not only help create and maintain a positive school climate but will also help students to become more confident, more motivated, and less likely to engage in behavior requiring disciplinary action.

Praise can occur in places other than the classroom and for groups as well as for individuals. Groups of students or the entire study body may be praised on various occasions. Opportunities occur frequently in assemblies, after such public events as a football game, or when visitors are in the school and comment favorably on student conduct. Praise, of course, should always be sincere and should only be given when it is deserved. But again, the tendency is to neglect rather than to overdo the business of praising.

One form of praise that can contribute markedly to a positive school climate is the expression of school pride. A school pride/spirit committee can be formed to develop means of promoting school pride. The committee might plan a series of motivational assemblies, or commission students to prepare posters, or investigate items of clothing or buttons that proclaim that the individual belongs to the school. In one school, students secured and sold buttons that said such things as, "At North, we care." In essence, students and staff use such mechanisms to praise the entire school.

The leaders of social movements, executives in industry, and others responsible for groups and organizations have long known the value of creating solidarity in the membership. Songs, slogans, clothing, and ideologies have been used to develop the sense of unity. Leaders know that the mere bringing together of people with a common interest does not mean that they have unity. As someone has said, if you tie two tomcats together by their tails and throw them over a clothesline, you will have union but not unity. Union, the bringing of people together, can be a monstrous headache. Unity, the creation of solidarity among those who are brought together, can result in an effective and rewarding organization. We will go one additional step and point out that uniformity, the creation of sameness as well as solidarity, is not a valid goal. As noted in the last chapter, the conflict of ideas is a creative force. In sum, then, school pride is a form of self-praise by the entire school community. It is a unifying mechanism. As such, it minimizes the potential for behavior that requires disciplinary action.

## BUILD GOOD HUMAN RELATIONS

This final principle is a general one that underlies all the activities of a human organization. Each of the principles discussed above contributes to the building of good human relations. Here we want to emphasize, however, the development of good interpersonal relationships among students rather than between students and staff.

The deliberate development of programs and activities that foster good human relations among students will prevent problems. For good human relations also contribute to the solidarity of the student body, and solidarity will tend to minimize behavioral problems. We have already noted the importance of a standing committee on student relations. This committee should play a vital role in any program of building the desired kinds of relationships among students.

There are some programs already available which might be used to develop good human relations among students. A school that faced court-ordered desegregation used the Outward Bound program as part of its preparation for an influx of black students. Small groups of students that represented a cross-section of the new, enlarged student body (age, sex, and race) were invited to participate in two-day Outward Bound experiences. The students in the groups were selected so that none had been friends prior to the experience. In the Outward Bound program, groups are placed in a strange environment (in this case, in a state wildlife area) and given a series of problems that require group cooperation to solve. For example, one of the initial tasks was getting each member of the group over a sheer, thirteen-foot wall. Members cooperated in a wide variety of other tasks, such as rock climbing, rappelling down a cliff, crawling deep into a small cave, and overcoming different natural and artificial obstacles. Friendships formed in the groups that carried over into the school and the classroom. Many of the students who participated had never before interacted closely and cooperatively with someone of another race.

Teachers can facilitate the development of good relationships by employing strategies in all classes that allow students to know each other, help each other, and solve problems together. Students should not sit in class after class and remain strangers to each other. But like every other teaching task, the achievement of this task demands thoughtful planning and deliberate effort. The planning and effort have their rewards, however, for to the extent that the teacher facilitates the development of good relationships between himself or herself and members of the class, solidarity, interest, and responsibility will prevail. Classroom control will be a joint effort rather than something which is imposed by the teacher on the students.

## SUMMARY

Both the authoritarian and democratic models of discipline can be carried to an extreme. In a human organization, discipline involves authority without authoritarianism. Rigid controls stifle the development of adolescents. Therefore, discipline must be seen as not simply conformity to the rules but as a process in which students internalize the values and norms that facilitate a free and orderly society.

An effective disciplinary process demands carefully conceived and clearly stated guidelines for rule enforcement. Such guidelines must respect student rights, provide for an appeal process, identify categories of infractions of varying seriousness, and define the role of parents and advisors in the disciplinary process. Schools must maintain and exercise the right of suspension in order to safeguard the learning atmosphere, but every consideration should be given to alternatives to suspension. Finally, the entire rule enforcement system needs periodic evaluation.

Preventive discipline—the active promotion of a positive school climate—is critically important. There are five general principles in preventive discipline. Open communication must be maintained. Whenever possible, discipline should be kept private. Students should be given responsibility so that they can develop self-discipline. The staff should be alert to every possibility to praise good behavior. And there should be the deliberate development of programs and activities that foster good human relationships.

# Endnotes

[1]J. Patrick Mahon, "Beyond Judicial Intervention: Student Discipline and the Courts," *NASSP Bulletin* 63 (February, 1979):68.

[2]Karl A. Menninger, The Human Mind (New York: Alfred A. Knopf, 1961), p. 344.

[3]Ted Blackman *et al.,* "Corporal Punishment, School Suspension, and the Civil Rights of Students: An Analysis of Office for Civil Rights School Surveys," *Inequality in Education* 23 (September, 1978):62.

[4]Knute Larson, *School Discipline in an Age of Rebellion* (West Nyack, New York: Parker Publishing Co., 1972), p. 90.

[5]Louis E. LaGrand, *Discipline in the Secondary School* (West Nyack, New York: Parker Publishing Co., 1969), p. 3.

[6]Edgar Z. Friedenberg, *Coming of Age in America* (New York: Random House, 1963), pp. 28–29.

[7]*Ibid.,* p. 46.

[8]Charles H. Madsen, Jr. and Clifford K. Madsen, *Teaching/Discipline: A Positive Approach for Educational Development* (Boston: Allyn & Bacon, Inc., 1974), p. 9.

[9]Larson, *op. cit.,* p. 84.

[10]George Orwell, *1984* (New York: The New American Library, 1949), p. 178.

[11]Quoted in Lester W. Anderson and Lauren A. Van Dyke, *Secondary School Administration,* 2nd edition (Boston: Houghton Mifflin, 1972), p. 366.

[12]Mahon, *op. cit.,* p. 69. For a discussion of a variety of legal issues relating to classroom management, including class suspensions and due process, see Daniel L. Duke, Robert Donmoyer, and Greg Farman, "Emerging Legal Issues Related to Classroom Management," *Phi Delta Kappan* 60 (December, 1978):305–309.

[13]Peter Roos, "Goss and Wood: Due Process and Student Discipline," *Inequality in Education,* Number Twenty, July, 1975, p. 43.

[14]*Ibid.,* p. 44.

[15]*Ibid.,* p. 45.

[16]Anderson and Van Dyke, *op. cit.,* p. 381.

[17]Larson, *op. cit.,* p. 97.

[18]See, for example, M. Hayes Mizell, "Designing and Implementing Effective In-school Alternatives to Suspension," *The Urban Review* 10 (Fall, 1978):213–26.

[19]See Merle McClung, "Alternatives to Disciplinary Exclusion from School," *Inequality in Education,* Number Twenty, July, 1975, pp. 61–62.

[20]*Ibid.,* p. 65.

[21]August B. Hollingshead, *Elmtown's Youth* (New York: John Wiley & Sons, 1949), pp. 185–92.

[22]Reported in Dale Findley and Henry M. O'Reilly, "Secondary School Discipline," in Leslie J. Chamberlin and Joseph B. Carnot, eds., *Improving School Discipline* (Springfield, Ill.: Charles C Thomas, 1974), pp. 129–30.

[23]Paul Tournier, *The Meaning of Persons* (New York: Harper & Row, 1957), p. 199.

[24]Michael Zunich, "A Study of the Relationships Between Child Rearing Attitudes and Maternal Behavior," in Alan L. Grey, ed., *Class and Personality in Society* (New York: Atherton Press, 1969), p. 80.

[25]Louis E. LaGrand, *op. cit.*, p. 143.

[26]*Ibid.*

[27]Charles H. Madsen, Jr. and Clifford K. Madsen, *op. cit.*, p. 146.

[28]Robert H. Lauer and Warren H. Handel, *Social Psychology: The Theory and Application of Symbolic Interaction* (Boston: Houghton Mifflin, 1977), p. 191.

[29]*Ibid.*, pp. 196–204.

# Chapter 8

# Rewarding
# Excellence

An office secretary was busily working on a rush project when a young executive came to her and insisted that she fill out a purchase report for him. "You can do it yourself," she told him. "It will only take you a couple of minutes." The young executive replied that he did not know how to type, and the secretary countered by saying that he should learn. The man said that typing was not his job: "And besides, my time is worth five times as much as yours."

At that point, the secretary became extremely angry. She shouted at the executive: "I've had enough of this superiority crap. Just because you're paid five times as much doesn't mean you're worth five times as much." The secretary's assertion of her own worth and her unwillingness to defer to the executive as a superior being caused him considerable discomfort. He backed off, grumbling about the problems of finding a decent secretary. His real problem, she told him, was that he wanted a rug to walk on, not just a decent secretary.[1]

The secretary's experience illustrates some of the points we want to make in this chapter about rewards in a human organization. First, all of us have a need for respect from others. The secretary felt that she was being treated in a disparaging way by the young executive and she rebelled against it. No one, whatever their position in an organization, should be treated with disdain. Whether secretary or executive, whether student or administrator, we all have, as human beings, certain needs, including the need for respect or approval by others. In a human organization, every member is treated with a basic respect and the dignity due to a human being.

Second, it follows that people should be rewarded for what they are doing and are capable of doing. A secretary is an important member of a business organization, and should be recognized as such. The secretary rightfully rejected the implication that executives are intrinsically more worthwhile creatures than secretaries. Secretarial excellence is important to the success of a business organization, as is executive excellence. "Excellence" can occur in numberless endeavors, all of which may be important to a particular group or organization. As this concept suggests, and as we shall discuss in detail below, rewards for excellence in a high school should not be thought of in terms of a small group of elites. In the last chapter, we noted that praise is a way of rewarding accomplishments in an informal as well as formal way. Praise from a teacher, advisor, or administrator on a one-to-one basis is one way to include all (or virtually all) students in the reward system. In this chapter, we will examine in detail some of the formal mechanisms for a broad system of reward.

Finally, the incident of the secretary and the executive illustrates a problem which we shall consider first—the dilemma of equality versus excellence. The secretary's response indicated that her encounter with that executive was but one of a series of experiences in which she was made to feel inferior. She rejected the notion of executive superiority. She felt that she had the right to equality in terms of respect and in terms of the value of her work. But if we treat people equally, can we also recognize individual differences and high levels of achievement? Does equality mean that we cannot recognize and reward excellence? Does the recognition of excellence mean that we inevitably reject the notion of equality? We will discuss this dilemma, its meaning for the high school, and the way to deal with it. We will then show how to reward excellence in a variety of ways and for a variety of reasons. Finally, we will discuss briefly some ways of motivating students to attain excellence and the value of the reward system we set forth.

# EQUALITY AND EXCELLENCE

Social life in general, and education in particular, contains many dilemmas. Some dilemmas occur at the point of a contradiction between ideology and reality. The ideology may affirm, for example, that every child should have an equal opportunity to get a good education, while the reality may be that children from lower socioeconomic backgrounds are unlikely either to attend a good school or to go very far in their education. Other dilemmas arise because of a contradiction between two values or two ideologies, such as the one we will deal with here—equality versus excellence.

## AN AMERICAN DILEMMA

In his provocative book, *Excellence,* John Gardner quotes from the diary of a Mrs. Clappe, the wife of a 19th century physician who lived in a mining camp during the California gold rush:

> Last night one of our neighbors had a dinner party. He came in to borrow a teaspoon. "Had you not better take them all?" I said. "Oh, no," was the answer, "that would be too much luxury. My guests are not used to it, and they would think that I was getting aristocratic, and putting on airs. One is enough; they can pass it 'round from one to the other."[2]

Gardner uses the story to illustrate our deep regard for the idea of the equality of people.

The notion of equality has been affirmed throughout our history, and various trends and developments have been evaluated in terms of how they square with equality. That which enhances equality is to be eagerly accepted, while that which reduces equality or contradicts it is looked upon with suspicion. In the 19th century, many writers lauded science and technology because they would help us achieve our goal of equality. In an address before the American Association for the Advancement of Education in the 1850s a teacher asserted:

> ... that science, in its very nature, tends to promote political equality; to elevate the masses; to break down the spirit of aristocracy; and to abolish all those artificial distinctions in society which depend on differences of dress, equipage, style of living, and manners.[3]

This is not to say that every American is equal to every other American in all respects. Gardner summarizes well what we have believed about equality:

1. All people are equal in matters relating to life and death. We do not distinguish among people in our concern for preserving life or in our care for the dying.
2. All people are equal in the area of civil rights. We are a nation of laws, and everyone receives equal treatment in the courts and possesses equal rights in the political process.
3. All people should have equality of opportunity. Not everyone will succeed, but everyone should have the opportunity. There are complexities and problems, of course, if we want to insure equality of opportunity to people of widely divergent backgrounds. But the commitment to realize the goal of equal opportunity has been strong, particularly among those who work in public education.
4. All people are not equal in terms of talent and motivation. Consequently, even given equal opportunities, all will not be equal in terms of achievement and rewards.[4]

The question of achievement brings us to the other horn of the dilemma—our value on excellence. We value excellence in a wide variety of things, including intellectual accomplishments, physical activities, moral character, and business success. Historically, the economic realm has been a favorite one for Americans to demonstrate excellence: "The comparatively striking feature of American culture is its tendency to identify standards of personal excellence with competitive occupational achievement."[5] Not only do we value excellence in various endeavors, but we believe in rewarding those who achieve excellence: "It has been part of the fundamental pathos of American culture to believe that virtue should and will be rewarded—and more particularly that such economic virtues as hard work, frugality and prudence should receive a proportionate reward."[6]

But how can we encourage and reward excellence while at the same time affirming our value on equality? In particular, if we insist on total equality, will we not rob people of their motivation to strive for excellence? On the other hand, if we stress excellence and reward highly the very few who make it to the top, are we not thereby disowning our value on equality?

The dilemma of equality and excellence can be resolved, according to Gardner, by a moderate equalitarianism that offers protection to some aspects of equality but does not attempt to ignore or minimize individual differences or outstanding individual achievements. We do not want a survival-of-the-fittest social order in which "excellence" means the besting and subordination of the many by the few, nor do we want an everyone-is-the-same social order in which competition and striving for excellence fade away.

## A HIGH SCHOOL DILEMMA

The same dilemma of equality versus excellence must be faced in the high school. Can we be democratic, emphasizing the value and dignity of each individual, and at the same time achievement oriented, recognizing and rewarding the attainment of excellence by certain individuals? The dilemma is reflected in recent concerns about grading. Should, as some insist, all students be able to "succeed" by being measured in terms of their personal objectives and goals rather than in terms of some more universal standard established by the school? Or should, as others argue, all students have equal access but compete for class rank and grades? Similarly, there are disagreements about the curriculum. Should there be college preparatory course for an intellectual elite, who receive the bulk of the school's attention and rewards? Or should all courses be equal, with no attempt made to differentiate students by ability?

The way the questions are phrased suggests that we cannot value high achievement and still preserve the worth and dignity of each individual, that we must choose between an emphasis on equality and a goal of excellence. Gardner uses comments from two teachers to set up the dilemma.[7] One said: "I regard it as undemocratic to treat so-called gifted children any differently from other children. To me all children are gifted." The other, a professor of education, argued: "The goal of the American educational system is to enable every youngster to fulfill his potentialities, regardless of his race, creed, social standing or economic position." One says that we must treat all students equally while the other says that we must establish the kind of system in which each individual can fulfill his or her own unique potential. Both goals are valued in American society. The dilemma arises if it is not possible to enable individuals to fulfill themselves without treating them differently.

Our efforts to resolve the dilemma plunge into deeper perplexities when we deal with the question of the meaning of equality. As noted above, no one argues that everyone must be equal to everyone else in every respect. The emphasis has been on equality of opportunity.

But there has been considerable debate over the meaning of equal opportunity:

> Does it mean that a child should have the opportunity to attend a nonsegregated school? Does it mean that all children should be schooled with equal amounts of money? Does it mean that the proportion of people of various kinds (racial minorities, women, different socioeconomic strata) in various educational levels should be the same as their proportion in the total population? Does it mean that each child should have access to the same quality and same amount of education? Does it mean that the same amount of education should yield the same payoff in terms of income or personal development?[8]

Does it mean that there should be no special programs for special needs? Does it mean an end to such practices as tracking?

Different people give different answers to the questions. Without addressing all of the questions and without trying to provide a definitive answer to the question of the meaning of equality, we will describe below a system that we believe allows a school to pursue both goals—equality and excellence. We do not believe that the goals are mutually exclusive. In a human organization, there is equal opportunity for each student. As we have shown in earlier chapters, all students can have the opportunity to participate in important decisions, to select from the full range of courses in the curriculum, to choose special programs such as out-of-school learning, and to work with other students of varying degrees of ability. An effective, comprehensive high school does not separate students into tracks or streams in all subjects.

On the other hand, a human organization can also set the goal of excellence at every level and in all activities. Indeed, excellence must be the goal. For if the modern high school is expected to attend to each individual and encourage the full development of each individual's talent and ability regardless of the level of his or her ability, the school is also expected to search diligently for those individuals in the school who have the capacity to achieve excellence. There is widespread agreement that the nation needs those exceptionally talented individuals in all areas of life to develop their abilities and assume responsible positions. As Gardner puts it, "the tone and fiber of our society depend upon a pervasive and almost universal striving for good performance."[9] He illustrates the point by noting that a missile could blow up on the launching pad because of various kinds of failures—incompetence of the designer or of the mechanic who was responsible for adjusting the last valve.

It is perhaps a truism to say that there are various kinds of excellence which are possible. However, the varieties of excellence may be obscured by the tendency to reward only particular kinds. The question for the high school administrator is, what is the range of excellence that we are rewarding? All schools recognize and reward academic excellence and athletic achievements. But if excellence is recognized only in these two categories, then the rewards can be gained by only an elite few.

The point is that there should be a variety of ways in which an individual can attain and be recognized for excellence. There should be a category of excellence attainable by every student. Not everyone will attain excellence, but everyone should be able to strive for it, including the student who is average academically and who has no athletic ability. Thus, the goals of both equality and excellence are maintained by broadening the range of activities in which excellence is recognized and rewarded.

## REWARDING EXCELLENCE

As we noted in the last chapter, there is a tendency to react to undesirable behavior and take desirable behavior for granted. We are more prone to correct than to praise. Furthermore, an administrator may be so engaged in dealing with various problems that he or she spends little time and thought on the matter of rewards. This is unfortunate, for desirable behavior, as the behaviorists have well taught us, needs to be recognized and rewarded, not enjoyed in silence. The following discussion of a reward system is not meant to be exhaustive. As with other aspects of the human organization that we have discussed, a reward system needs to be constructed in accord with the local situation. We will show the basis for the system and the variety of ways in which the school can recognize and reward students for excellence.

## THE BASIS: DIVERSE COMPETENCIES

In our discussion of the curriculum, we noted that there has been a tendency to assess students in terms of ability measures for entry into various offerings and to ignore some of the benefits of letting student interests play a role. We argued for a more balanced use of both criteria in planning programs. The ability/interest matrix can be converted to another matrix which is useful for examining the school's stance toward excellence. The matrix consists of academic skills (primarily language and mathematics) on the one hand, and what we will call other competencies on the other hand. The other competencies will vary from one school to another, but they include many and diverse skills, ranging from technical skills, such as welding or woodworking, to the skills demanded for excellent performance in service projects. Our schools tend to be skilled in using the yardstick of academic skills. We have a good many formal tests that measure these skills. But we do not have much information about students' other competencies. In fact, we do not typically even ask what they are or how they can be measured. There are, of course, some exceptions to the neglect of the other competencies. In many schools there is an awareness of the competencies involved in the performing or expressive arts. And in some schools there is recognition of student leadership. But these do not exhaust the range of competencies which are important.

In a discussion of the relative importance of various competencies, a high school principal in a southern state told one of the authors that his students tended to score below the national averages on standardized tests. This caused many people in the community to be very critical of the school and to overlook many of the other achievements of his students. To illustrate, he pointed out with obvious pride that a number of local industries openly expressed preference for hiring graduates from his school. The principal was not denying the importance of the basic skills of literacy and mathematics. Nor was he denying the legitimacy of concern about the lower scores of his students. At the same time, he felt that due weight should be given to those other competencies that allowed his graduates to become productive, loyal, and ambitious workers.

It is certainly possible that this principal's school, given the socioeconomic and cultural background of the students, is in fact a superior school. That is, it may be a school that is pervaded with a spirit of striving for excellence in many ways, without minimizing the significance of those few who achieve academic excellence. It may be that the yardstick used by many people in the community to measure the school is too narrow. Schools with high *average* scores on standardized tests are not necessarily doing the best job of developing the potential of the individual student or the student's ability to become a lifelong learner. To measure every student constantly and exclusively by the yardstick of language and math skills may demean many students, diminish their motivation to excel in something, and overlook the social worth of those other competencies which the students have or could develop.

Our argument here is in no way intended to minimize the importance of academic excellence. It is rather intended to recognize the fact that academic excellence is not even an option for every student. The modern comprehensive high school is expected to serve more than an intellectual elite. It must, therefore, have a reward system that recognizes the social worth of other competencies as well as those we measure on standardized tests. We emphasize the other competencies because schools know how to reward academic excellence, but tend to ignore the other competencies. Having made the point, we will look first at the rewarding of academic excellence.

## REWARDING ACADEMIC EXCELLENCE

Typically, schools have several important means of rewarding traditional academic excellence: honor rolls, selection of valedictorians and salutatorians, and honor societies. In one school, these traditional rewards were broadened by creating an honors program that included all subjects taught in the school. Essentially, each department in the school established criteria for the attainment of honors. The student who wants to strive for honors in a particular subject area must take a minimum number of courses, including a prescribed number at the advanced level, and achieve a 3.5 (on a 4.0 scale) grade point average. It is important to note that all departments provide an honors program—industrial education and business as well as the more traditional areas of language and mathematics. Those students who meet the standards of excellence are recognized by:

(1)   a certificate, which is awarded in an assembly; and
(2)   an entry on the student's permanent record indicating the subject area or areas in which honors were attained.

Some students excel in several subjects. Many are able to excel in one. The program achieves at least two important goals:

1.   It recognizes the value of excellence in a broad range of subjects, in metal working, for example, as well as in the typical college preparatory courses in science or math.
2.   It provides a means for the advisor or teacher to communicate high standards to all students, helping many of them to set goals which are meaningful to them personally and, at the same time, are socially recognized as valuable.

Obviously, the above program broadens the notion of academic excellence. But we know of no reason why any subject area in a high school should be excluded from an honors program. The above program also illustrates the point that even where a particular kind of achievement is being recognized (such as by the honor roll) it may be fruitful to explore new ways or new programs in which excellence is recognized and rewarded. In the human organization, there is an ongoing search for a structure and for practices and policies that better facilitate the achievement of goals. The achievement of excellence by members of the organization will be facilitated by the striving for excellence in organizational structure and practices.

## REWARDING OTHER COMPETENCIES

The achievement of excellence in areas other than the academic should be given the same recognition. A school can conduct an annual honors assembly where awards are given for a variety of other competencies. In one school, for example, Senior Honors Awards were presented to 50 students out of the class of 700. Among the awards given were:

(1) outstanding leadership in one or more areas of student activity;
(2) outstanding scholarship—one for each subject area;
(3) outstanding service, given to those students who have exemplified the spirit of service and humanitarianism;
(4) special achievements, for those who do not fit in one of the above categories but who have achieved something above the ordinary; and
(5) outstanding athletic achievement.

It is important to develop categories for the reward system, either the above set or one more suited to the local situation. The aim of the categories is to insure that excellence will be rewarded in a variety of activities, not simply in scholarship and athletics.

To enhance the opportunity for all students to demonstrate their talent, their leadership, and their willingness to serve, the school should develop a service program. Some schools that have begun such a program have found that interest fades after a short time and have dropped the service projects. We believe that this is a mistake. In some cases, interest in service programs may be continual. More likely, there will be cycles of high and low interest, reflecting certain differences in successive generations of students. The service program should always be available to students; it should not be dropped merely because a particular cohort of students expresses little interest.

What is involved in a service program? In essence, the program challenges students to develop a service project as either an individual or as a group. The student council can develop a catalog of service projects to assist students in developing their own ideas. The service projects are numerous, limited only by the imagination of the planners. For example, projects are possible in the areas of

(1) education, such as tutoring;
(2) consumer protection, such as a bicycle safety program;
(3) political or civic activities, such as voter registration, the develop of political information programs, or volunteer rides to the polls during an election;

(4)  environmental activities, such as an anti-litter campaign or a beautification project at the school or in the community; and

(5)  special assistance to particular groups, such as fix-up projects for retired people.

The student council can manage the program with the assistance of school administrators. Among the materials necessary for an effective, efficient program are descriptive brochures, a catalog of suggested projects, and application and completion forms for program administration. The brochures can describe the origin and purpose of the program along with explanations of how to participate. For example, the brochures may note the historical importance of the concept of volunteer service in the United States, and point out that the high–school program is based on the premise that students can make important contributions to others in the community.

There should be clear instructions in the brochure for participation in the program, such as those shown in Figure 8.1. The brochures are given to all advisors, who give them in turn to their advisees. The advisory system is the primary means of providing the information and communicating the challenge of the program.

---

PARTICIPATING IN THE SERVICE PROGRAM

The program is sponsored and managed by your Student Council Service Committee in the Student Center.

1.  Talk with your advisor or sponsor about the program; look at the Catalog of Service Projects which is available in the Student Center or Advisement Center.

2.  Talk with your friends about a group project or challenge your organization to participate.

3.  Submit an application for a service project to the Student Council for approval. Applications are available in the Student Center or Advisement Center.

4.  Report to the Student Council office when the project is completed.

5.  Wear your service pin proudly and encourage others to join.

---

Figure 8.1
An Example of Instructions for Participating in a Service Program

A catalog of suggested service projects should also be made available to all advisors. Staff members and members of the Student Council should be available to discuss service project ideas with students in advisement and classroom settings. It should not be necessary for a student to have a definite idea in mind. If the student finds the notion of a service project appealing, a brainstorming session can be held to generate ideas.

Finally, forms should be available for students to apply for a project and for completion reports at the end of the project. Figures 8.2 and 8.3 illustrate useful forms. Once a student has completed a service project, he or she is awarded a service pin to wear. The pin can be a motivation to others to participate. (Research has shown that blood donations increased after donors were given red-drop pins to wear.) At the end of the year, the Student Council can give a summary

---

## APPLICATION

Name:_____(leader's name if a group—attach a roster of all members)

Address:_____Telephone:_____

Project Description (include nature of service, need for service and where it will occur):

Dates of Project:

Approval by Student Council and Administration:

_____    _____
Administrator                Student Council Officer

Special Conditions of Approval:

---

Figure 8.2
Sample Application for Student Service Project

## COMPLETION REPORT

Name:_____

Project Description:

Date Completed:

List of Participants in Project:

Total Number of Hours:

Evaluation of Effectiveness of Project:

**Figure 8.3**
Sample Completion Report Form for Student Service Project

report of service projects to the Board of Education. This report becomes a part of the graduating class's gift to the school and the community.

There is one additional point about the service program that demands attention—its larger significance. Service programs can be treated as a concession to those who have no other talents or as an idea that is nice but largely peripheral to the goals of the school. We believe that they should not be treated in such ways. In fact, we would argue that service projects make a significant contribution to a major goal of every school—the development of concerned, effective citizens. The nurturing of individual development and achievement must be carried on in the context of concern for the social well-being. It is possible that individual development can become atomistic, self-centered, and even destructive. Dostoyevsky portrays one of his characters as "very sensitive about everything that concerned himself" but "very stupid about the feelings and sensations of others."[10] One of the aims of education is to produce individuals who are sensitive to issues and needs that go beyond their own personal pleasures and pains. That aim, indeed, is essential to the goal of individual fulfillment. As Gardner points out, the individual must have a society in which he or she can both lose and find himself or herself. Such societies emerge and survive only when people attend to the welfare of their society. "In this sense every free man lives for himself but also lives for his society. His goal must be not only individual fulfillment but the enrichment and strengthening of his society."[11]

In sum, the service program makes a significant contribution to the goals of the school by involving students in that enrichment and strengthening of society which is so important to both the student and the society. Those who administer the program should be aware of its significance, and communicate that significance to the student body. As the fifth point in Figure 8.1 rightly says, a student may wear the service pin proudly.

REWARDING THE GIFTED

Providing a qualitatively different education for the gifted and specially talented is another means of rewarding excellence.[12] As we noted in the introduction, some observers feel that the gifted are among the more neglected groups in high schools today. From our point of view, it is important to understand that special provisions can be made for gifted students without creating an atmosphere of elitism or neglecting other kinds of rewards for other students.

Intensive study of gifted children can be traced back to the work of Lewis Terman in the 1920s. His work helped to create a climate that made it acceptable to treat gifted children differently and to recognize them as a special resource. One outcome was the formation of the American Association for Gifted Children. More specific impetus to educating the gifted was provided by the National Defense Education Act of the 1950s. Increasingly, it was recognized that democracy is not well served by ignoring or downplaying the special abilities of the gifted child. As Passow put it, depriving the gifted of "opportunities to develop and use their gifts does not result in upgrading the attainment of their less able peers. Such meaningless and misguided egalitarianism contributes to the development of no one in particular."[13]

Who are these gifted children who need the qualitatively different education? The following definition has been widely accepted:

> Gifted and talented children, identified by professional qualified persons, are those who by virtue of outstanding abilities are capable of high performance. They require differentiated educational programs and/or services beyond those normally provided by the regular school program in order to realize their contributions to self and society. Children capable of high performance include those with demonstrated achievement and/or potential ability in any of the following areas, singly or in combination:
> 1. General intellectual ability
> 2. Specific academic aptitude
> 3. Creative or productive thinking
> 4. Leadership ability
> 5. Visual and performing arts
> 6. Psychomotor skills
> 7. Culturally different gifted[14]

The definition is broad in scope. It is not restricted to high performance on traditional IQ or achievement tests.

There is still the question of how the gifted student is to be identified. A screening process is recommended that uses a number of criteria and methods, including teacher and peer nominations and various intelligence and achievement tests. We simply do not know enough to depend upon any single measure. Once the gifted are identified, however, there are various programs which can be made available, ranging from those that merely provide additional enrichment activities to those that offer a completely separate facility. In between these extremes, a school can select from a considerable number of programs which have been used in schools throughout the country. Four basic enrichment arrangements have been used:

> *Grouping:* clusters; special classes; part-time groups before, during, after school or on Saturdays; seminars, mini-courses; resource or demonstration centers; itinerant or resource teachers; field trips and cultural events; special summer sessions.
> *Vertical Acceleration:* double-grade promotion; advanced placement, ungraded or multi-age classes; tutoring, correspondence courses, credit by examination; independent study; extra classes for extra credit; early college admission.
> *Horizontal Acceleration:* individual or group research projects, study groups, part-time classes, clusters within regular classes, mentorships, interest clubs, summer school.
> *Guidance:* individual conferences, group meetings, career and vocational counseling, community programs and sponsorships, scholarship societies, mentorships.[15]

Twenty years ago, the White House Conference on Children and Youth recommended that *all* schools make special provisions for educating the gifted "including opportunities for intellectual freedom, individual inquiry, decision making, critical analysis, concept formation, originality, creativity and communication."[16] The recommendation has not yet been implemented, though an increasing amount of attention is being given to the gifted. In a human organization, the special provisions are essential. Rewards for excellence must be available to all categories of students, and a fundamental way of rewarding the gifted student is the provision of a qualitatively different education.

## REWARDS AS PUBLIC RECOGNITION

If, as we noted in the last chapter, discipline should be largely a private affair, rewards should be generally a public matter. Opportunities should be provided for students to share their achievements and interests with others. Students will experience some intrinsic rewards from participating in various programs and activities, of course. But the importance of public recognition is too well known to argue the point. In addition to its value for the students who are rewarded, public recognition helps create a climate in the school of liveliness, creativity, and achievement.

We have already mentioned a number of ways in which public recognition for excellence can be given—the provision of special programs and assemblies for the distribution of various kinds of honors and awards. There are a number of other ways in which talent can be put on display, publicly recognizing the achievement of various kinds of excellence:

(1) performance by school groups in special assemblies, such as choral and instrumental music and plays.

(2) special talent shows to give unique talents an opportunity. This is particularly appropriate where certain talents may not be used in a conventional dramatic or musical production.

(3) special activities to give students opportunities to express their cultural heritage. Particularly where there are a number of minority students in a school, a foreign festival day or an Afro-American week can be a rewarding experience.

(4) the provision of several areas, preferably in more public spaces such as lobbies or libraries, where students can exhibit their work. All kinds of work can be exhibited, including welding or metal projects, electronics, designs from beginning art students

or portfolio exhibits of advanced honors students in art, and special cultural displays reflecting interests or backgrounds of the students.

Many schools do provide some of these opportunities for students to display talent and achievement. But too often the assemblies are called infrequently and then for athletic achievements only or for an outside group to perform. And too often a walk through the school reveals emptiness—no signs that students are busily producing works of high quality.

The significance of assemblies, exhibits, and special activities such as an Afro-American week cannot be stressed too much, especially if students are involved in the process of managing the activity. Students will respond to the achievements of their peers if it is obvious that all achievements are valued. Unquestionably, school spirit can be developed around first-rate athletic teams. But school spirit can also develop—and in a more lasting way—if various kinds of excellence are rewarded and valued.

## MOTIVATING TO EXCELLENCE

There is an old anecdote about a farmer who was sitting on the steps of his deteriorating house. A stranger came by and asked how the man's cotton was coming along. The farmer said he didn't have any; he didn't plant it because he was afraid of boll weevils. "Well," said the stranger, "how is your corn?" "Didn't plant none," was the reply, "afraid there wasn't going to be enough rain." "What did you plant?" asked the stranger. "Nothing," said the farmer. "I just played safe."

Every teacher knows students like the farmer, the apathetic individuals who always seem to seek the path of least resistance. A danger in a school that seeks to be humane is to lower expectations to meet the "needs" of such students. Another danger is to be satisfied as long as students and teachers seem satisfied, regardless of whether either group has achieved the best in terms of their potential. Likert pointed out that the human organization maximizes productivity. The point of a human organization is not simply to make people feel good, but to bring about high levels of achievement. By its very nature, a human organization tends to motivate, because people are valued, are involved in the decision-making process, are given responsibility, and are rewarded for their participation. More particularly, we may note four aspects of a high school that motivate students to excellence: the reward system itself, realistic opportunities, teacher expectations, and the advisory system.

## THE REWARD SYSTEM AS MOTIVATION

We have suggested that all schools in fact do have a system for rewarding excellence, but may not be fully aware of what it is or of how it is affecting the school's climate. Periodically, the administrators should explicitly identify the kinds of excellence which are being, and which should be, rewarded. We have argued that a well-developed reward system will recognize a broad variety of achievement, and that this will, in turn, create a climate that motivates all students, not just those capable of the highest scholastic and athletic achievement. In other words, the reward system not only recognizes achievement, but also stimulates achievement. As some studies of the motivation of professionals have shown, recognition may be more important than responsibility, money, opportunities for advancement, or the work itself in motivating the individual to achieve excellence.

## REALISTIC OPPORTUNITIES

Excellence will not be attained by everyone, but some kind of excellence should be attainable by everyone. This is the point of broadening the reward system, to recognize and reward the varieties of excellence that may be achieved. The attainment of excellence then becomes realistic for every student. The bulk of students are then not automatically excluded because of a narrow definition of excellence that includes only athletic prowess and high scores in literary and scientific areas.

Many Americans have castigated the poor because, they say, the poor are unwilling to work hard and thereby solve their own problem. But studies have shown that, given realistic opportunities, the poor are as highly motivated and willing to work as anyone else.[17] Similarly, we believe that when students are given realistic opportunities to achieve excellence, they will attempt to do so. This is the point of recognizing and rewarding varieties of excellence. To reward academic excellence means that there are realistic opportunities for some students, while the opportunities exist for others in athletics, service, or special achievements of various kinds.

## TEACHER EXPECTATIONS

"Set high goals," advises a corporate manager of training. "Men like to work for a successful leader. They like to be a part of an organization that's going places."[18] Effective executives and managers have long known the significance of expectations for behavior. Let people know that you expect high levels of achievement and you are much more likely to get those high levels of achievement. For when people know that a good deal is expected of them, they are much more likely to set high goals for themselves. Likert found that subordinates in a sales organization were unlikely to set high performance goals for themselves unless their superiors had high aspirations for each salesperson and for the organization.[19]

In schools, teacher expectations seem to have considerable effect upon student performance. In their noted study of a California school, Rosenthal and Jacobson found that the expectations of school teachers about the intellectual abilities of their students was reflected in the students' measured IQ scores. A student who was expected to do poorly tended to get low scores and vice versa.[20] The authors know one teacher who begins each new class by telling the students: "You probably don't know how to read, because you have never been taught how to read. And since you don't know how to read, many of you won't make it in this class." Such an attitude is unlikely to elicit much in the way of excellence from the students.

The teacher should set standards for each student, expecting each student to do his or her best. Students who are learning to write simple business letters or to fill out job applications can be expected to complete the assignment without a single spelling error, for example. The "excellence" of some students may be the mediocrity of others, but it is no less an achievement. Thus, the teacher's expectations are both general and particularistic. In general, the teacher expects the best from each student. In particular, what is best from various students will differ considerably. In order to fulfill this task, the teacher must be sensitive to and knowledgeable about each student. The teacher can get help from advisors, since he or she often has too many students to get to know each one sufficiently well.

## THE ADVISORY SYSTEM

In addition to helping teachers set high but realistic expectations for each student, the advisor in the participatory advisement system we have discussed plays a crucial role in motivating students to excellence by his or her personal relationship with advisees. In fact, the advisor is one of the school's primary means of communicating high expectations and helping each student make a realistic self-assessment and set significant, achievable goals.

The advisor can be a kind of mentor for each advisee, and the mentor relationship is often a critical aspect of an individual's development, particularly of those aspects of development that involve high aspirations and achievement. We recognize, of course, that a student's socioeconomic background, including family and friends, is strongly related to aspirations and achievement. Nevertheless, some students overcome the handicap of a deprived background. And even those who come from a more favorable background can be motivated to higher levels of achievement through their personal relationship with an advisor. As Robert Ellis has noted, the young person who is going to be upwardly mobile or is going to retain the favored status of his or her parents needs someone or a number of people who will serve four functions: a goad, a coach, an incentor, and a sponsor. The goad stimulates the young person to aspire to high positions. The coach helps the young person to gain the necessary skills. The incentor encourages the young person to continue his or her career and educational plans in spite of any obstacles and setbacks. And the sponsor can open doors which might be partially closed but which are necessary for the young person to achieve his or her aspirations.[21] An advisor can serve one or more of these functions for an advisee.

We would emphasize once again that the attainment of excellence means very different things for different students. The advisor is in a unique position to gauge the kind of excellence attainable by various advisees, and to help each advisee achieve his or her best even when the best is minimal by the standards of others. Consider the experience of a girl diagnosed as mildly mentally retarded who participated in a child development center as an aide. Reports from her supervisor indicated that she was very patient, expressed great warmth toward children and was exceedingly dependable. At the end of her semester experience she was awarded a certificate of achievement. The girl's advisor shared in her sense of accomplishment and sent a note of praise to the girl's parents. The entire family had a new sense of the girl's ability to make a contribution. The girl may never be able to secure a high school diploma, but she can still find areas in the school's program in which she can excel and have a sense of her own worth as an individual.

A related problem in which an advisor's knowledge and personal relationship with a student is invaluable, is the case where expectations have been set too high. A young person may fail to measure up to his or her parent's dreams, or even to his or her own expectations. A student may be disappointed because he is not a scholastic honor winner. Another may be disappointed because she is not meeting graduation requirements. In such cases, the advisor may plan a key role in reawakening some hope. Shattered expectations need to be replaced, not simply abandoned. They need to be replaced with more realistic expectations, in many cases. In conferences with defeated parents or students, an advisor can effect significant, positive changes. Sometimes this can be done by a simple act, namely, finding from the student's record or recent experience one positive indicator of the student's worth and talent. The indicator might be a test score that shows high ability in one particular area, or a positive report from the student's employer or supervisor in out-of-school learning, or a piece of work from a class that met high standards. Parents and students alike will respond quickly and positively when some sign of the student's worth and ability is given.

## EFFECTS OF REWARDING EXCELLENCE

Virtually any principal can talk about the effects of having a winning athletic team, particularly a championship team. Such a team has an impact on the school and the community. Everybody wants to be associated with winners and achievers. With a winning team, people can be heard talking about the record in various places in the community. School spirit and unity and community pride are all enhanced (and sometimes may plummet when the personnel of the team change and the winning ways no longer prevail).

What if this phenomenon were not limited to athletics? What if you could hear people proudly describing and associating themselves with other accomplishments? What would happen if the school were to recognize, reward, and publicize various other achievements, such as

a young woman who was selected to dance in the civic ballet,
the students who organized a volunteer clean-up campaign,
the students who won competitive scholarships to leading universities,
the choir selected to perform at a special occasion,
the young man who won a writing award in national competition, and
the student whose art work was selected for exhibit at a university?

Such achievements, and many more, can generate the same pride in the school as a winning team in some sport, and, in addition, will associate the name of the school with excellence.

In other words, an effective reward system has a number of important and desirable consequences. As we noted above, students are motivated to attain excellence. School spirit and pride are developed. The reputation of the school is enhanced in the community. Interpersonal relationships may improve because of the climate of achievement that is created.

Both the formal and informal reward mechanisms have positive consequences. For example, the praise of a teacher can motivate students, develop pride, and enhance the reputation of the school, and sometimes can accomplish all three at once. A metals teacher known to one of the authors has the habit of calling several students aside each time a visitor comes into the shop area. He shows the visitor the current work of the students and explains what techniques they are developing. The teacher displays an obvious pride in the students' work, always stressing what is being achieved. This attitude noticeably affects his students, who frequently stay after school hours to put the finishing touches on special projects. Each year, the teacher's students set up a display of their work in the school library. The displays have been judged by observers to range from very good to remarkable work. The teacher plays a vital role in setting high standards, providing for recognition of student achievement, and endowing the work of his students with dignity. For him and his students, metal working is a challenging and worthwhile activity that merits the goal of excellence.

The reward of excellence, then, should be a pervasive theme in a human organization, an informal as well as formal procedure. The formal aspect includes such things as public recognition, news releases and announcements, special assemblies, certificates and letter awards, honor awards of various kinds, and scholarships. The informal aspect occurs as achievements are praised and aspirations are established in advisement and in classrooms.

But if the reward of excellence is to be a pervasive theme rather than a sporadic affair, the principal must accept a major part of the responsibility for establishing and maintaining the reward system. The principal is the primary spokesperson for articulating the achievements of faculty and students to the school and the community. In addition, the principal should build the concept into the objectives of inservice training programs conducted for advisors and teachers. One useful activity in advisement team meetings and in departmental meetings is the sharing of "success" stories by staff members. For instance, an art teacher knew that a young girl in his print making class was having considerable turmoil at home. Her troubled relationships with her parents were reflected in her behavior at school; she grew increasingly depressed and hostile. The teacher recognized her artistic ability, and encouraged her each day to work on a particular design. She produced, in time, an excellent piece of work. The teacher showed the principal the design. The principal, in turn, requested a copy to hang in his office. The girl's response to this recognition was dramatic. She began to apply herself energetically to completing and framing two copies, one for the principal and one for her parents. The girl's gift to her parents was a gesture that opened up communication between them and between the parents and the school. The recognition and rewarding of an excellent piece of work stopped the process of degenerating relationships and established a basis for rebuilding.

An important element in this incident was the teacher's reputation for setting exacting standards. His recognition and praise was not a ploy to manipulate the girl; it was a genuine expression of his evaluation of her work. At the same time, the teacher was sensitive to the girl's situation and he seized the opportunity to reward her when she produced a work of excellence. By sharing the story with others, he helped stimulate greater efforts by his colleagues to encourage and reward excellence.

Athletes and scholars are important heroes in our society. But we need a greater variety of skills and achievements and personal qualities than those of the athlete and scholar. All kinds of excellence, therefore, should be identified and rewarded. The task of rewarding cannot be left to chance. It is a crucial element of a human organization, and the principal plays a vital role in the successful implementation of the reward system.

## EVALUATING THE REWARD SYSTEM

Every aspect of the human organization must be periodically evaluated. Both the formal and informal aspects of the reward system need to be evaluated to determine whether the system is indeed a pervasive theme and whether the varieties of excellence are being identified and rewarded. We would suggest three aspects of evaluation, as follows.

First, establish an IIC study group, as described in Chapter 6. The study group will be charged with gathering information on the reward system and making recommendations for improvement. Among other things, the study group should include recommendations for:

(1) using the media in the school and the community more effectively in order to recognize outstanding achievements;
(2) establishing a program to make full use of exhibit areas in the school and in the community for the display of student work;
(3) using the assembly program to recognize achievement and honors more adequately, and to give performing groups and individuals the opportunity to display their talents.

Second, administrators should review the school's inservice program to insure that activities are provided which allow the teachers and advisors opportunities to:

(1) understand the concept of rewarding excellence in a human organization and to identify its relationship to other activities and to school environmental concerns;

(2) set goals for the recognition and praise of student achievement as advisors, teachers, administrators, or counselors (including the critically important informal system of praise and reward); and

(3) develop methods and strategies for helping students to make realistic self-assessments and to set meaningful personal goals.

Third, administrators should periodically develop reports on the school's achievements. These reports should be given to the staff and to the community to develop pride in what was accomplished and to associate the school with the attainment of excellence. There should be a sufficient number of achievements in any school to make reports at least annually, and probably more often than that. As the reward system becomes more effective, the number of achievements should increase and the reports will become more frequent.

Earlier, we made the point that most people are quicker to criticize than to praise. One of the goals of evaluation is to help staff members to be as quick in praise as in criticism. Some people, perhaps most people, have the idea that excellence is its own reward. But very few of us have sufficient self-confidence or sufficient expertise to determine when we have achieved excellence. And even if we did, the lack of recognition and praise from those we value would quickly dull the sense of gratification. We are all social creatures. We all need recognition. We are all stimulated to further effort by recognition. Those who evaluate the reward system, therefore, should aim at the goal of insuring that each student receives his or her due.

## SUMMARY

All of us have a need for respect from others and for recognition of work we have done. The need for the recognition and rewarding of excellence seems to contradict our value on equality. Nevertheless, a school can simultaneously pursue both goals—equality and excellence—by broadening the range of activities in which excellence is recognized and rewarded.

The basis of the reward system is the recognition of diverse competencies. Students should be rewarded for nonacademic as well as academic achievements, and should be given every opportunity to find an area in which they can achieve excellence. This means that every group of students is recognized for achievement—the gifted, the academically distinguished, those skilled in arts and crafts, those who distinguish themselves in service projects, athletes, and so forth. In general, rewards should be a public affair.

Attention must also be paid to motivating students to excellence. The reward system itself will motivate. In addition, students need to have realistic opportunities for attaining excellence, high teacher expectations for performance, and an advisement system that provides each student with a mentor.

An effective reward system has important, positive consequences for the school. Students are motivated. School spirit and pride are developed. The school's reputation in the community is enhanced. And interpersonal relationships in the school may improve. In order to maintain an effective system, periodic evaluation is necessary.

# Endnotes

[1]The incident is related in Ingrid Bengis, "The World of the Secretary," *Mother Jones*, February/March, 1977, pp. 47–48.

[2]John W. Gardner, *Excellence* (New York: Harper & Row, 1961), p. 11.

[3]Denison Olmsted, "On the Democratic Tendencies of Science," in Thomas Parke Hughes, *Changing Attitudes Toward American Technology* (New York: Harper & Row, 1975), p. 144.

[4]Gardner, *op. cit.*, p. 12.

[5]Robin M. Williams, Jr., *American Society* (New York: Alfred A. Knopf, 1954), p. 390.

[6]*Ibid.*, p. 416.

[7]Gardner, *op. cit.*, pp. 74–75.

[8]Robert H. Lauer, *Social Problems and the Quality of Life* (Dubuque, Iowa: William C. Brown, 1978), p. 438.

[9]Gardner, *op. cit.*, p. 132.

[10]Fyodor Dostoyevsky, *The Brothers Karamazov*, trans. Constance Garnett (New York: The New American Library, 1957), p. 324.

[11]Gardner, *op. cit.*, p. 145.

[12]The material in the following paragraphs largely follows Barbara Pannwitt, "Lest the Gifted Be Unseen: Qualitatively Different Education," *NASSP Curriculum Report* 8 (December, 1978):1–4.

[13]Quoted in *ibid.*, p. 2.

[14]*Ibid.*, pp. 2–3.

[15]*Ibid.*, p. 4.

[16]*Recommendations, Composite Report of Forum Findings: Golden Anniversary White House Conference on Children and Youth* (Washington, D.C.: U.S. Government Printing Office, 1960), p. 23.

[17]Leonard Reissman, "Readiness to succeed: mobility aspirations and modernism among the poor," *Urban Affairs Quarterly* 4 (March, 1969): 379–95. See also Robert H. Lauer, "Unemployment: Hardcore or Hard Shell?" *Urban and Social Change Review* 6 (Fall, 1972): 7–10.

[18]Guy B. Ford, *Building a Winning Employee Team* (New York: American Management Association, 1964), p. 73.

[19]Rensis Likert, *The Human Organization* (New York: McGraw-Hill, 1967), p. 63.

[20]Robert Rosenthal and Lenore Jacobson, *Pygmalion in the Classroom* (New York: Holt, Rinehart & Winston, 1968). This study has been subjected to considerable criticism, and some efforts to replicate the results have failed to support them. Nevertheless, there is sufficient evidence about the effects of

276

expectations to insist upon their importance as a motivating factor. For an excellent discussion of some of the issues and the research see Theodore X. Barber, *Pitfalls in Human Research* (New York: Pergamon Press Inc., 1976).

[21]Robert A. Ellis, "Some New Perspectives on Upward Mobility," in Edward Z. Dager, ed., *Socialization* (Chicago: Markham, 1971), pp. 57–59.

# Chapter 9

# Space: The Architecture of a Human Organization

Why architecture? What does the building have to do with the creation and maintenance of a human organization? Why should a secondary administrator be concerned with such matters? The physical environment may be taken for granted until we are suddenly thrust into a setting where our senses are assaulted by the sights and smells of deterioration and deprivation. Consider, for instance, Jonathan Kozol's description of what it is like to walk into a ghetto school:

> You walk into a narrow and old wood-smelling classroom and you see before you thirty-five curious, cautious and untrusting children. . . . Nobody seems to know how many teachers they have had. Seven of their lifetime records are missing: symptomatic and emblematic at once of the chaos that has been with them all year long. . . . You check around the classroom. Of forty desks, five have tops with no hinges. You lift a desk-top to fetch a paper and you find that the top has fallen off. There are three windows. One cannot be opened. . . . The general look of the room is as of a bleak-light photograph of a mental hospital. Above the one poor blackboard, gray rather than really black, and hard to write on, hangs from one tack, lopsided, a motto attributed to Benjamin Franklin: "Well begun is half done." Everything, or almost everything like that, seems a mockery of itself.[1]

In such a situation, one very quickly becomes aware of the importance of the physical environment. Normally, however, the impact of the physical environment is more subtle, though not less important. We will begin our discussion of the architecture of the human organization, therefore, by looking at some of the effects of the physical environment which have been identified by researchers. This will provide the necessary background for examining some important architectural and spatial aspects of high schools.

## SIGNIFICANCE OF THE PHYSICAL ENVIRONMENT

We use the term "physical environment" in the same sense as environmental psychologists do—to indicate "the man-built or man-modified and the natural" environment of the individual.[2] Our concern will be only with the "man-built and man-modified" and not with the natural environment.

## THE PHYSICAL ENVIRONMENT AS MEANING

In the past few decades, a number of researchers have shown that the physical environment has meaning. That is, the environment is not merely a context in which behavior occurs but is an influence upon behavior because of certain meanings which it inevitably has. In an effort to ferret out the varied meanings of the built environment, researchers have looked at such things as architecture and spatial arrangements, and have concluded that directives for behavior lie in the physical environment. Speaking of both the built and the natural environment, Kevin Lynch argues that the environment has an impact that is similar to law and custom, for it

> tells us how to act without requiring of us a conscious choice. In a church we are reverent and on a beach relaxed. Much of the time, we are reenacting patterns of behavior associated with particular recognizable settings. A setting may encourage a behavior by its form—a staircase has a shape that is made for going up or down—but also by the expectations associated with it—until recently it was not seemly for adults to sit on stairs. When place changes rapidly, as in a migratory move, people no longer "know how to behave." They must expend effort to test and choose a new form of behavior and to build group agreement.[3]

As Lynch indicates, the meaning of the physical environment varies from one culture to another and among subcultures within a society. The cultural variation has been explored by the anthropologist,

Edward Hall, among others. According to Hall, there are four kinds of what he calls "informal space," each of which has a near and a far phase—intimate distance, personal distance, social distance, and public distance.[4] At intimate distance, "the presence of the other person is unmistakable and may at times be overwhelming." The close phase includes such things as love-making and wrestling while the far phase (6 to 18 inches) may occur in crowded public settings. Intimate distance typifies conversation among some peoples, but is considered inappropriate by most Americans. The other kinds of distance get progressively greater as we move from personal to public and characterize different kinds of interaction in different settings. The point Hall makes is that all animals, including humans, exhibit territoriality. "The specific distance chosen depends on the transaction; the relationship of the interacting individuals, how they feel, and what they are doing."[5] Furthermore, the specific distance chosen will vary by culture.

If cultural meanings attach to the spatial arrangements of people as they interact, they also attach to the aspects of the built environment that surround the interacting people. People may not be conscious of it, but they are influenced by such things as a building's layout, the appearance (including the aesthetic qualities) of a building, the arrangement of furniture and other furnishings in rooms, and the lighting and temperature. A teacher who worked in a relatively new and well-planned school spent a day in another high school in the district working on a special project. The teacher later reported that he had felt oppressed throughout the day without quite knowing why until it occurred to him that the halls were narrow and the classrooms in which he worked were windowless.

Before looking at some of the effects of particular aspects of the physical environment, we want to emphasize the point that we are not suggesting any deterministic impact of the environment. It may not be possible to avoid a sense of oppression in a badly designed building, but that does not mean that the teacher will work poorly or inefficiently. On the other hand, a well-designed building will not insure a productive and humane school. Sommer has argued for the spatial freedom of the open classroom, but notes that the spatial freedom itself will not guarantee educational innovation:

> Presented to an unsure and inadequate teacher, it will result in greater efforts at discipline in order to keep people together and "on the same track" once the fixed rows of chairs, which greatly aided in discipline, are eliminated. The spatial freedom will only help those teachers already committed to individual or small group instructions or willing to try it.[6]

## THE BUILDING AS ENVIRONMENT

One psychologist has scored architects for their failure to design buildings for people, arguing that poorly designed buildings "tend to produce frustrations and illnesses in the users. Those that are well designed tend to produce greater health and well-being."[7] Furthermore, he says, the building and its furnishings tell people something about their value and worth. People's self-esteem may be affected by the buildings in which they live and work. In one unemployment office, clients became less hostile after the reception and interviewing areas were carpeted. The carpeting suggested that the clients were viewed as people of worth and dignity. The new meaning provided by the alteration helped change the behavior.

All kinds of buildings have been studied in terms of their effects upon people, including individual homes, public housing units, hospitals, offices, apartments, and schools. In general, the studies support the idea that the design of a building will facilitate some kinds of behavior and inhibit some kinds, and may affect as well certain feelings and attitudes of those who occupy the building. A building may be very functional for one purpose but dysfunctional for another purpose. For example, inflation in recent years has led to the rise of a number of grocery stores that offer low prices by eliminating many of the "frills" of other stores. One purpose is achieved—lower prices. But another purpose—making shopping a pleasant experience—is lost. Some people refuse to shop in the stores in spite of the lower prices because they dislike the oppressive atmosphere.

Every aspect of the building can have meaning. Not only the general design, but the interior decoration also affects behavior and feelings. Studies have shown that people perceive the temperature of a room to change when the color is changed, even though the temperature actually remains the same. Thus, the color of a room, as well as the actual temperature, may bear upon the comfort of the occupants. In addition, color has been found to affect people's perceptions of such things as a room's spaciousness, complexity, and social status.[8] In one study, a hodometer, which measures where people go in a room and the time they spend in varying locations within the room, was used to test the effects of two different colors.[9] The room was located in a museum. For one part of the study, the carpet and walls were light beige, while for the other part they were chocolate colored. When the room was beige, people who came into the room explored less (in the sense that they used less of the floor space as measured by the hodometer). When the room was chocolate, however, people took more steps and covered almost twice as much of the room's area, but spent less time in the room.

Color combines with the so-called "ambient" environment of a room (noise, temperature, odor, and lighting) to make the room a desirable, neutral, or undesirable place for people. "The ambient conditions required for satisfaction and appreciation vary from room to room because they are a function of the purpose for which a room was designed. Thus, depending on the purpose of a particular room, different aspects of the ambient environment can be manipulated to produce an atmosphere that, in turn, will elicit the desired behavioral state in the occupants of the room."[10]

We have already offered one caveat, namely, that the physical environment is not deterministic. Now we will offer another: our knowledge of the effects of the physical environment and, in particular, of buildings and their furnishings, is not as precise as the above discussion might suggest. It is not yet possible to say to an architect, "Design a building in which every student and staff member will feel optimally comfortable at whatever tasks they are engaged in." The effects of the physical environment intersect with those of the social environment, and different people will react somewhat differently to the same physical environment. Nevertheless, we know enough to be able to say that administrators who are concerned to build a human organization cannot ignore the physical environment with impunity. The design, decoration, and furnishings of the organization's building can facilitate or impede the goals of the human organization.

## SPATIAL ARRANGEMENTS AS ENVIRONMENT

It is not merely the kind but the arrangement of furnishings that affects our behavior and feelings. A number of studies have investigated the effects of seating arrangements on interaction. Sommer notes that most airport terminal buildings have seating arrangements that make it virtually impossible for two people to converse comfortably for any length of time. In fact, he says, terminals are "perhaps the most sociofugal public places in American society."[11] (Sociofugal arrangements impel people toward a room's periphery, whereas sociopetal arrangements tend to bring people together into the room's center.) The reason is simple—"to drive people out of the waiting areas into cafes, bars, and shops where they will spend money."[12]

Sommer himself set up a number of experiments in which he investigated the seating preferences of people who are conversing. First, he asked subjects to sit on two couches in a lounge and discuss a particular topic. The couches were positioned to face each other at varying distances. The people preferred to sit across from each other until the couches were more than three feet apart, when they preferred to sit together on one couch. In a follow-up study, he used chairs instead of couches. Subjects tended to prefer to sit across from each other as long as the distance was equal to or less than the distance between adjacent chairs.

The point is that even if spatial arrangements do not preclude people from engaging in certain activity, they may make that activity less comfortable. As in the case of seats in airports, however, the tendency is not to make an activity more or less comfortable but to affect the kind of activity that occurs. As Duncan Joiner has pointed out, "there are many examples of formal situations where spatial relationships are used to reinforce social distinctions and to mould the kinds of social interaction to be expected within the spaces."[13] Joiner provides the example of office space which conveys at least two kinds of information—information about the office's occupant and information about how that occupant would like visitors in the office to behave. For example, the arrangement of a desk in the office tends to divide the room into private and public zones, as shown in Figure 9.1. Furthermore, the desk may act as a barrier between the occupant and visitors or may be arranged, along with other furniture, so that no physical barriers exist between people in the office. A more formal atmosphere is suggested by a desk set up as a barrier (Fig. 9.1, A and C), while such arrangements as those shown in Figure 9.1, B and D, suggest that the occupant of the office will interact more informally with visitors. Some doctors who were concerned about breaking down the formality (and anxiety) in their relationships with their patients dealt with the problem by arranging that patients would approach the physician from the side and sit by his side during their conversation.[14]

Other aspects of the office also contribute to the sense of formality or informality of the interaction. Moreover, such things as the size and interior decoration of the office may be related to the status of the occupant. Since space is not unlimited, its allocation can be a form of reward (and lack of reward). In general, then,

> office spaces are used and organized in a way which establishes interaction boundaries, sets the pattern of interaction with which the occupant expects visitors to comply and fosters impressions about the role and status of the occupant in his organization.[15]

We would only add that office spaces may also tell visitors something about their worth and value (as in the case of the clients of the unemployment office that we noted above).

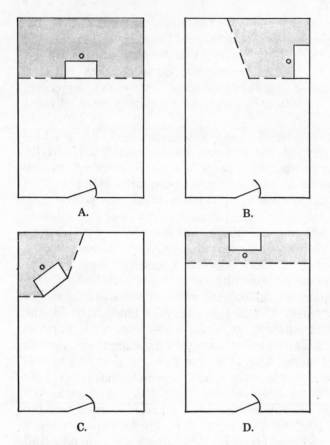

**Figure 9.1**
Private (shaded) and Public Areas of Offices with Varying Desk Positions

## THE HIGH SCHOOL AS PHYSICAL ENVIRONMENT

Our examples in the preceding section have been largely from non-school settings because the research has tended to focus more on such settings. Nevertheless, the principles apply to schools. That is, the high-school building, including its design and its furnishings, is a physical environment. As such, it has the various kinds of effects discussed above. Getzels, although speaking primarily about the elementary schoolroom, expresses well the impact of the school as a physical environment:

The classrooms we envision for our children represent not only conceptions of spaces for learning but also our conceptions of the learner. . . . The classrooms we build for our children are not only places where the lessons intended by the teacher are taught. These classrooms teach lessons of their own; they tell the child who he is supposed to be (or at least who we think he is) and how he is supposed to learn.[16]

Getzels goes on to say that one kind of classroom may tell a child that he or she is "an empty organism" who learns by the commands of the teacher through the dispensing of rewards and punishments. Another kind of classroom may tell the child that he or she is "an active organism learning through the solution of problems that satisfy his needs." Other classrooms tell children that they are basically social creatures who learn through interaction or that they are stimulus-seeking creatures who learn because of an intrinsic need to learn.

In other words, the school, like any other building, is not a neutral place in which activity occurs, but a physical environment that helps shape the behavior or the activities that occur within it. Unfortunately, too many of the schools that we have inherited (that is, that were built long before we ourselves made use of them) and too many schools still being built seem out of touch with the needs, feelings, and experiences of adolescents. In particular, many schools imply in their organization and in their specific arrangements of rooms and furniture that high-school students cannot be trusted, that students are not respected as persons with needs and feelings, and that students are not ready to be responsible for some of their own learning. Rather than promoting personal growth, these physical structures inflict control, limit privacy, make social activity difficult, and restrict learning patterns by imposing uniformity in classroom spaces and arrangements. In the early part of the 19th century, the English system of "batch-process education" was introduced into the United States. "A batch of students, fastened to a teacher, in a box, established itself as the norm for the next hundred years, and the configuration of school buildings became set in a rigid mold that is now as familiar and American as Thanksgiving turkey."[17]

As rapid changes have occurred in society over the past few decades, the roles of teachers and learners have also changed. With the knowledge explosion, teachers have become less and less the dispensers of information. Few teachers feel comfortable with the old philosophy of "you sit still, while I instill." Students must participate in their own learning. Most important, they must be taught how to learn. That is, they become self educators. But the schools we have inherited are in many ways incongruous with new educational patterns. In 1970, the administrators of nearly a third of the 700 large high schools surveyed were "substantially constrained from designing new programs because of limitations in their physical facilities."[18]

As given, then, many of our buildings are nonadaptive (note that we do not say "unadaptable") for new programs, and may be unresponsive to the various needs of adolescents. One teenager eloquently described this kind of problem:

> The very nature of the high school is dour and unpleasant and seems to invite destruction. Whether it is old or new, its floors are most often tiled, its halls are usually beige or pink or tan or gray or light green. It may be lined with that coldly evil ceramic brick.... The classrooms are arranged as tightly as a baseball diamond: one large desk facing 30 small ones. As the new protective measures are put into effect the schools being to look and function more and more like early industrial revolution factories.[19]

The student goes on to suggest that many students feel that the schools cannot be changed and that some will use vandalism as a way of "forcibly stopping the educational machine."

The above observations should be carefully considered by anyone who feels that students rarely notice or care about the buildings in which they learn. Furthermore, the sterile and gray school building will seem equally dull and unaccommodating to the teachers and administrators who work in them. Yet the physical environment of education, as depressing as it often is, too often is accepted as a given. It is perceived to be implacable by those who work in it. It may even form a rationale for why the school is not a better place in which to learn. Instead, the building should be viewed as an element which can be changed, as a tool or resource for attaining educational goals.

In the case of a new building, of course, the administration faces a challenging opportunity to create a physical environment that optimizes learning. The opportunity will be lost unless careful thought and planning are given to the task. Educational specifications for school buildings are extensive and detailed but limited to sheer housing and functional considerations. The educator's input to planning facilities and spaces typically consists of facts determining square footage needed for instructional areas, statements about program relationships bearing especially on desired proximity, descriptions of some particular teaching methods and their requirements, and similar practical or technical elements.

For example, Anderson and Van Dyke show the educational specifications for a mathematics-science classroom.[20] The specifications contain ten different sections. The first is a general description of the space, including subjects taught and grade levels. The second discusses the functions of the space, including purposes and types of activities. The third outlines some general design considerations such as size and shape, type and arrangement of seating, and lighting and acoustics. The remaining sections, shorter than the first three, are these: any special design considerations such as safety and health; utilities; special needs in the space such as lighting, windows, or waste disposal facilities; chalkboards, tackboards, and other means for displaying materials; furniture and equipment; storage; and any additional information needed by the architect.

Anderson and Van Dyke also offer eight "miscellaneous suggestions" for the principal who is involved in planning a school building, including preparing a dummy schedule of classes, securing information about new instructional materials and equipment, visiting other high schools to observe their facilities, preparing a chart of interrelationships between various departments and teachers, and so forth.[21] These are excellent suggestions. We do not intend to minimize their importance, nor the significant role that administrators must play in specifying the technical and functional considerations of the physical plant. Nevertheless, we know enough about the impact of the physical environment to say that if nothing more is done, administrators have not fulfilled their total responsibility. The educational specifications must include the social and psychological requirements of the building as well as the functional and technical matters.

In the next sections, we will examine the social and psychological elements in terms of certain themes that characterize a humane high school. Many of the ideas we will discuss will relate to instructional effectiveness and efficiency. But most will relate to the "feeling" aspects of the school building, aspects that bear upon the developmental and human needs of the school's occupants. Our discussion will apply to both the planning of new facilities and the renovation or alteration of old facilities. Obviously, inherited facilities do not allow the options which are open to planners of new buildings, but the old facility is not implacable or "unforgiving" (see below). Dramatic effects can sometimes be achieved with old facilities through relatively inexpensive and creative use of color, wall space, graphic design, and the arrangement of furnishings. The point is that adopting the goals of a human organization should include careful consideration of the impact of the physical plant. The goals of a human organization can be facilitated or impeded by the design and use of buildings and space:

> ... in some kinds of design such as the design of jobs and games, we can speak of actualizability. ... A "rich" game like bridge, poker or chess challenges and rewards the novice or the expert. Can spaces lead to actualization? Permit it?[22]

## ARCHITECTURAL AND SPATIAL THEMES IN A HIGH SCHOOL

We would not presume to design anyone's building. As with other programs we have discussed, any design must be adapted to the local situation. Our emphasis throughout has been on the ideals and goals of a human organization, and we have shown the kinds of programs and policies that can achieve those ideals and goals. Here we shall follow the same procedure. We will discuss the architectural and spatial themes that are harmonious with a human organization and we will provide some illustrations from particular high schools. As noted above, it is important to keep in mind that the discussion refers to the restructuring or remodeling of old buildings as well as to the design of new buildings. Some exciting things have been done with older buildings. In fact, older buildings offer possibilities that are not even economically feasible with a newer structure. The age of the building does not preclude the administrator from creating a physical environment compatible with a human organization.

## INTERACTION

Students are not mere receptacles, to be bussed in and stuffed with information each day. Students are developing social creatures, who learn and grow through their relationships with others. One theme of the humane high school, therefore, is interaction. That is, the opportunities for student-to-student and student-to-teacher interaction should be maximized. Various architectural and spatial arrangements can facilitate such interaction.

We believe that schools should legitimate interaction by providing places and times for students to meet, to talk, to listen, and to explore and practice the ways that people learn to get along with each other:

> The development of social skills depends, among other things, on gaining a growing network of *one-to-one* meetings. As an individual one cannot meet a crowd, an entire class, a whole school. That first step of strangers saying hello is a delicate one. It requires time and the right circumstances. . . . In schools there is much talk but little dialogue.[23]

Some of the efforts to develop social skills among students occurs in the classroom and in extra-curricular activities. But much can occur

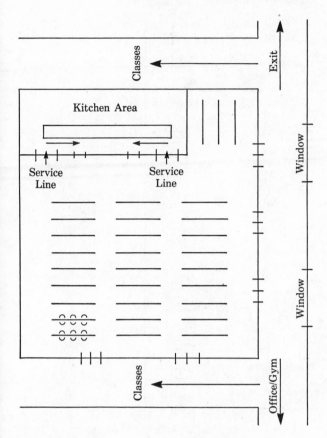

**Figure 9.2**
A Formal, Controlled Cafeteria Space

throughout the day whenever opportunity and time allows if spaces are provided that facilitates one-to-one and small group conversation.

As an example of a space designed to promote meeting and talking, consider the cafeteria. Figure 9.2 shows a cafeteria that will maximize seating efficiency and the control of movement. The seating is all of one type—rectangular tables for groups of four to eight, uniformly placed to prescribe traffic and service lines. In one school, this space was given a dramatically different look and feel by removing the walls into the hallway and by using a variety of seating arrangements. Since the halls led to other public facilities and the cafeteria was in a zone designed for noisier, public activities, the removal of the wall presented

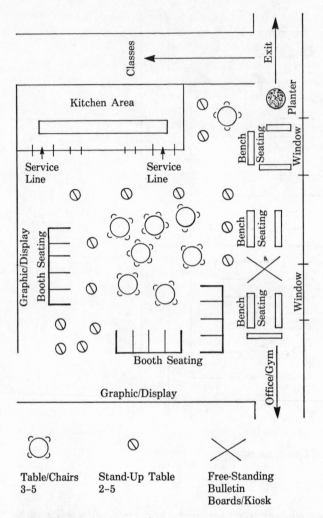

**Figure 9.3**
Cafeteria Space Designed to Maximize Interaction

no serious problems. The final design, shown in Figure 9.3, achieved a number of goals:

1. The space creates much more visual interest through its size, its variety of furnishings, and its wider vista (including the view outside).
2. The variety of seating and talking places encourages circulation and freedom of movement. Students have options in this space,

room to negotiate and explore social relationships more easily. Shopping malls have become popular social centers for teenagers for many of the same reasons—a place to gather, a place to move from one conversation to another, and a place to stand and view the social scene. The stand-up tables in particular provide a greater sense of freedom to some students. Most of the seating, with the possible exception of the booths, offers greater flexibility both in the variety of social groupings possible and in options available to a single student in a short period of time. If they choose, students in this setting can move from group to group very naturally because circulation is integrated with the furniture and the furniture itself is more approachable. Groups around tables will grow and diminish in size within short time intervals. The other design (Figure 9.2) implies rigidity, restricted movement, and little choice of seating arrangements or of group size.

3. Faculty supervision is less obtrusive in this environment and more likely to become part of the social interaction.
4. The effect of the arrangement is that students are told that a high value is placed on the social functions of the school. In particular, student interaction is valued and students are encouraged to interact in a pleasant atmosphere.

The promotion of social skills as achieved by the cafeteria can be done in other spaces as well. The effective classroom teacher can encourage students to work together, to evaluate each other's opinions and work. The sensitive teacher continually rearranges classroom furniture as activity changes, letting the desk arrangement suggest the kind of interaction expected during a particular time. Teachers' fears of losing control will inhibit flexibility and cause the retention of a formality and constraint in the classroom that can prevent the free expression of ideas and meaningful dialogue among students. Such fears are often based on a realistic appraisal of a particular situation, of course. But as the school becomes a human organization, as students develop self-discipline and accept their responsibility for a good learning environment, teachers can use spatial arrangements to allow considerable flexibility in the kinds of interaction that take place in the classroom.

With respect to interaction between students and teachers and other staff members, we have noted a number of ways in which a school's structure can provide such interaction. We also pointed to the need for setting apart space as well as time for such interaction. Here we want to emphasize the importance of another kind of student-teacher interaction, namely, the interaction in the classroom. The effective teacher will encourage the expression of opinions, speculation, and disagreement as well as questions. Many teachers, of course, value classroom dialogue with their students, but most are probably not aware of how classroom spatial arrangements bear upon the probability of student participation.

For many years, a number of different observers have argued that the traditional row-and-column seating arrangement in the classroom may inhibit maximum student participation and satisfaction. Now, however, we have experimental evidence to support the argument. For instance, Koneya looked at the effects of row-and-column seating arrangements on high, moderate, and low verbalizers.[24] He found a "triangle of centrality" that accounted for most student verbalizations. Furthermore, given a choice, students who were high verbalizers (that is, who tended to speak frequently in small group discussions) tended to choose central seats in a row-and-column arrangement. And both moderate and high verbalizers had higher verbalization rates when they were placed in central seats than when they were placed in noncentral seats. An implication of the experiment, notes Koneya, "is that there is a chance that individuals with 'moderate' and 'high' verbalization inclinations may be involuntarily excluded from or included in the interaction of a large group in row-and-column seating by virtue of their location at times contrary to their intentions."[25]

This is not to say that row-and-column seating is always inappropriate, but to point out that the teacher can use a variety of arrangements for differing purposes. Teachers need to be aware of the effects that diverse arrangements are likely to have. If participation is desired, circular seating will maximize that participation. If listening to a lecture is in order, row-and-column seating may be preferable. Spatial arrangements affect interaction independently of students' normal inclinations. One of the authors recalls (with a shudder) a high school teacher who insisted on minimizing or eliminating interaction between students in her classroom. She achieved this quite well by the simple expedient of a row-and-column seating arrangement with all desks facing away from her desk. She was behind every student every day, and each one knew that she could detect the slightest sideways movement of a head. The students in her room were not inclined under normal circumstances to ignore each other, but they largely did so in her class. Her arrangement also minimized interaction between herself and her students, for no one spoke until spoken to by the teacher. She worked some years before the social psychological studies of space began, but she knew and applied the principles to achieve her ends. Fortunately, those who prefer other ends can also use the principles.

## PARTICIPATION

Participation by all parties has been a continuing theme in this book. The theme should continue in architectural and spatial considerations. If new facilities are being planned, participation should be incorporated into the planning. As Holt has said, "most enlightened planners" will agree that students, parents, and community residents should be involved in the life of the school, including the planning of a new building.[26] One way to get broad participation in planning a new facility is the "charrette," a number of which have been supported by federal funds. (Holt defines charrette as an "intensive group planning effort"—Ed.) In the charrette, the majority of participants are community residents. Community leaders guide multidisciplinary groups (educators, architects, public officials, students, businesspeople, etc.) in an intensive study of community problems in an open public forum. "Primary emphasis is given to educational facility and program as the natural catalyst for revitalization of the total community."[27] The charrette was used, for instance, in East Baltimore in 1969. Participants were supposed to concentrate on a new high school but

> discussions soon spread to an analysis of total community needs, and the high school was viewed as a focal point for a neighborhood center which might encompass the following: family health center, neighborhood city hall, creative arts and recreation center, restaurant, movie theatre, bank, pharmacy, bookstore, supermarket, childcare center, and possible housing for staff and students.[28]

Some of the ideas were not legally feasible as long as educational funds had to be used. But a HUD grant allowed some nonschool elements to be accepted, so that "the completed project will be a true neighborhood center with day-care facilities, city hall, job-placement center—all with the high school as its nucleus."[29]

The novel ideas that emerged from the East Baltimore charrette illustrate once again the creative potential of the participatory process. But, granted the many benefits of a participatory organization, how can the completed or remodeled building contribute to participation? In essence, the interior of the building can invite students to participate in various activities (including interaction with other students) and students can help create such an inviting atmosphere. Thus, a self-sustaining process is created: students participate in creating the kind of environment that encourages further participation.

A student responded to the cafeteria shown in Figure 9.3 by remarking that it was cosmopolitan and fascinating—like an airport terminal. He was not responding merely to the large amount of space or to the arrangement of furnishings. Rather, he was struck by the overall impression given by the area. The cafeteria was rich in information in terms of access to graphics and to a variety of social interaction. The graphics were the result of an emphasis on student use of the remaining wall space for designs, posters, and signs. Also, bold colors and live plants were used to communicate a warm and inviting atmosphere (again, note that these are elements associated with modern shopping malls). Incidentally, the school uses live plants liberally in its library and instructional areas as well as in the cafeteria. Sometimes a visitor will express surprise that the plants have been able to thrive for six or more years in the school. Similarly, student work on display is not vandalized. The school is not free of vandalism, but the vandalism that occurs is directed toward more institutional items like bathroom stalls and not at plants or student work that is publicly displayed.

The development of wall space for display and the free-standing bulletin boards (kiosks) in the cafeteria illustrate a most important aspect of the interior—the development of spaces that invite use, display, and expression. In classrooms, halls, libraries, and cafeterias a visitor should find extensive evidence that the spaces are occupied by productive users. The participation of students in creating an inviting environment is crucial. It not only encourages further participation in activities, but also shows that the school values and desires to preserve student work. On the other hand, having students do work and then throwing it away teaches them that we have a low regard for their achievements. Whatever a student creates may have considerable personal value to that student and may be an important part of that student's self-evaluation. One art teacher we know insists that each of his students prepare at least one object for display. This is an excellent way to develop a sense of self-esteem and achievement in students. Of course, the school administrators must recognize the importance of such practices and insure the availability of space for the display.

In sum, the school's interior should invite students to participate in various activities. A library can be arranged to invite, or to discourage, students to browse and read. A cafeteria can be arranged to invite, or to discourage, interaction and movement. The availability of space for the display of student work encourages that work and places students in an environment that they have helped to create. In these and other ways, the theme of participation can be affected by architectural and spatial arrangements.

## FLEXIBILITY AND FORGIVENESS

No one can confidently predict the course of education in the future. We need, therefore, to be able to adapt our facilities to new methods and new ideas. We need flexibility. And we need to be able to change our minds and change our facilities. "The unpredictable nature of our future needs requires a forgiving behavior in facility design."[30]

An important form of flexibility is the provision of a variety of spaces—spaces that accommodate one-to-one activity, small groups, groups of 20 or 30, and assemblies of varying sizes. One of the biggest problems with the typically designed eggcrate school with the uniform classrooms for groups of 20 or 30 students and one teacher is that there are few negotiable options. Even if instruction is generally organized on a 25 to one basis, teachers and students may generate needs for varying kinds of space.

It is possible, of course, to carry flexibility to the extreme, producing a plan that is not really appropriate for any specific activity. As Sommer pointed out:

> The architect who tries to serve all masters may serve none well. The high school auditorium that must serve as a gymnasium, dance hall, and theater is likely to fail in all capacities. There is a point at which the price of flexibility is too high in terms of functional efficiency. Since teaching methods are changing, and it is difficult to forecast where things are going, the best alternative to infinite flexibility and "loose-fitting space" is to provide for many different sorts of space so that a new activity can be accommodated somewhere within the existing structure.[31]

The attempt to be totally flexible has occurred in some buildings which were essentially wraps or coverings of large, open spaces that users were not prepared or equipped to negotiate. In some instances, the areas have been "landscaped" with furnishings, panel systems for visual and some acoustical treatment, plants, and graphics. In spite of the landscaping, the openness can present unresolved sound problems, problems intensified by the inability of a large number of people to cooperatively control various interferences. Furniture and panel systems are most effective in providing visual privacy and in defining territory in functional terms. One-to-one and small group activities are accommodated more effectively in open, landscaped areas. Problems arise when larger groups are negotiating the use of an area. For example, a teacher who speaks loud enough to be heard by 30 is likely to be an interference for other groups in the area, particularly if there are other groups of equal size. While two groups might easily adjust to each other in one area and even learn to take advantage of the flexibility and options available in it, more than two begin to have trouble controlling or negotiating each other's noise.

There are exceptions to the above critique. Larger open spaces seem to be quite effective in areas of art instruction, for instance. In fact, art instruction is greatly enriched when students of different abilities and students who are exploring different media can see each other work. Observing the process and the product of other kinds of work is an effective learning mechanism in art.

Flexibility is important, then, but it can be overdone. The kind of flexibility needed is that provided by a variety of spaces of different sizes, not that of the "wrapped space" type of building. "Forgiveness" is also a form of flexibility. It relates to the capacity of the user to change the use of some spaces from that for which they were originally designed. The facility "forgives" the designer or planner of his or her original intent. In one school, for example, the planners placed the large open library in the heart of the building and idealistically arranged the space so that normal traffic circulation and the book collection itself were integrated. The books were on open stacks throughout the large area with several entrances and exits. After about a year it was evident that spreading the stacks across a large area was not workable for a number of reasons:

1. The library user found it inefficient to use the stacks.
2. The stacks were so spread out that users were often finding it inconvenient to return books to shelves or report to the check-out counter.
3. The amount of space was so great that the library staff was not able to be sufficiently accessible to help students or to supervise library work.

The problem was resolved by pulling stacks into the least exposed portion of the space, condensing the collection into one efficient and usable area. The librarians moved their desks into the open areas immediately adjacent to the stacks in order to be accessible to students and teachers. A check-out station was placed conveniently near the stacks. A large portion of the space, that intersected by traffic, was furnished for study spaces for individuals and small groups. The remainder of the area was converted to a counseling/advisement center (it was one of the few areas in the school large enough to bring both functions together). The new arrangement works extremely well for each of the activities. In fact, the entire area looks as if it were designed that way. The original idea was a good one, but it turned out to be impractical. The school's administrators, fortunately, did not view architectural mistakes as irreversible. They forgave the original and unworkable intent, capitalized on the flexibility of the space, and created area for a variety of activities.

## AESTHETIC PLEASANTNESS

There is concern in a human organization to maximize the well-being of all participants. Maximal well-being demands a concern for aesthetic pleasantness. As Bennett has argued, in designing spaces for people one must be concerned always about four factors: health and safety, effects on performance, comfort, and aesthetic pleasantness.[32] There is some experimental evidence that performance is affected by the pleasantness or unpleasantness of the physical environment and that people can easily evaluate the attractiveness of their environment. But while various studies show how people react, "they do not tell the designer what to do. 'Spaces evaluated highly are pleasant, beautiful, interesting, and exciting. So how do I achieve these things?' "[33]

Obviously, the question cannot be answered with certainty at this point. But we have suggested a number of things which we believe will contribute to the aesthetic pleasantness of the physical environment:

(1) the use of bright colors and avoidance of dull, repetitive grays or greens associated with cold institutions;

(2) the use of graphics throughout a building to denote function and direction as well as to create interest;

(3) the use of live plants in various areas such as classrooms, halls, library, and cafeteria;

(4) the use of displays and exhibits in all appropriate spaces (most of which should be student work);

(5) furnishings that invite use and don't simply become ugly with use (e.g., occasional use of soft elements as contrasted with the sterile ceramic tile look that is indestructible but uninviting);

(6) provision of flexible spaces which can be manipulated and personalized to a degree so that they reflect the individuals and groups that use them.

Aesthetic pleasantness is tied up with the feeling that you belong in a space and the space belongs to you. It is a space, ideally, that you have helped to create so that it fits your needs and reflects your individuality. Thus, orderliness but not uniformity is one goal of various spaces such as art labs, classrooms, science areas, and library seating arrangements. In one school, a group of gifted students and their teacher were provided with a small, unfurnished area in the library for their meeting place. The group was permitted to furnish and decorate the area with any items they could find in the school that were not in use already and did not belong to others. The students created an area out of broken, cast-off furniture, posters, live plants, and creative bulletin boards that became a favorite space in the school. Many students enjoyed "looking in." It was a space at once unique and personal, warm and friendly. It was an area that belonged to that group of students and reflected the needs and individuality of each of them.

As the above example suggests, aesthetic pleasantness does not necessarily demand a good deal of money. And recycled space, particularly when students participate in the recycling, may have more aesthetic pleasantness to students than built space. In New York City, an alternative high school was created out of an old printing plant at about one-fourth the cost of a new building. Students began attending within six months from the time of the initial planning:

> And attendance, incidentally, is at a 70 percent level; a triumph, considering that the school's population is composed of drop-outs and push-outs from the city's regular high schools—but not a surprising one to the school's planners, who assert that the conventional school building is often counterproductive functionally and psychologically. In contrast, these recycled schools—perhaps because no one is guarding them as community monuments—are freer, more relaxed, more human.[34]

## A CONCLUDING COMMENT

Form and function are closely related. If one agrees that the high school should adopt the goals of a human organization (the *what* of the school), it follows that the physical environment (the *where*) should also be a matter of concern. The physical environment can facilitate or impede the ideals and goals of the human organization. In a 1972 conference that brought architects and educators together it was discovered that both groups "wanted buildings that would be less awesome, less forbidding, freer. Above all, they were both seeking to create space or place or school as a climate for diversity, for trust, for engagement with people and the pleasures of the mind."[35] We agree with the goals, and believe that the goals can be achieved by attending to the themes discussed above.

## SUMMARY

The physical environment has an impact upon human behavior. School administrators must not overlook the importance of the environment they are providing for students. A major part of the environment is the building in which people must function. A building's design can facilitate some kinds of behavior and inhibit others, and can also affect feelings and attitudes. The building's furnishings and the spatial arrangements within the building also influence behavior and feelings.

"Batch-process education" earlier in our history resulted in buildings which are, in many ways, dysfunctional to contemporary education. Students do notice and care about their physical environment. The contemporary administrator faces the challenge, therefore, of providing an optimum environment. To respond adequately to the challenge, the administrator should think of the school in terms of certain architectural and spatial themes that are congruent with a human organization. These themes can be expressed in terms of four key terms: interaction, participation, flexibility/forgiveness, and aesthetic pleasantness.

# Endnotes

[1]Jonathan Kozol, *Death At An Early Age* (New York: Bantam Books, 1967), pp. 190–91.

[2]Norman W. Heimstra and Leslie H. McFarling, *Environmental Psychology* (Monterey, Calif.: Brooks/Cole, 1974), p. 5.

[3]Kevin Lynch, *What Time Is This Place?* (Cambridge, Mass.: The MIT Press, 1972), p. 40.

[4]Edward T. Hall, *The Hidden Dimension* (Garden City: Anchor Books, 1966), pp. 113–29.

[5]*Ibid.*, p. 128.

[6]Robert Sommer, *Personal Space* (Englewood Cliffs: Prentice-Hall, 1969), p. 105.

[7]Calvin W. Taylor, quoted in *Intellect* 106 (September, 1977):101.

[8]Heimstra and McFarling, *op. cit.*, p. 31.

[9]*Ibid.*, p. 32.

[10]*Ibid.*, pp. 33–34.

[11]Sommer, *op. cit.*, p. 121.

[12]*Ibid.*, pp. 121–22.

[13]Duncan Joiner, "Social Ritual and Architectural Space," in Harold M. Proshansky, William H. Ittelson, and Leanne G. Rivlin, eds., *Environmental Psychology*, 2nd edition (New York: Holt, Rinehart and Winston, 1976), p. 224.

[14]*Ibid.*, p. 227.

[15]*Ibid.*, p. 229.

[16]J. W. Getzels, "Images of the Classroom and Visions of the Learner," *School Review* 82 (August, 1974):537–38.

[17]Robert Propst, *High School: The Process and the Place* (New York: Educational Facilities Laboratories, 1972), p. 11.

[18]*Ibid.*, p. 12.

[19]*Ibid.*, p. 14.

[20]Lester W. Anderson and Lauren A. Van Dyke, *Secondary School Administration*, 2nd edition (Boston: Houghton Mifflin, 1972), pp. 505–511.

[21]*Ibid.*, pp. 511–13.

[22]Corwin Bennett, *Spaces For People: Human Factors in Design* (Englewood Cliffs: Prentice-Hall, Inc., 1977), p. 20.

[23]Propst, *op. cit.*, p. 39.

[24]Mele Koneya, "Location and Interaction in Row-and-Column Seating Arrangements," *Environment and Behavior* 8 (June, 1976):265–82.

[25]*Ibid.*, p. 281.

[26]James Holt, "Involving the Users in School Planning," *School Review* 82 (August, 1974):709.

[27]*Ibid.*, p. 715. See pp. 717f for some other methods of involving the users in the planning.

[28]*Ibid.*

[29]*Ibid.*

[30]Propst, *op. cit.*, p. 34.

[31]Sommer, *op. cit.*, p. 108

[32]Bennet, *op. cit.*, pp. 11–23.

[33]*Ibid.*, p. 17.

[34]Ruth Weinstock, *The Greening of the High School* (New York: Educational Facilities Laboratories, 1973), p. 52.

[35]*Ibid.*, p. 49.

# Envoi

In a play called "The Black Stranger" the Irish government has set men to work digging roads. Road building is a sign of vitality in a society. It suggests that the outcome of the hard work of construction will be a new level of prosperity. But in this case, the digging of roads is occurring in the midst of the famine of the mid-nineteenth century. In desperation, having no other solution in mind, the government has decided on the road-building project without having any purpose or destination for the roads. One young man discovers this, and says to his father in despair, "They're makin' roads that lead to nowhere."

The incident is a kind of parable of educational innovations over the past decades. There has been a lot of activity, and the activity could have suggested a new vitality and new levels of effectiveness. But to many observers, it seems that it was just a building of roads that led nowhere. Educational innovation seems peculiarly prone to failure. A sociologist says that educators "have been perhaps the most successful professional group in avoiding modern technology," and he quotes as support the conclusions of some Stanford professors:

In the early 1920's, shortly after radio broadcasting was proved to be economically feasible, Robert Hutchins is said to have predicted that this new technology would undoubtedly have a dramatic impact on education. Subsequent events have shown that his assessment of the educational potential of radio was probably correct but, for a variety of reasons, the potential did not materialize. In the early 1950's instructional television was introduced with a similar fanfare. However, with a few notable exceptions, its potential also failed to materialize. It seems that more recent innovations such as computer-aided instruction and satellite-based educational delivery may come to a similar fate. Why is it that these technological aids to education seldom seem to live up to their potential?[1]

The criticism has been leveled in popular articles as well as in the professional literature. In December, 1978, an article entitled "Remember those bold ideas to improve schools? What happened?" appeared in a popular magazine. The article begins by pointing out that there are many ideas for dealing with the problems of American schools:

But change doesn't come easily. Innovations often surface with great fanfare and promise, occupy our attention for awhile, then seem to sink without much trace.[2]

The article proceeds to discuss some of the pitfalls encountered in a variety of recent innovations, including computer-assisted instruction, vouchers, open-space schools, and performance contracting.

The kind of school we have described is innovative. Is this just more fanfare? Is this one more innovative scheme that will ultimately be thrown into the educational graveyard of impractical ideas? Obviously, we believe that the answer to such questions is "no." But we would like to buttress our answer by making three important points in these concluding pages.

First, the kind of school we have described is idealistic, but it is not unrealistic. We have not presented a utopian scheme. We have, perhaps, laid considerable stress upon the value of such a school and upon the benefits to be gained by all participating groups. But we have also noted that the school that strives to be a human organization will not be problem free. Our educational headaches will not disappear. There will still be difficult decisions to make, painful experiences to deal with, and frustrating situations to cope with. At the same time, a human organization can address the dilemmas we discussed in the introduction and can provide a context in which the development of all participants is maximized.

Furthermore, *everything we have discussed in this book has been successfuly implemented at one or more schools*. In essence, then, we would agree that we have portrayed a school that is idealistic in the sense that it differs dramatically from the typical school and in the sense that it may be difficult to create such a school. At the same time, we would argue that our portrait is realistic because we have acknowledged that problems occur in the humane school (indeed, we have discussed mechanisms for dealing with various kinds of problems); that a school, like an individual, is always striving toward the ideals rather than attaining and functioning in an ideal state; and that various schools have successfully implemented the programs, practices, and policies that we have described.

Second, it is important to recognize the interdependence of the various elements we have described. Marcus Aurelius advises us to "meditate often upon the bond of all in the Universe and their mutual relationship. For all things are in a way woven together and all are because of this dear to one another."[3] Many thinkers have similarly stressed the interdependence of all being. We will not take a stand on that question, but we would stress the applicability of the notion of interdependence to the high school as a human organization.

In other words, we view what we have offered in this book as a package deal. Does it work? If a school attempts to implement only one part of the system, it may or may not work. The kind of school we have discussed can be brought into operation gradually, but it is important to recognize the interdependence of the various elements and ultimately to incorporate them all into the school. For example, it would be difficult if not impossible to have the kind of responsive curriculum we have discussed without the participatory advisement system. A responsive curriculum demands special knowledge of each student and a staff member who can work closely with each student. In like manner, effective preventive discipline requires the kind of staff-student interaction that is provided by participatory advisement.

We view the advisement system as the heart of a humane high school. It is through the advisement system that a broad curriculum becomes responsive to individual student needs; that students learn decision-making skills; that students maintain the kind of relationship with a staff member that addresses the problem of alienation and helps students develop self-discipline; that excellence is stimulated, identified, and recognized; and so forth. The advisement system is crucial, for if it is working properly every student in the school has at least one staff member that knows and cares about that student.

John Gardner tells about a 19th century actor who was watching a small boy. The boy was looking at a number of older boys who had gone out to play. The small boy wanted to join them, but was afraid they would not accept him. When the older boys began coming back to the house, the actor said to the small boy, "Let's hide behind the curtain and they won't know where we are." The boy looked at the actor sadly and said, "Suppose they don't care?"[4] The boy's anxiety is reflected in the searching eyes of masses of people in the modern world who ask the question, "Does anyone care what happens to me?" The participatory advisement system is designed to say to every student, "Yes, we care, and here is a particular person who shall care especially about you." As such, it is the foundation for a human organization.

Finally, we need to make the point that building a human organization is a process. It requires time both to build the structure and to experience the benefits. Likert makes this point about business organizations when he calls time a "key variable" in evaluating the effectiveness of different systems of management. He notes that some researchers have found no relationship between productivity and type of management system while others have found a strong relationship. One reason, he argues, is that some researchers did not allow sufficient time for the human management system to work and it "apparently requires an appreciable period of time before the impact of the change is fully manifest in corresponding improvement in the end-result variables."[5] In one case, it took one and one-half years after the structure of the human organization was implemented for substantial changes in productivity to be realized. In the case of the high school, some of the benefits we have described have only been realized after a number of years of working with the structure. Once the decision has been made to build a human organization, the administrators and staff must be willing to work with the structure for a period of time before realizing some of the goals for which the organization was created.

In sum, we believe on both theoretical and empirical grounds that molding a high school into a human organization is not only desirable but a contemporary imperative. We make no claim that the task is an easy, quick, or simple one. But it is both possible and practical. We close, therefore, with some additional words of ancient wisdom from Marcus Aurelius:

> Do not because a thing is hard for you yourself to accomplish, imagine that it is humanly impossible; but if a thing is humanly possible and appropriate, consider it also to be within your own reach.[6]

# Endnotes

[1]William M. Hastings, *How To Think About Social Problems* (New York: Oxford University Press, 1979), pp. 89–90.

[2]"Remember those bold ideas to improve schools? What happened?" *Changing Times*, December, 1978, p. 20.

[3]Marcus Aurelius, *Meditations*, trans. A. S. L. Farquharson (London: J. M. Dent, 1961), p. 37.

[4]John W. Gardner, *Self-Renewal: The Individual and the Innovative Society* (New York: Harper & Row, 1963), p. xv.

[5]Rensis Likert, *The Human Organization* (New York: McGraw-Hill, 1967), p. 81.

[6]Marcus Aurelius, *op. cit.,* p. 34.

# Index

Ability/interest matrix, 132, 257
Accessibility of advisors, 238–239
Accidental education, 149–150
Achievement tests, 5, 6
ACT college aptitude examination, 63
Ad hoc committees, 215
Administrative assistant, counselor as, 100–101
Administrators, 56, 91
  commitment of, 84
  views of counselors, 105
Adult Basic Education programs, 182
Advisees, 48–50, 69–70
  assignment of, 70
  goal setting, 48–50
Advisement
  calendar, 41–48
  conference area, 78
  conference schedule, 75–77
  leadership group, 72
  and staff-student relationships, 237–238

team leaders in decision-making
    process, 212–213
  teams, 74
Advisor-advisee relationship, 42
Advisors, 68–69
  conferences, sample materials, 82–84
  resources for training, 79
Advisory system, 269–271, 304
Aesthetic pleasantness, 297–298
Affirmative action programs, 32
Alienation, 189–193
  treating symptoms of, 192–193
American Association for the
    Advancement of Education,
    253
American Association for Gifted
    Children, 264
American School Counselor Association,
    89, 93
Apprenticeship experience, examples,
    150
Aristotelian theory, 95

Attitudes, formation of, 55, 66–68
Authoritarian organizations, 189–193
Authoritarianism, 190–192

"Back to basics," 7
Basic skills, 7–8
Board of Education, 263
Brainstorming, 48–50

California Commission for Reform of
    Intermediate and Secondary
    Education, 127
California School of Mechanical Arts, 88
Career information program, sample,
    112–113
Career planning/preparation, 38–39
Change
    in advisor assignment, 70
    agent, 61–62
    approaches to, 59–62
    initiating, 55–56
    multistage process, 53–55
    principles of, 61–62
Change-of-Advisor form, 71
Civil Rights movement, 32
Classroom innovations, 61
Client-centered therapy, 95–96
College Entrance Examination Board, 5
Color of room, 281
Commons program, 244
Communication
    inservice training, 239
    maintaining open, 237–242
Community action projects, 156
Community-based programs, 153
Community class, 155
Community learning program, 169–178,
    183
    agreement with community sponsor,
        175
    catalog description, 170
    forms/materials, 173–175
    functions of supervisors, 170–171
    implementing, 172
    improved family relationships, 177–178
    outline of responsibilities, 173–174
    random survey, 176–178
    supervisory functions, 170–171
Community outreach program, 159–169,
    175, 178
    student journals, 178–181

Community services, 93
Compartmentalization of responsibility,
    92
Comprehensive high school, 33–34,
    91
    curriculum, 122–123
Compulsory school attendance laws,
    151
Conant, James Bryant, 123–125, 145
Conflict resolution, 240–242
Conformity in schools, 3
Contemporary education, dilemmas of,
    6–10
Control, maintaining, 220–222
Control-oriented schools, 223
Cooperatively Planned Unit (CPU),
    139–141
Counseling
    behavioral, 98–99
    developmental, 96–97
    nondirective, 89
    samples of functions, 111–113
    theories of, 94–99
Counselors, 73
    administrative assistant, 100–101
    client-centered therapy, 95–96
    deliberate psychological educators,
        109–110
    existential therapy, 97–98
    high school development, 89–92
    history of, 88–89
    information and program specialists,
        110–113
    model advisor, 107–108
    nonparticipation of, 96
    participatory advisement system,
        106–115
    role of, 87–115
    student advocates, 101–102
    students view of, 105
    support personnel, 108–109
    teachers view of, 105–106
    theories of, 94–99
    therapists and facilitators, 103–104
    training of, 92–94
    trouble-shooters, 102–103
    work load, 113–115
Counselor/student ratio, 100, 104
Court-ordered desegregation, 24, 90
Criminal offenses, 230–231
Crisis-oriented counseling programs, 73